In Search of Frankenstein

In Search of Frankenstein

**Exploring the Myths Behind
Mary Shelley's Monster**

Radu Florescu

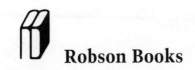

Robson Books

First published in Great Britain in 1996 by Robson
Books Ltd, Bolsover House, 5–6 Clipstone Street,
London W1P 8LE

British Library Cataloguing in Publication Data
A catalogue record for this title is available from
the British Library

Set in Trump Mediaeval by Columns Design Ltd,
Reading.
Printed in Great Britain by St Edmundsbury Press,
Bury St Edmunds, Suffolk

Contents

Acknowledgements

This book owes a heavy debt gratitude to the collaboration of my faithful friend and colleague Dr Matei Cazacu, Professor of Romanian history at the Sorbonne and a senior researcher at the prestigious Centre National de Recherches Scientifiques (CNRS) in Paris. I am also indebted to Alan C Barbour, a noted film historian, and to Ian Holt, specialist on the Horror film and scriptwriter, for an updated chapter on the Frankenstein films and the Filmography, an essential ingredient of the Frankenstein story, which in essence ensured its popularity more than the books among the public at large. I am also grateful to Joseph Stone for his insights on the Gothic novel.

Beyond these chief contributions, my indebtedness is quite extensive, and should I per chance have missed the name of any collaborator, their satisfaction will be that of the true scholar who prefers anonymity. My deep appreciation goes to the sisters Ramu and their descendants, the owners of Montalègre, who so graciously gave me their time in touring what was left of Mary Shelley's Chapuis, and to Françoise Ramu, for her contribution in elucidating the history of Villa Chapuis since Shelley's departure. To the former Mayor of Nieder-Beerbach, Eric Naut, I owed my initial inspiration, based upon his educated hunch, substantiated by local folklore, that Mary Shelley visited Castle Frankenstein and became acquainted with the story of the Alchemist Dippel.

To local historian and journalist Walter Scheele, I owe the extensive work and archaeological excavations he conducted with the help of Mathias Bührer, the present Director of the Castle, both at the site and at the Hesse Archives in Darmstadt, opening up many interesting new speculations on the Shelley visit, and obtaining access to the *Primavesi* collections of prints of the castle as it existed in Shelley's time.

Among my Genevan friends, my gratitude goes to Claire Elaine Engel, who was good enough to make time for a lengthy chat on the Shelley connection with Chamonix, where she summers each year, and on the legendary summer of 1816 about which she has written by far the most scholarly interpretation. I am also grateful to Ms Engel for certain unique pictures from her private collection, including that of Byron's boat, which she graciously made available. To former Dean Gagnebin of the faculty of Arts and Sciences at Geneva University, I owe many leads introducing me as he did to other scholars and showing me what was left of the Hôtel d'Angleterre at Sècheron, presently a public park. I thank Jean-Claude Hentsch, the direct descendant of Charles Hentsch, Byron's banker and real estate specialist, for his numerous informative letters and conversations concerning his famous forebear; Idelette Chouet of the Geneva University engraving collection who was most kind in cutting the red tape which enabled me to reproduce many of the pictures in this book; Freddy Baud of the automaton museum at l'Aubersson for having, on a busy visitors' day, allowed me to watch Chapuis's film on the history of the automaton; Raymond Barde, the son of the well-known specialist on the history of the Genevan 'campagnes', who gave me the kind of tour of the old city that only a lover of the old houses really can; his daughter Marie-Françoise, a television actress, who bore a remarkable resemblance to Mary Shelley, who was kind enough to perform on the site of Villa Diodati; the assistant former mayor of Cologny, Mr Brundlein, who was good enough to draw our attention to some little-known incidents of Mary's stay in the village; Dr Binz of the Geneva archives, who kindly located the police document attesting to Mary's presence in Geneva; André Chevalier of the cinemathèque in Lausanne for his lengthy interview on Frankenstein in films; Mr Blaise Evard of the Lausanne radio network, who took the risk of shocking the Genevan and Lausanne public with the revelation that the vampire and the artificial man were both born in their peaceful neighbourhood and Emanuel Bălăceanu, presently director of the Bruxelles office of the Credit Commercial de France, and at the time a brilliant young journalist from the *Tribune de Genève*, our anchorman in Geneva who did the same for the press.

In Germany, our indebtedness goes to Dr Erchardt of the Darmstadt archives, who provided us with the essential bio-graphical guide to the Frankenstein family; Dr Eberhard Bauer, the chief archivist of Prince Wittgenstein at Laasphe; Dr Munderlich, his assistant; Georg Krenmitz, assistant at the University of Munster; Marcel Poirard of the Bibliothèque Royale Albert I of Belgium; W Leist, reference librarian at the University of Giessen; Professor Gündisch, formerly from Cluj University and presently residing at Castle Horneck in Gundelsheim on Neckar (for information on the Transylvanian Frankensteins). We also thank Baron Georg Frankenstein of Ulstadt for his expression of interest in our work.

I am also deeply indebted to: Anne Marie Armelin, who worked on the Shelley genealogy; Ornella Volta, author of *Frankenstein and Co* who generously donated some of her Frankenstein film reproductions; Richard Chiampa, one of my brilliant former students, who helped elucidate the mean-ing of cryonics (he undertook a journey to Houston especially for me); Doreen Mouton, whose artistic talents helped re-create the atmosphere of Frankenstein's Genevan environ-ment; Mrs J Jaffee, the former head reference librarian at Boston College, for swiftly obtaining impossibly difficult books and for her help on the Golem legend; Elizabeth Miller, Professor of English literature at St John's Memorial University in Nova Scotia, for her help in updating the Frankenstein bibliography; Michael Callis for his research on the Trach family who assumed the name Frankenstein (being born in the Castle area), and distinguished themselves as artists in the early nineteenth century, painting Mt Blanc, and Chamonix and Frankenstein's Cliff in the White Mountains of New Hampshire. Finally, I would like to thank Nick Stein of the ABC Kane production, who showed enough faith in my theory to persuade the network to produce a 'special', which has been shown three times in the US, focusing on Castle Frankenstein as an important source of inspiration for Mary Shelley's famous work. I would also like to say a special thanks, to Sir David Frost for his tribute in words of encouragement on a variety of television shows and newspaper articles.

For patient research in a wide diversity of fields too numerous to be itemized, I am specially indebted to Pat Lambdin Moore whose enthusiasm has already impressed me in the search of Dracula and who is presently embarking on a book on Von Kempelen, a nineteenth-century mechanical chess player she first encountered doing research for my book. For my wife, Nicole, this book is particularly meaningful since it marks the occasion for her conversion from traditional typist to mastering the awesome computer, the writing instrument of the twenty-first century – a conversion triggered by editing the chapter on the man-machine theme in this book. This augurs well for husband–wife collaboration for future books and should in turn help expedite an author with a medieval frame of mind to the mechanistic twenty-first century.

At a more personal level, I would like to thank my brother who was good enough to put up with the liberated community that I imposed upon him during a certain Genevan summer (which bore some similarity to Mary's own); the Marquise de Virieu, who so kindly offered us the splendid setting of her château for inspiration; to my son John, the Director of Paradine Productions in the US, who produces Sir David Frost interviews on PBS and was responsible for much of the photography. Finally my gratitude goes to Louise Dixon, the Editor of Robson Books, who believed that this search, begun in America some years before, would be just as successful in England and made this book possible in record time. I will also light a candle to my copy editor Audrey Aitken for her helpful comments in bringing this book up to date.

Introduction

This book originates in dissatisfaction with Mary Shelley scholarship concerning the origin and the name of her novel, *Frankenstein* – which has now haunted the world for over 150 years.

Given the implantation of artificial organs, the latest experiments in freezing bodies in preparation for a hypothetical future life, the advent of the era of the test-tube baby, genetic engineering, the cybernetic revolution and thinking machines, the Frankenstein myth has become more topical than ever before. Cartoonists have exploited the well-known effigy of Mary's monster to castigate a great variety of politicians from Pakistan's Bhutto to Dr Kissinger; theologians, sociologists, behaviouralists, feminists, physicians and philosophers confront us with the scientist–monster themes at different intellectual and moral levels. Writers of science fiction terrorize our generation with the haunting spectre of Frankenstein robots taking over planet earth. Recently artificial intelligence, in the form of an MIT-built computer called Deep Blue, commanded international headlines as it came close to defeating the internationally known chess champion of the world: Gary Kasparov.

At a more popular level of public consciousness, advertising men are peddling millions of dollars' worth of Frankenstein gadgetry, ranging from the bald and fanged monster doll that loses its pants as it blushes to Frankenstein masks, popular during Hallowe'en, key chains and mystery games. For the movie zealot, the Frankenstein Society, such magazines as *Frankenstein Castle* and the inevitable funnies enjoy great success. At the site of Frankenstein Castle near Darmstadt in the state of Hesse, Germany, which is connected with Mary Shelley's original inspiration, popular Hallowe'en festivals are beginning to draw the attention of American GIs and other tourists interested in the origins of the story. Students of genealogy and those fascinated by the name have linked Frankenstein to a number of landmarks in the State of New Hampshire and a CD Rom on that theme has recently been produced (by Michael Callis), drawing tourists to the Mt Washington area. In the movie world, the Frankenstein theme continues its partnership with Dracula from its early origins during the silent movie days to the latest production of Coppola and Branagh, with Robert de Niro, undoubtedly the most famous of the Frankenstein actors, playing the monster in the horror epic *Mary Shelley's Frankenstein* (1995). Even those who feel they can avoid the monster by staying at home are mistaken, for they have had their privacy invaded by innumerable Frankenstein commercials, re-runs of classical movies and, within the last year, by documentaries revealing the true story (one of which, *The Real Frankenstein* by ABC Video, played twice on the Discovery Channel in 1996, was anchored by Sir David Frost, and put particular emphasis on the theory of the author of this book). This Frankenstein phenomenon (which would require a doctoral dissertation to account for) is not limited to the United States or even the English-speaking world; it has been manifest in virtually every nation. The Frankenstein theme is a popular one in France (*Mary Shelley's Frankenstein* had better reviews in France than in America) as it is also in Germany – even in Romania where the latest Branagh film played far longer than Coppola's *Dracula*. In the Far East, Shri Sant Ji Maharaj, the Indian religious leader of over three millions disciples is, according to the *Washington Post* (14 September 1971), often in the habit of donning a Frankenstein mask as a diversion.

While the Frankenstein explosion, like a runaway horse, is

cavorting unbridled upon the world stage, true scholars of Mary Shelley have also of recent date multiplied efforts to reveal 'the true story' in a number of biographies, monographs, scholarly and semi-scholarly articles. They include: Muriel Spark, *Mary Shelley* (Constable, 1987, a revised version of her 1972 biography entitled *Child of Light*), Emily Sunstein, *Mary Shelley: Romance and Reality* (Little, Brown, 1989), Anne K Mellor, *Mary Shelley: Her Life, Her Fiction, Her Monsters* (Routledge, New York and London, 1988). A good deal of controversy has arisen by way of the challenge of feminist authors who tend to highlight Mary Shelley's originality, whittling down the influence of her male entourage, including Shelley the poet, by focusing on the 1818 edition of the novel as opposed to the 1831 version, in part edited by Shelley (Marilyn Butler, *Mary Shelley's Frankenstein, or the Modern Prometheus 1818 Text*, Oxford University Press 1994).

In terms of periodicals, interest ranges from the prestigious *Shelley–Keats* journal to magazines of wide circulation such as *Life* and *Ms*. At a different level, in movie literature, largely because of the efforts of Forrest Ackerman, Donald Glut and other Boris Karloff enthusiasts (the actor who has immortalized the Frankenstein monster mask made by Jack Pierce), *Frankenstein* is widely read. To compound the confusion, a number of films, plays and works of fiction have been written (by Derek Marlowe and Brian Aldiss, among others) on the story about the story.

In the process of this large-scale exploitation of Frankenstein, the general public has become hopelessly confused. This confusion can be illustrated by a questionnaire which the author gave to one of his legends classes at Boston College in which the students reflected the general trend of the reading public: more than 50 confused the monster with its creator, Dr Frankenstein; only about $1/4$ of the class knew that Mary Shelley was the true author of the original novel; none were aware of the fact that she was also the daughter of one of the great feminist of all times, Mary Wollstonecraft, who is currently enjoying quite a unique 'rediscovery' (no less than three biographies within the last three years). Like Bram

Stoker, the author of *Dracula* who died in virtual obscurity (to the point that his recent biographers felt obliged to append the word *Dracula* to the title (Ludlam, Farson etc.), Mary Shelley also seems to have been condemned to live in the penumbra of her immortal monster. Although Bram Stoker's relative obscurity is readily understandable, Mary Shelley's anonymity is difficult to account for, since she was the daughter of two famous parents, the wife of a great poet and a literary celebrity even as a teenager.

Some of the explanation for Mary's comparative obscurity and perhaps the reason for the divorce existing between fact and fiction, the authentic story and the myth, may well lie in the barrier that presently exists between the academic world and the general reading public. On the one hand, the genuine scholar publishes the results of his doctoral dissertation for a university press, writes in the jargon of the academicians often encumbered by subjective and literary criticism and involves himself in controversial polemics (the recent feminist approach is a good case in point). Consequently, he or she appeals to a relatively small audience. The popular writer, on the other hand, who aims at the masses by failing to mention his sources, often does not convey credibility. It is this author's conviction that, in spite of the number of good Mary Shelley's monographs that have recently been published, a definitive popular biography of Mary Shelley is yet to be written.

We have attempted to steer somehow between these two courses. This book is not a biography of Mary Shelley but an attempt to pry into the origins and meanings of Frankenstein. It is written for the general public in a language that the layman will readily understand. At the same time, we hope to have exhausted not only the available written sources concerning Mary Shelley and Frankenstein but have had recourse as well to extensive field work and to local historians for the solution of certain problems.

Why has a Romanian scholar, an expert on East European History and a specialist on Dracula embarked upon the subject of Frankenstein? The ultimate answer to this question will be largely revealed in the pages to come. For the time being, we shall merely state that the vampire and artificial monster themes are historically connected from the date of that common birth in 1816 to Coppola's latest *Bram Stoker's Dracula* and his *Mary Shelley's Frankenstein* horror billing. Beyond this logic, the author confesses that once introduced to the subject, he could hardly prevent a total immersion and even developed passionate feelings for this attractive teenager whose literary career began at her famous mother's tombstone.

Yet a final circumstance helped to bring the author close to his subject. While in Italy, Mary developed a platonic love for a certain Prince Mavrocordato (the Romanian branch of that family is related to the author) who was, in fact, responsible for arousing her interest in the cause of Romanian and Greek independence for which the authentic Dracula had fought and died over 500 years ago.

1

The Geographical Background of the Search

The impetus for a book on Frankenstein came to me on a TV panel show, when, short of time, the M C dismissed me with, 'Professor Florescu, after Dracula you have but little choice: your next assignment inevitably must be the search for Frankenstein.' At the time, I cursorily dismissed his light remark from my thoughts.

By coincidence I had been spending my summers on the shores of Lake Léman, where my brother, an English banker, lived in a villa a few miles northeast of the city of Geneva, in the village of Corsier. My intuition, sharpened by my search for Dracula,[1] combined with a recently developed taste for the occult and a more forcible passion for old books, led me often to antique book dealers. That summer I returned one evening from a dealer in the old city with what I thought was a priceless collection of ghost stories, translated from the original German by an amateur, Jean Baptiste Eyriès. The book was entitled *Fantasmagoriana, or Collection of the Histories of Apparitions, Spectres, Ghosts, etc.*, published in Paris in 1812.[2] As I discussed my purchase with a scholar of English literature, who happened to be visiting us that evening, he remarked: 'I believe these were the stories read aloud by Lord Byron on the stormy night of June 16, 1816[3] to Percy Bysshe Shelley, Mary Wollstonecraft [Shelley, the poet's future wife], Claire Clairmont [Mary's stepsister], and Byron's eccentric, Italian-born physician, John William Polidori. According to a well-established legend, known to every English school-child, the reading of these stories led to Lord Byron's famous proposal at the end of the seance that "We will each write a ghost story."' It seems that Percy Shelley and Claire Clairmont immediately lost interest in the contest; Byron wrote a fragment, 'The Vampyre', which he later appended to his poem *Mazeppa* and which Polidori later expanded into his story of *The Vampyre*. Polidori, according to Mary, wrote about a skull-headed lady who was punished for peeping through a keyhole; Mary Shelley wrote one of the most terrifying stories of all time, and the first genuine work of science fiction – *Frankenstein, or the Modern Prometheus*. Polidori's *The Vampyre* became the logical precursor to Bram Stoker's equally durable and inimitable *Dracula*. Since that time the inseparable villains, Frankenstein and Dracula, have inhabited the domain of publishing's bestseller list, and have attained immortality on stage and screen.

My Mary Shelley 'syndrome' had begun; my first symptoms were daily visits to the Bibliothèque publique et universitaire, located just by the old city walls of Geneva. I read several biographies;[4] her *Letters*;[5] and most intently, her Journal: *History of a Six Weeks' Tour through a Part of France, Switzerland, Germany, and Holland: with Letters Descriptive of a Sail round the Lake of Geneva and of the Glaciers of Chamouni*,[6] published one year before *Frankenstein*, in 1817.

As I examined these books, the familiar twentieth-century Genevan landscape, well-travelled by me over the years, assumed a totally new character. All of the familiar images dimmed and vanished entirely from view, as the sprawling modern metropolis assumed the more humble proportions of the 'old city' and as the surrounding countryside donned the gentler mantle of the early nineteenth century. Hidden behind three ramparts and extensive counterscarps, the austere international capital of Calvinism was accessible only by three gates, hermetically sealed when the tocsin rang the alarm at 10 p.m. Even the approaches by lake were closed by a system of locks and barrages. Beyond the city walls flickered the lights of the numerous cottages in neighbouring villages and the more ambitious mansions or 'campagne'. Although most of Mary Shelley's Geneva has long since disappeared, the Alpine and lacustrine setting, some of the flora and fauna, parts of the old city and isolated islands of brick, stone and mortar have survived from that time. So have some of the names, familiar to me now through my reading. Surviving as well is a rich body of local folklore that has raised the story of that haunted summer of 1816 to the status of a legend.

Apart from reading, a number of coincidental (one might call them uncanny) occurrences drew me closer to the central drama. Villa Diodati, the scene of the drama, was located only three or four miles to the south, in the village of Cologny. A chance acquaintance had introduced me to the owner of Diodati: a Madame Simone Washer, the widow of a Belgian industrialist. From the formidable vantage point of the terrace, immortalized by Byron and Shelley, I could scan on the distant horizon of the opposite shore the 'dark and sulky Jura' mountains, so often described by Mary, though they were bright and cheery the day I saw them. As I gazed southwards, the city of Geneva and the harbour lay at my feet. Words can hardly convey the thrill that I experienced when I entered the main living room where the 'seances' were held during the summer of 1816, or explain my eerie feeling when I gazed at the mirror that dominates the fireplace and that probably had reflected the shadows of the fivesome. To the left of the hallway, on the ground floor, was Byron's bedroom, now converted into a study. Going upstairs by a narrow stairway, I could not resist peering into an ornate and elegant bedroom facing the lake where Polidori probably had composed the initial lines of his story about the skull-headed lady.

If Villa Diodati gave birth to the vampire story, the much humbler 'Campagne Chapuis', sometimes called 'Montalègre' by Mary, was the birthplace of Frankenstein. Chapuis is still a familiar name in the area, but the property at Montalègre was sold by Jacques Chapuis in 1829 to a family called Chapalay, who in turn re-sold it to François Alexandre Ramu in 1863. Ramu's heirs still own the property.

Dr Gagnebin, a former Dean of the College of Arts and Sciences at the University of Geneva, and also a well-known scholar of Rousseau, put me in touch with one of the present owners of the property that Mary Shelley and Percy Bysshe had rented in 1816. Mademoiselle Françoise Ramu brought the story of campagne Chapuis up to date: When her father purchased the property in 1863, it encompassed the small 'campagne' which Chapuis had recently refurbished for summer rental purposes. There was in addition a building to the south, where the Ramus presently live, that could have been a stable or a barn at the time, and several other smaller outbuildings, two of which can still be seen below, on the edge of the lake. There was also a small harbour, or perhaps two, which belonged to the property, where Byron and Shelley anchored their famous sailboat. As the Ramu family grew, the grandfather decided to build a more spacious villa, visible just to the north; it is now rented. Since the space available for new buildings was limited, the older Ramu decided to pull down campagne Chapuis in 1883. Out of piety for the memories enshrined in the original Shelley–Chapuis house, Monsieur Ramu instructed his gardener to rebuild the structure – the stones, tiles, and wood had been meticulously preserved. This was done within the year, and the Chapuis house was resurrected virtually unchanged in its quaint square and simple Swiss styling in the neighbouring village of Collonges, at the intersection of a place called Pointe de La Bise. Hardly any Shelley scholar is aware of this fact.

As I was about to rush out, camera in hand, to immortalize this extraordinary revelation, Mademoiselle Ramu stopped me and said: 'The resurrected campagne Chapuis no longer exists, though we shall be glad to place pictures of the original house where Mary Shelley stayed at your disposal.' As if the present story isn't bizarre enough, there is a sequel. In 1970, the son of the former king of Italy, Prince Victor Emmanuel, bought the rebuilt version of the Shelley house, had it pulled down once again, and built a villa in its place that has shocked lovers of traditional Swiss architecture. It took me ten minutes by car to reach the location.

All that is left at Montalègre today of Mary's 'dear Chapuis' is the house next door – the former stable or carriage house, now a quaint and unpretentious two-family dwelling where the two Ramu sisters lived, and which they occasionally rent. 'One English tenant,' one of the sisters told me, 'complained that the house was haunted.' On further inquiry, the sisters admitted that there had been a strange psychic manifestation in the house, particularly on the second floor, and that steps had been heard on the stairways at night – but Françoise Ramu added reassuringly, 'It is a friendly, poetic, Ariel-like ghost.'[7] I quickly understood the allusion, without further explanation, that 'Mary and Percy Bysshe strolled in the very room in which we now are standing'. When I made some reference to the main characters in Mary's novel, Victor Frankenstein and his monster, there was a blank look of consternation in the gaze of both sisters, and a shudder, as if I had mentioned the unmentionable!

Beyond the Ramu house, itself now greatly altered, all that is left from the Shelley period are the foundations, the cellar locked by a heavy, rusted iron door (how tempted I was to step within!), a terrace, an old stairway leading down to another building, a well, a stone bench, two other structures on the edge of the lake (they can still be seen from the Geneva road) and a few chestnut trees, which, judging by their size, have survived from that period. The basement originally stored the Chapuis wines. During World War II it was converted into an air-raid shelter just in case Swiss neutrality was violated. The view from Chapuis of the Jura mountains in the sunset was not as breathtaking as the panorama from Diodati, as the house sat much lower on the hill. Framed as it was by coniferous trees, which easily could have dated from Shelley's time, the landscape seemed peaceful and bucolic, as reflected in the works of the nineteenth-century English painter Francis Danby, who rented Montalègre shortly after the Shelleys left.

There was still another coincidence in my search: my

Map of
LAKE LÉMAN

brother's neighbour at Corsier was Jean Claude Hentsch, a member of a prominent Swiss banking family whose direct ancestor, Charles Hentsch, was Byron and Shelley's banker, friend and admirer – he wrote a poem in Byron's honour shortly after the poet's departure. It was Hentsch in fact who negotiated the Diodati rental and who was a frequent visitor at the villa afterwards, just as the English poets were always welcome at his fastidious estate of Mon Repos across the lake at Sécheron. Charles Hentsch was undoubtedly a confidant of the English poets, and this intimacy is amply revealed by the fact that he inherited the famous sailboat owned by Byron and Shelley. The boat (the first such sailboat on the lake) had made history by braving the treacherous waves and winds of Lake Léman. Unfortunately it was to die an ignominious death, rotting away in Charles Hentsch's harbour at Mon Repos.

Much folklore survives among the natives of Cologny and neighbouring villages, which probably has contributed to the preservation of that summer's legend. The descendants of Byron's boatman, Maurice, who had a knack for embroidering stories, are still alive. Vernes-Prescott, a reputable Swiss writer who professed to have known the English poets as a child, gathered some of these anecdotes together at the end of his long life (he was in his eighties at the time).[8] In some prominent circles of Cologny it is still whispered that genteel young ladies had to be kept indoors at night when the unorthodox group lived at Diodati and Chapuis.

A more enticing anecdote concerns an incident[9] that transpired recently in the municipality of Cologny, where a young lady, a relative of the mayor, was getting married in the Cologny church. After the wedding a banquet was held at the Town Hall. The event climaxed when the mayor suddenly produced a worn and mouldy lady's slipper, evidently dating back decades. 'This,' said Mayor Guempert, 'was the shoe of Mary Shelley when she lived at Chapuis during the summer of 1816.' According to the tale, the vine-growers in the area – observing a path of trodden flowers and beaten grass leading from Diodati to Chapuis, concluded that a prowler was about. Staying awake one night to apprehend the trespasser, they spied in the early morning the shadow of a young girl leaving Diodati through a back door and walking down the hill toward the lake. They could not help laughing. Startled, the young lady started running, and in the process, lost a slipper. The peasants retrieved it and in the morning brought it to the lost-and-found section of the municipality of Cologny, where it remained unclaimed. I tried in vain to locate the shoe. Perhaps it was taken as a trophy by the bride or bridegroom in question. Although the problem of the identity of the prowler will never be finally resolved, most scholars will agree that the lost shoe did not belong to Mary Shelley, but to her stepsister Claire Clairmont, Byron's mistress, who was nightly stealing between the two villas.

In Geneva itself, only the 'old city' was of interest to me. It was exciting to discover that Mary's description of Geneva to an unknown addressee, written in June 1816, was still largely valid – nothing much had changed.[10] The Municipal Archives still keep the police record of the Shelleys' stay; the remains survive of Dejean's Hôtel d'Angleterre at Sécheron, where Mary, Shelley, and Claire, as well as Lord Byron and Polidori, first stayed upon reaching the vicinity of Geneva in 1816. It took a great deal of footwork and questioning to locate a small plaque on the busy rue de Lausanne across the lake from Cologny. The main hotel has long since disappeared, but various smaller buildings, including the building bearing a plaque with Shelley's name engraved among a list of famous guests, remain in the beautiful Parc de Mon Repos, which belonged at one time to the Hentsch family.

Diodati is very visible from Sécheron across the lake, and it is easy to envisage the 'wicked' English tourists peering through telescopes, which the innkeeper Dejean had placed at the disposal of his guests, trying to catch a glimpse of the famous poet Byron and the Shelleys.

Many souvenirs of the summer of 1816 persist. They are to be found scattered around the lake, beyond Geneva and Cologny. The *Tour du Lac*, undertaken by Byron and Shelley from June to July[11] to visit Hermance, Clarens, Meillerie,

Chillon, and Ouchy in search of Rousseau and the historian Gibbon, created its own legend and had immense literary repercussions. Although it was not connected with *Frankenstein*, I could not resist the temptation of spending the night at the Hôtel de l'Ancre at Ouchy facing the harbour, where Byron had composed his *The Prisoner of Chillon*. As was the case everywhere we went, all trace of the more ethereal Shelley had been lost.

Many of the families that are descended from some of the prime actors on this early nineteenth-century stage have survived; so have their mansions, castles and estates, some of them virtually intact. One of the best preserved is the estate at Coppet, the property of the descendants of the financier Necker and his daughter, Madame de Staël, where Byron and Polidori were frequent visitors. The castle of Nyon, located fifteen miles beyond Coppet, was at the time owned by Victor Bonstetten, a well-known scholar of English literature and an intimate of the Diodati household. The Diodati family itself has survived, even though the villa has been sold. On questioning some of the heirs of these imposing names, I received the unmistakable impression that there was the greatest reluctance on their part to admit even the remotest connection with *Frankenstein*, the monster, or its author. As I asked permission to reproduce pictures of Coppet and Madame de Staël, the direct descendant and present owner of Coppet, the Marquis d'Haussonville, politely responded that he failed to see any connection between Madame de Staël and Frankenstein's monster.

The monster and his creator are also permanently entrenched in the shadow of icy Mont Blanc, in the town of Chamonix (Mary spells it Chamouni), just across the French border, where Mary Percy, and Claire toured in the week of 21 July.

Needless to say, I retraced her steps, a two-and-a-half-hour trip by car, taking the road she had taken: the valley of the Arve, Sallanches, and Servoz. As is the case with Geneva it is difficult to carve out Mary's little village of Chamonix from the sprawling winter and summer resort that now extends in all directions. The Hôtel de La Ville de Londres, where Mary stayed, still exists. I developed the habit of seeking hotel registers wherever the couple stayed, a habit that was spurred by the knowledge that during the early nineteenth century it was customary for guests to add a comment or even a jest to their name, age, nationality and permanent domicile. In 1840 when Mary revisited Geneva she stayed at the comfortable Hôtel des Bergues overlooking Mont Blanc and Mont Salève. The Director informed me that Mary's signature had been inscribed in the *Livre d'Or* without comment. When Byron had registered at the inn at Sécheron in May, he had incurred the wrath of Mr Dejean, the Swiss proprietor, by jokingly inscribing his age as '100'. During the trip to Chamonix, Shelley had carried the joke one step further by registering at the Hôtel de La Ville de Londres as an atheist.[12] Visiting the same hotel in late August, Byron had amended Shelley's entry, and the whole episode escalated to the status of a *cause célèbre*. That particular guest book aroused a good deal of curiosity thereafter. In time the whole register mysteriously disappeared from the hotel archives and, despite my intensive research, I could not find a trace of Shelley's signature in Chamonix.

The influences of Swiss, Genevan and Alpine geographies are very apparent in the writing of *Frankenstein*. They are also evident both in Mary's and in Shelley's letters and in *The History of a Six Weeks' Tour*. At least one of the personalities in the drama of 1816, Claire Clairmont, describes herself as proud of her 'Swiss ancestry'. When we checked on that ancestry we discovered that the names that are most often attributed to Claire's parents – Vial and Gaulis – are prominent Swiss names, and often occur in the Geneva and Lausanne telephone directories (Clairmont was most probably an adopted name). It should therefore come as no great surprise (as it was to many of our Genevan friends) that the main characters of the novel as well as the principal setting are Swiss, and specifically Genevan.

Although the name Frankenstein may be an exception, most of the other characters in the novel bear Swiss names that are familiar in the area: Caroline Beaufort (Frankenstein's mother), Henry Clerval (his best friend), Justine Moritz (the maid), etc. Frankenstein possessed a townhouse in Geneva and a campagne at Bellerive, a small township in the vicinity of Cologny. 'When I was 13 years of age,' states Frankenstein, 'we all went on a party of pleasure to the baths near Thonon,' to this day still a popular spa. The monster had killed William, Frankenstein's brother, in Plainpalais. Once an insalubrious marsh and a field for drilling soldiers, Plainpalais is now used as a parking area, or for festive occasions. Frankenstein passed by Lausanne, where he 'contemplated the lake ... and the snowy mountains.' Lausanne is an ancient university town, fifty miles northeast of Geneva.

Frankenstein knew, as did Mary Shelley, that after 10 p.m. 'the gates of the town were already shut' and hence he, too, 'was obliged to pass the night at Sécheron, a village half a league to the east of the city.' He 'saw the lightning playing on the summit of Mont Blanc ... the Juras, and the Alps of Savoy ... the village of Copêt ... and the Môle, a peaked mountain to the east of the lake' (just north of Mont Salève), these were all familiar sights to Victor Frankenstein. Frankenstein finally caught a glimpse of the monster with a fierce countenance 'hanging among the rocks of the nearly perpendicular ascent of Mont Salève, that bounds Plainpalais on the south', a bleak and steep mountain that dominates the city of Geneva. Justine Moritz was falsely accused of murder 'at the house of an aunt from Chêne, a village situated at about a league from Geneva'. (It now lies within the suburbs of the city.) Frankenstein pursued the monster in the 'ravine of the Arve' and directed himself 'to the valley of Chamouni', passing 'the bridge of Pelissier', like Mary Shelley in her journey. Then, finally, the creator found the monster 'beside the sources of the Arveiron, which take their rise in a glacier'. (The Mer de Glace is still an awesome sight, although the glacier has been less impressive in recent years.)

Finally the monster revealed his cruel predicament and his desire for a mate, on the site of Montanvert, just below Mont

Blanc (still a favourite excursion site that you can reach by a small cog railway). When Frankenstein returns from his peregrinations abroad at the end of the novel, he reaches 'the pleasant banks of Montalègre' (where Mary Shelley stayed). The monster, however, having been deprived of a mate, pursues his revenge and kills Frankenstein's bride, Elizabeth, at the Inn of Evian (a favourite French watering place on the edge of the southern shores of the lake just beyond Thonon). As our investigation proves, the geographic background of the novel is evidently Genevan, reflecting Mary's three-month stay there in 1816.

What of the origin of that extraordinarily durable name Frankenstein? Mary Shelley wrote some years later in her *Rambles in Germany and Italy* ' "What's in a name" – You know the quotation: it applies to things known; to things unknown, a name is often everything: on me it has a powerful effect; and many hours of extreme pleasure have derived their zest simply from a name.'[13]

There are, of course, numerous definitions and connotations of the name 'Frankenstein'. When someone says, 'I am creating a Frankenstein', it generally conjures up the notion of a soulless monster destroying its creator. A distinction was drawn initially between the creator (Frankenstein) and his nameless creature. When George Canning first alluded to Frankenstein in the House of Commons only a few years after the publication of the book in 1818, arguing against the liberation of the West Indian slaves, he deliberately eschewed the name, though the inference was quite clear. 'To turn him [the slave] loose in the manhood of his physical strength, in the maturity of his physical passion, but in the infancy of his uninstructed reason, would be to raise up a creature resembling the splendid fiction of a recent romance.'[14] Since the monster had no name, it was tempting to associate him with his creator. Charles Sumner, the American statesman, speaking at the time of the American Civil War, compared 'the Southern Confederacy with the soulless monster of Frankenstein. The wretched creation of a mortal science without God; endowed with life and nothing else; forever raging madly, the scandal to humanity; powerful only for evil; whose destruction will be essential to the peace of the world.'[15] The beginnings of a definition as well as of a confusion (monster and creator) were already inherent in that citation. It was slightly later that a conservative English Parliamentarian and a man of science, Sir John Lubbock, speaking to the House of Commons against certain new liberal reforms, stated that he 'believed it would be impossible to control the Frankensteins we have ourselves created'.[16] The cycle was completed: the monster had exchanged places with the scientist, and the word had acquired new meaning.

It seems incredible that few biographers of Mary Shelley, or critics of the novel, should have attempted to offer a satisfactory explanation of the origin of the name Frankenstein, for it was not just a quaint polysyllabic German name stemming from Mary's imagination. Of course, there are a few unsatisfactory theories.

W E Peck gives the explanation that 'The names Frankheim and Falkenstein from Monk Lewis's tales probably supplied Mary Shelley ... with the title for her romance.'[17] Mary's journal indicates that she read Lewis's *Tales* in 1815. She may also have been impressed by the eerie quality of some castles with a 'stein' ending that she had seen in her voyage down the Rhine in 1814 – like Castle Ehrenbreitstein. (*Stein* is simply the German word for *stone*.) A subtler explanation was given by 'literary detective' Samuel Rosenberg in an answer to a letter referring to his original article in *Life* magazine, written on the occasion of the 150th anniversary of the publication of the novel *Frankenstein*: Author Rosenberg states that Shelley at the age of 18 wrote *St Irvyne* whose hero, a seeker of eternal life, he named 'Wolfstein'. Shelley also regarded Benjamin Franklin, who dabbled in electricity, as a modern Prometheus [the life-giving god of the Greeks, whose name was used as a subtitle for *Frankenstein*]. This suggested to Rosenberg that 'Franklin' [Promethean], plus 'Wolfstein' [searcher for eternal life] equalled 'Frankenstein', or the modern Prometheus.[18]

It is interesting to note in passing that Mary's signature was found in 1957 in a three-volume book entitled *Recollections of a Pedestrian*, by an obscure author named Thomas Alexander Boswell.[19] The chief hero of the novel was a German traveller called Frankenstein, who shared some characteristics with Mary's Victor Frankenstein. I found a copy of that rare volume at Houghton Library in Cambridge, Massachusetts, but unfortunately it was published in 1826, *after* the publication of Mary's *Frankenstein*.

After many false starts, a footnote in Donald Glut's *The Frankenstein Legend* provided a clue: 'There was a legend about a monster in the Castle of the Frankensteins in Darmstadt, Germany ... it is possible that Mary Shelley had encountered the legend in her readings. But neither she nor her husband had ever visited Germany.'[20] That Mary Shelley went to Germany, however, is evidenced by the title of her journal *History of a Six Weeks' Tour Through a Part of France, Switzerland, Germany, and Holland*. She travelled by boat down the Rhine and the fact that the valley made a profound impression on her is described not only in the travelogue but also in the novel *Frankenstein*. On their trip down the Rhine, Victor Frankenstein and his friend Henry Clerval had agreed to 'descend the Rhine in a boat from Strasburgh to Rotterdam ... We saw many ruined castles standing on the edges of precipices, surrounded by black woods, high and inaccessible.'

The first serious discussion I had on the possibility of the existence of a Frankenstein family was with the noted scholar and specialist of the Gothic novel, the late Sir Devendra P Varma, on the occasion of our both receiving an award at the annual meeting of the Dracula Society of America at the Alexandria Hotel in Los Angeles. Our discussion started by reviewing various place names bearing the name of Frankenstein on a map. The two Frankenstein place names that seemed most relevant to Mary's travels were located in the Rhineland, where we knew she had been, on the stretch between the cities of Mannheim and Mainz. We dismissed the one located in the Pfals near Kaiserslautern; it was located too far from the river. The other Frankenstein, a castle or burg, was situated to the south of the city of Darmstadt, only eight or nine miles east of the Rhine. Having pinpointed the location, I agreed to meet with Professor Varma at Castle Frankenstein in the summer of 1973 – he was to proceed up the river from Holland, duplicating the journey of Byron and Polidori in 1816; I was to sail down the river from Rheinfelden, following Mary and Shelley's 1814 canoe trip down the Rhine. The rendezvous with Professor Varma at Castle Frankenstein never materialized – we unfortunately missed each other by a matter of hours.

Several weeks earlier, I had received a letter from Matei Cazacu, a brilliant Romanian scholar, now a senior researcher at the Centre national de recherches scientifiques (CRNS) in Paris, who had become absorbed in the career of a Baron Frank von Frankenstein (the name Frankenstein was tantalizing). He had been elected leader of the German Saxons of Transylvania in the seventeenth century and who also had a reputation for dabbling in alchemy. Baron Frankenstein was buried in a vault of the Evangelical Church of Sibiu, in Transylvania, where his effigy can still be seen. Not far away lie the earthly remains of Dracula's only son, Mihnea the Bad, who was assassinated in front of the church on 12 March 1510. Is it not an odd coincidence that these two tombs should lie in such proximity – as Dracula was one of the bitterest enemies of the Germans of Transylvania, whom he impaled in great numbers. (Many of Dracula's crimes were committed in the vicinity of Sibiu.)

Cazacu, who had just been granted a research fellowship to the prestigious school of archivists, the Ecole des Chartes, Paris, wanted to study the link, if any, between the 'Transylvanian' branch of the Frankenstein family and the owners of the castle on the Rhine. Thus, from entirely different tangents, we met on the densely forested heights of Magnetberg at the site of the Frankenstein castle, just outside of Darmstadt, on 10 August 1973. There, I persuaded my colleague to abandon or postpone his own research and to collaborate with me on my search for Frankenstein.

Dominating the Rhine valley with its grotesquely terraced donjon and weathered battlements, the thirteenth-century castles of the Barons Frankenstein looked as tortured by time as Dracula's famous fortress, which we had scaled only six years before. Burg Frankenstein was much better preserved, however. We were to discover that the castle had a fascinating history accompanied by a body of local folklore including tales of a series of calamities that felled various members of the Frankenstein family. We heard the legend of Knight Georg and the dragon-monster, idylls of romance, and stories of ruthless vengeance; more to the point, we heard tales that the castle and its surroundings were centres of alchemy and necromancy.

That evening we dined on German sausages and beer with the former Mayor of Nieder-Beerbach (a small village located at the foot of Castle Frankenstein), at a small inn a few miles away called Dippelshof which has since been converted into an elegant country club. We told the mayor that we were seeking more information on the Shelleys' connections with Frankenstein. The mayor related to us the local lore that Mary Shelley and the poet had visited the castle in 1814 and may have spent some time at the very inn where we were dining. 'Do you know,' he whispered, 'that exactly 300 years ago, on 10 August, 1673, there was born in the castle of the Frankensteins, a remarkable alchemist, Konrad Dippel, who, though unrelated to the Frankensteins, occasionally signed himself Frankensteiner by virtue of his birth at the castle – a custom at that time.'

The mayor told us that it might be well worth our while to investigate Dippel's career in some detail. Like all respectable alchemists, he, of course, discovered the secret of converting metals into gold – people at the castle are still seeking for gold – but in addition he was interested in things far more diabolical; he thought he had discovered the secret of immortality and wanted to create human life. Some of Dippel's experiments were undoubtedly carried out within the castle walls, and perhaps at this very inn, which was owned by his brother. The mayor was convinced that Mary Shelley was aware of the Dippel saga.

If indeed Mary was inspired by local lore in the writing of *Frankenstein*, why didn't she reveal it in her *Letters* and *Journal*? Why the conspiracy of silence among the tiny group who left testimonies? Even Claire Clairmont is silent in her *Journal*. Some scholars have made note of the fact that neither Mary nor Claire kept accurate records of their journeys. Place names are handled in a cavalier fashion; quite often they are misspelled. More seriously for scholars, there is at least some suspicion that the two stepsisters were secretive, and that they deliberately withheld information when it was in their interests to do so. It is equally mysterious that virtually the whole of the crucial summer months of 1816 have disappeared from both Mary's and Claire's journals. Are we to assume then that facts are neatly arranged to suit the author's dramatic intent?

Most of Mary's biographers have also observed in her writings her heavy reliance on her experiences: on things heard, or seen. Mary herself admitted her dependence upon geographical settings actually observed and on personalities either known or described to her. Could it be that Mary deliberately destroyed all traces of her sources for this particular story to establish a reputation for the kind of creativity she really lacked – and that Claire abetted the plot?

Considering the volumes that have been written on *Frankenstein* and the many biographies that have been published of Mary Shelley, not to mention the tomes on Percy Bysshe Shelley and Lord Byron, there is little justification for writing yet another book on Mary Shelley and the novel *Frankenstein*. But this is not just another book: the project was initially conceived on the basis of a 'hunch' that there was a *new* dimension to the origin of the Frankenstein story, and that, if the hunch were based on extensive research both in Germany and Switzerland, and that if information was unearthed that had escaped the attention of scholars, it might be proven. We do *not* offer our theory as the *sole* explanation for the writing of the novel. There were undoubtedly many influences at work on Mary that can be traced from her early childhood to the summer of 1816. We are not convinced by the accepted view, which Mary herself would have us believe, that Frankenstein was the result of a 'nightmare', in itself the indirect consequence of a proposal to each write a 'ghost story'.

The next chapter introduces the reader to the key personalities in this extraordinary story, beginning with Mary Shelley's mother, Mary Wollstonecraft – history's first genuine feminist. Her death, when Mary was born, may be one reason, among many, why her tombstone at St Pancras's cemetery in London has acquired such symbolic importance. Mary's elopement in 1814 with the married poet Shelley, accompanied by Claire Clairmont, through war-ravaged France, Switzerland, and Germany, that probably included a visit to Castle Frankenstein – a visit that we shall attempt to prove – is examined in Chapter 3. We reveal to the public for the first time in Chapter 4 the history and mythology of the Barons Frankenstein, and the extraordinary career of the alchemist Konrad Dippel 'the Frankensteiner'. This chapter is based on our research in Darmstadt, and contains much historical fact as well as local folklore.

Although the summer of 1816, during which much of *Frankenstein* was written, has been studied thoroughly,[21] we shall re-examine it from the perspective of the local history and its Genevan context. The complex relationships between the Diodati (Byron and Polidori) and the Chapuis households (Mary, Percy Bysshe, and Claire Clairmont) are explored in Chapter 5, and the relevance of the various 'seances' and 'proposals' to the conception and writing of *Frankenstein* is reassessed in this chapter.

Chapter 6 studies the haunting legacy of that summer of 1816 in terms of the premature or violent deaths (or suicides) of all the male members of the Diodati group, as well as the suicides of some of its peripheral members; Mary Shelley died of brain cancer in 1851, aged 54, while Claire Clairmont lived to the venerable age of 81 (she died in 1879).

The complete story of Mary and Shelley's attempt to publish the novel, the history of the various editions, the reaction of the critics to the work of a nineteen-year-old woman, and Mary's reaction to the success of her work has never been told. Chapter 7 tells that story, and the history of the many Frankenstein plays, giving Mary's reaction to the variations on her plot during her lifetime.

The impact of the monster on the Gothic novel is presented in Chapter 8, along with an analysis of the influences on Mary Shelley of the most salient novels of the Gothic horror tradition. The chapter also investigates the literary sources of Mary Shelley, putting her extensive reading list in an interesting perspective.

An insightful analysis of the great Frankenstein films, the great monster roles of Karloff and Lugosi, Lee, Boyle, Branagh and de Niro and the great make-up men is given in Chapter 9, supported by an extensive Filmography.

No author has, to our knowledge, placed the novel *Franken-stein*, in essence a reflection of the scientific, medical and occultist discoveries and hopes of the early nineteenth century, within the general framework of the alchemist's attempt to create life, from the beginning of time. Chapter 10 traces the history of the human efforts and frustrations in trying to play God up to Mary Shelley's time, and evaluates Mary's exploitation of the theme of the artificial man.

Finally, even though the moralist may legitimately anathematize Mary's Promethean presumption, our twenty-first century cybernetic revolution, the advent of the age of the computer, the semi-artificial man and genetic manipulation will justify a few concluding remarks on Mary Shelley's prophetic vision.

When we visited Dracula's castle in the Transylvanian Alps several years ago, before our research on Dracula began, it represented but a forgotten, meaningless, empty shell, like many other ruins scattered throughout the Transylvania countryside. It has, since the first publication of *In Search of Dracula*, become one of Romania's favourite tourist sites – in 1995 the first World Dracula Congress met in Bucharest and new tours are planned for 1997, the centennial year of

Stoker's *Dracula*. In the same way that I had known Villa Diodati long before I became interested in Mary Shelley during my years of residence in Geneva: Diodati was just another imposing mansion, not very different from countless others bordering the lake in the fashionable suburb of Cologny. It was only when I became aware of the drama that unfolded there, and when I began to associate a series of gripping events with that house, that its bricks and walls came to life. These are some of the satisfactions of the local historian, and only the dullest minds can fail to experience the kind of pleasure and excitement derived from the most minute local discovery, akin to that of the Alpinist scaling a new summit.

There is a certain ill-defined psychic quality about a place – houses do have souls of their own – particularly those marked by strong impressions, which a privileged few can sense after the passing of decades, or even centuries. The two American lady tourists whose sensitivity to strong impressions was such that they re-lived a scene from the French Revolution at the Place de La Bastille years afterwards is a good case in point. Although we could not reconstruct a 'ghost', somehow I felt close to Mary Shelley's spirit when walking in the ruins of Chapuis, or watching the sun set on the darkened Jura across the lake, casting its deep shadows around me.

There is an added advantage to the study of history at its source. Although I am not a geographical determinist – man is not necessarily what he eats – mountains, lakes and rivers, sunshine and storms, mould the patterns of thought in a definite way. There can be no question that Lake Léman, the old city of Geneva, the Jura, Mont Blanc and the castle on the Rhine have left their firm imprint on the novel *Frankenstein*.

This book is primarily intended for the general reader. Our experience with *In Search of Dracula* has suggested that a picture is well worth a thousand words. We offer a rich selection of photographs, reproductions, maps, genealogies and movie stills, drawn from various archives and collections. Some of these are unique: the pictures of Diodati and Chapuis, among others, are from private sources and have not been published elsewhere. The rich geographic context of the novel *Frankenstein* has given us ample pictorial opportunity to exploit it by using original engravings from the period. This also has never been done before. We hope that the visual wealth of this study will encourage the reader to travel in Mary Shelley's and in Frankenstein's footsteps.

To our many Genevan friends who have made this book possible we owe a note of apology. Local literary historians have long been proud of the fact that the summer of 1816, in its Genevan context, has been one of the most productive and brilliant in English literary history. Countless literary pilgrims have flocked to the shores of Lake Léman, seeking the Alpine and lacustrine setting that had inspired Byron's Third Canto of *Childe Harold*, *The Prisoner of Chillon*, and Shelley's 'Ode to Immortality' and 'Mont Blanc'. Somehow, Mary Shelley's *Frankenstein* and Polidori's *Vampyre* are almost always absent from the impressive list of English classics produced during those three months. Or, if they are mentioned at all, they are mentioned in a whisper, or as a footnote. Some years ago, when I highlighted these two works on a broadcast on Radio Lausanne by stating that the 'two greatest and most durable horror stories of all times were born on the shores of Lake Léman', the statement caused a tempest in a teapot. This fellow Florescu had already given Transylvania a bad name by associating it with vampirism; was he now going to convert Switzerland, with its quaint and quiet mountain scenery, its peace-loving reputation, its rigid Puritan standards, its impeccable democratic tradition, its healthy banking and tourist instincts and its watchmaking into a monster land? What, the monster and the vampire, these insidious and villainous literary and film companions, born in the bucolic countryside of Cologny? We were giving Switzerland, and to a lesser extent the Rhineland, an evil reputation. Letters of protest poured in. All those connected with the story, even the present Frankenstein descendants, dissociated themselves from Mary Shelley's Victor Frankenstein and his grotesque monster. The Baron simply wrote to us that his family's link with the castle bearing his name ended with its sale. So great is the fear created by the name *Frankenstein*!

Notwithstanding all these protests, we cannot avoid the conclusion that Mary Shelley's Victor Frankenstein, though of German descent, was by disposition and upbringing thoroughly Genevan, and that his monster made his first victim in the heart of the city, at Plainpalais!

2

The Tomb of Mary Wollstonecraft and St Pancras Cemetery

For Mary Shelley the memory of her famous mother became an ideal; as a young girl, she sought refuge at her mother's quiet tombstone in St Pancras Cemetery, London, to pursue her fantasies. Later, she would be joined there by Shelley, and the two lovers would remain in the ambience of the grave, perhaps reading the volumes of Mary Wollstonecraft to each other, perhaps engaging in flights of imagination, being interrupted only by dawn.

Mary Wollstonecraft

Mary Wollstonecraft Godwin (1759–1797) died a few days after Mary Shelley was born, from complications during her delivery. The delivery on 30 August 1797, in a shabby little room in the Godwin house, at 29 the Polygon in Somers Town, a suburb of London, had seemingly been normal. Mary had insisted on 'natural childbirth' and, assisted only by a midwife, had fully intended to be up and about the following day, as she had been after the birth of her first daughter, Fanny Imlay. The ten days that followed – tersely described in Godwin's diary – became a tragedy. The midwife had not completely removed the placenta in delivering the baby, and fragments of it began to poison the womb; internal haemorrhage set in and Mary began to sense great pain. Godwin went immediately to summon a physician, Dr Poignard; at Mary's request, Dr Fordyce was also summoned, but it was too late for surgery; the patient was too weak.

The tide of life ebbed and flowed during the next few days, and between physicians, midwife, nurses, and friends there were never less than five or six people in attendance. Godwin never left his wife's bedside. On Friday, 1 September, Mary's condition was still hopeful and she was able to sit up in bed. The following day she bore herself well until evening when she began to feel weak. On 3 September 'every muscle of her body trembled, the teeth chattered, and the bed shook under her.'[1] To dull her senses she was given copious draughts of wine. On the fifth day, puppies were brought in to suck the overflowing milk that had given her breasts such acute pain. On another occasion she wanly turned to her solicitous husband and cried, 'Oh Godwin, I am in heaven!' Godwin replied: 'You mean, my dear, that your physical sensations are somewhat easier.'[2]

By Thursday, 7 September, Mary began losing her struggle for survival, and seemed resigned to the inevitable. Godwin simply noted this cruel reality in his diary with the comment, 'Dying in the evening', and the following day, 8 September, he added, 'idea of death'. Death occurred two days later on Sunday, 10 September. Godwin had only enough strength to scribble the actual time. There followed in Godwin's diary three rows of dots – I took the trouble to count them. There were 38 dots in all – exactly Mary's age when she died. The official cause of death was septicaemia fever.[3]

Mary Wollstonecraft was buried the following day at the cemetery of St Pancras Church where she and Godwin had so recently been married – in March – though her remains eventually were transferred to St Peter's Church in Bournemouth. In St Pancras a forgotten monument still stands in the middle of the park that replaced the old churchyard, carrying the following inscription:

MARY WOLLSTONECRAFT GODWIN
Author of
A Vindication of the Rights of Woman
Born 27th April 1759
Died 10th September 1797

The effect on Mary Shelley of her mother's untimely death cannot be overestimated, for Mary Wollstonecraft set an example for her daughter, both in her lifestyle and attitudes, and in her writing. To understand fully the author of *Frankenstein*, then, one should be familiar not only with the story of her mother's career, but with the members of the Godwin household.

Although one recent biographer, Claire Tomalin,[4] displays a conspicuous lack of warmth towards her subject, Mary Wollstonecraft's life can hardly be examined dispassionately. In many ways the tenor of Mary's life was set by her bitter youth. Her father, Edward John Wollstonecraft, a manufacturer-turned-farmer, was mean, uninspiring, drank heavily, cursed, and kept his family in line by constant thrashings. Her mother, Elizabeth, was a sturdy Irishwoman, herself somewhat of a tyrant, who bore him six children in quick succession. Mary's childhood environment was tumultuous, but its effect was to develop in her a strong character: her family was poor; her father constantly shifted occupations and abodes.

Probably the happiest period of Mary's childhood was when the family was established in a comfortable house at Barking in Essex. Mary was six at the time, and spent much of her time outdoors; she apparently cared little for dolls or the usual amusements of little girls.[5] Her education, it seems, began around her sixteenth year, when her family moved to Hoxton, near London;[6] here Mary became acquainted with her deepest friend, Fanny Blood, after whom she named her first daughter. It was Fanny who first awakened her love of study, and would inspire her genius, until her death – also after childbirth – in Lisbon in 1785, Mary at her side.

At the age of nineteen, Mary left home to take a position as a lady's companion at Bath. (She was later to take a job as a governess to the children of Lord Kingsborough, an Irish noble-man.) Although away from home, Mary's loyalty to her family never ceased, and she continued to send money to her family, especially her two sisters, Eliza and Everina. (She even opened a school in Newington Green at which Eliza assisted.) Mary was soon summoned home from Bath, however, to attend her failing mother, nursing her to the end. As she died, Mrs Wollstonecraft uttered words that were to remain with Mary throughout her life: 'A little patience, and all will be over!'[7]

A talent for writing probably saved Mary from premature suicide. Some literary critics have dismissed her dozen books, travelogues, articles, and studies as 'sentimental nonsense' and Mary as 'a hack writer'. Nevertheless, her *A Vindication of the Rights of Woman*[8] was considered revolutionary when it was first published in 1792, and made Mary Wollstonecraft famous, especially within liberal circles. (Mary had dedicated her book to Talleyrand.) Mary was at this time a frequent visitor to the publisher Johnson's house, and there she met Thomas Paine and William Godwin. Earlier she had met the Swiss psychedelic painter, Henri Fuseli, while they were both translating for Johnson, and contributing to the *Analytical Review*. In fact, it is probably because of the love that developed between Mary and Fuseli, complicated by the fact that Mrs Fuseli and Mary were good friends, that the Fuselis and Johnson did not accompany Mary to Paris in 1792, as originally planned. (Mary's *idée fixe* of finding her paradise in Switzerland, evidently inherited by her daughter, probably stemmed from her relationship with Fuseli.)

Mary left England for France at the end of 1792 travelling alone, and, as an 'enemy alien', she threw herself into the maelstrom of the French Revolution, witnessing the last days of the French monarchy and the Reign of Terror. She joined a small circle of Anglo-American liberals in Paris – Tom Paine was in Paris at the time – and befriended, among others, the uncrowned queen of the Girondins, Madame Roland. As Paris became too bloody for her tastes, Mary moved a few miles out of the city to the village of Neuilly, where she was looked after by an old gardener. While at Neuilly, Mary became increasingly involved with a tall and ruggedly handsome American, Captain Gilbert Imlay (1755–1796), whom she had met earlier at the house of an acquaintance in Paris. Originally from New Jersey, Imlay had all the qualities that please a woman; he stood in sharp contrast to the more polished circle of cosmopolitan liberals with which Mary had travelled.

Imlay had fought in the American revolutionary war, had explored the 'wilds' of the Western Territories, and was an author in his own right. He had written *A Topographical Description of the Western Territory of North America* (1792), an account of his expeditions. When he met Mary, the expatriate had his mind set on business ventures and political intrigue, although he was an equally thorough sensualist and shared Mary's belief in free love.[9]

Although Mary's early years with Imlay seem to have been happy, their life was soon punctuated by Imlay's long absences. Imlay moved to Le Havre; Mary pursued him with letters, finally moving there herself. Here, a girl was born on 14 May 1794, whom Mary named Fanny. Imlay remained with her until August, then moved to London. Mary soon moved to Paris, and from there inundated Imlay with a flood of passionate, self-righteous, and pitiful letters. It seems, however, that though their affair had disintegrated, Imlay did not entirely desert her. His letters to Mary during this period are alternately affectionate and business-like. When Imlay finally wrote that he would like her to come to him, she obliged, arriving in London in April 1795. Here Imlay had provided a furnished house for her and Fanny, and he soon sent Mary on a business trip to Sweden and Norway on his behalf. That he looked upon Mary as his wife can be proved by a document in which he authorizes Mary to conduct business on his behalf:[10]

May 19 1795

Know all men by these presents that I, Gilbert Imlay, citizen of the United States of America, at present residing in London, do nominate, constitute, and appoint Mary Imlay, my best friend and wife, to take the sole management and direction of all my affairs ...

Mary Wollstonecraft's travelogue from this period, *Letters Written during a Short Residence in Sweden, Norway, and Denmark*,[11] represents some of her best writing, and was one of Mary Shelley's favourite books. It also reveals the extraordinary pluck, perhaps born of despair, of a professional woman, willing to travel alone with a small child at the height of a war – a situation almost unheard of in the eighteenth century.

Although the mission was a commercial success, Mary returned to London in 1795 to find Imlay involved with an actress. Faced with the bitter reality of this rejection, she attempted suicide by plunging into the Thames, jumping from Putney Bridge. Only the buoyancy of her dress and the gallantry of a witness, who dived after her, saved her life. The suicide note she left for Imlay reads as follows:[12]

I shall make no comments on your conduct or any appeal to the world. Let my wrongs sleep with me! Soon, very soon, I shall be at peace. When you receive this, my burning head will be cold.

I would encounter a thousand deaths, rather than a night like the last. Your treatment has thrown my mind into a state of chaos; yet I am serene. I go to find comfort; and my only fear is that my poor body will be insulted by an endeavour to recall my hated existence. But I shall plunge into the Thames where there is the least chance of my being snatched from the death I seek.

God bless you! May you never know by experience what you have made me endure. Should your sensibility ever awake, remorse will find its way to your heart; and, in the midst of business and sensual pleasures, *I shall appear before you*, the victim of your deviation from rectitude. [author's italics]

Mary, as we have mentioned, had first met William Godwin in September 1791, while a guest at the house of her publisher, Johnson. That brief encounter had not augured well for a meaningful relationship. Judging from Godwin's notes, it would seem that not only was the political publicist unimpressed by Mary's writings (for offences against grammar and other minute points of composition), by her negative, censorious way of looking at people and events of the day (in contrast to his optimism), but he was particularly angered that Mary monopolized the conversation with Paine, who was 'not by instinct a great talker'. They parted, mutually displeased with each other. They met again in 1796 after Mary's return from Scandinavia. By this time Godwin had apparently changed his mind concerning Mary's writing. Referring to Mary's travelogue, he wrote: 'If ever there was a book calculated to make a man in love with its author ... this appears to me to be the book.'[13]

With Imlay relegated to her past, Mary began to take solace in conversing with the austere philosopher, visiting him frequently at his lodgings at Hatton Garden near Somers Town. Although theirs was never a passionate relationship, affection grew into love out of genuine, mutual respect, as well as Mary's desire to find a stable home for Fanny. Godwin describes the progress of their courtship as follows:[14]

> The partiality we conceived for each other was in that mode which I have always regarded as the purest and most refined style of love. It grew with equal advances in the mind of each. It would have been impossible for the most minute observer to have said who was before, and who was after. One sex did not take the priority which long-established custom has awarded it, nor the other overstep that delicacy which is so severely imposed. I am not conscious that either party can assume to have been the agent or the patient, the toil-spreader or the prey, in the affair. When, in the course of things, the disclosure came, there was nothing, in a manner, for either party to disclose to the other. ... It was friendship melting into love.

Neither, of course, believed in marriage, and they continued to live separately. It was only when Mary became pregnant that she insisted on marriage in order not to expose the future child to the vicissitudes to which poor Fanny had been exposed. They were married in a private ceremony at St Pancras Church on 29 March 1797.[15]

Although others have highlighted the impact of William Godwin upon Mary Shelley's work, he was probably a lesser influence on her life and work than was her mother. The admiration for her father, which she formed early in her life, was never completely shaken, however, in spite of countless disappointments.

William Godwin

William Godwin was born 3 March 1756, in Cambridgeshire, the son of a Dissenting minister. His family was large – thirteen children in all – and his early training was essentially religious. At the age of twenty-three he entered Hoxton College, where he finished his education. Leaving college he began a career as a minister, but moved to London by 1783, and began to support himself by writing.

Steeped in French philosophy, and an active sympathizer with the principles of the French Revolution, William Godwin was a very compelling and influential philosophic radical of late eighteenth-century England; his many followers considered him a demigod, a philosopher-king, and compared him to Voltaire, who ennobled all that he touched. Godwin's reputation, however, was essentially based upon a single work: *An Enquiry Concerning Political Justice and its Influence on General Virtue and Happiness*, published in 1793,[16] just a year after *A Vindication of the Rights of Woman*. The work is generally considered a classic, and had some impact on eighteenth-century English social and political thought, presenting, as it did, the more radical views of French revolutionary philosophy on morals and government. Like his wife, Godwin wrote massively (no less than thirty books in all), on a great variety of subjects which included fiction, biography, children's books, and the occult. Apart from *Political Justice*, two books made a particular impact on Mary Shelley: *The Adventures of Caleb Williams* (1794),[17] which argued the principle that man is the most formidable enemy of man, and *St Leon: A Tale of the Sixteenth Century* (1799),[18] the history of an alchemist seeking 'the philosopher's stone'. Interestingly enough, the travels of St Leon, like those of Bram Stoker's hero, led him to Transylvania, where he encountered a genuine native, Prince Bethlem Gabor, a Hungarian aristocrat, Nadasdy, who bears the name of the husband of the Blood Countess, Elizabeth Bathory (indicating that Godwin, like Stoker, was familiar with East European history). Although Godwin's *Lives of the Necromancers* was not published until 1834[19] – long after *Frankenstein* – the subtitle of the book indicates that it was an account of the most eminent persons in successive ages who have claimed for themselves, or to whom has been imputed by others, the exercise of magical power. The work indicates that such topics as necromancy, alchemy, Rosicrucians, Albertus Magnus, Cornelius Agrippa, Paracelsus, astrology, and witchcraft were familiar to the Godwin household.

In addition to writing, Godwin became the spiritual mentor of an élite of brilliant men of letters and science, who gathered at his house. These included the poet Samuel Taylor Coleridge, the author of *The Rime of the Ancient Mariner* and the poem 'Christabel', whose strange association with the Frankenstein legend will be developed in Chapter 5, and Sir Humphry Davy, a celebrated natural philosopher and chemist, who died at Geneva in 1829.

Notwithstanding the prestige of William Godwin the political scientist and mentor, Godwin the man exhibited few endearing qualities: he was generally cold and calculating, passionless, and undemonstrative, and is reported to have lacked a sense of humour. His unattractive personality was compounded by his homeliness; he had a thick, vulgar nose. He was, however, bound to truth and justice in his relationships as well as in his principles.

With the outbreak of the war against France in 1793, and the excesses of the French revolutionaries, Godwin was considered a subversive by the British government. His prestige, as well as the royalties from his books, fell rapidly, and his unending financial woes began.

Within a year of Mary Wollstonecraft's death, Godwin had proposed and been rejected three times.[20] He finally married his next-door neighbour, Mary Jane Clairmont, in December of 1801, a widow with two children – Charles and Claire. It is reported that Mary Jane first introduced herself to Godwin with the words, 'Is it possible that I behold the immortal Godwin?'[21]

Although the background of Mary Jane 'Clairmont' is obscure, it seems that she had not been married prior to her involvement with Godwin, and that her two children were illegitimate. It is believed that she was born on 27 April 1778 (same day, but not year, as Mary Wollstonecraft, and her daughter Claire), and that she was of Swiss ancestry. The name 'Clairmont' is certainly an assumed name. She had had a liaison with a Swiss merchant, Charles Gaulis, who was the son of a Syndic of Lausanne. (The family still survives in that city.) Mary Jane's own maiden name was either Val or Devereux; probably the former as the name is still current around Lake Léman. After the death of Gaulis on a business journey in 1796, Mary Jane moved to England. Claire and Charles Clairmont were thus probably Swiss on both sides and from the Geneva area.

The birth of a son William in 1803 only exacerbated the complicated relationships in the Godwin household. Fanny Imlay (born 1794) was the eldest of the stepchildren, a shy, introspective, sensitive, and kind girl whose suffering was reflected in the sad expression on her rather plain face (she was to commit suicide in 1816). The next to the oldest child was Charles Gaulis (the eldest son of Mary Jane Clairmont), who was born in 1795. Charles was a difficult child who eventually became tutor to the sons of the emperor Franz Joseph. There followed a daughter, variously called Claire, Clara, or Mary Jane, who was born in 1798. With her black hair, olive complexion, cherubic face, and dark eyes, she looked distinctively Latin, and was passionate, violent, prone to fits of hysteria, as well as generous, indefatigable, romantic, adventurous – and conceited. Claire fancied a stage or singing career – she had a beautiful singing voice. Even as a young girl, Claire envied the moral and intellectual superiority of her stepsister Mary.

Mary Jane Clairmont has been described as a vile-tempered and foul-mouthed infernal 'bitch' who wore green spectacles; her critics bore down hard upon her obscure origins. Making allowances for these unfavourable family circumstances, for Godwin's difficult character and lack of paternal instincts, and taking the increasingly tight financial situation into account, it is almost a miracle that Mary Jane managed as well as she did. She was by no means unattractive, and could be a good hostess and housekeeper. Although not an intellectual, she was practical, and had a certain gift for business. Since Godwin's books were no longer selling, she persuaded her husband to open a children's publishing house and library. The business did not make them rich, but it helped make ends meet. Mary Jane also used her language talents to translate many Swiss or German children's tales into English: such was the classic *Swiss Family Robinson*, translated from the book of Johann Rudolf Wyss, originally published in Zurich in 1812.[22] She was also probably familiar with the compilations of the Brothers Grimm, who had collected old folkloric tales from the German peasants and had published them from 1812 on. A tale about a Knight Georg, who kills a monster at Castle Frankenstein, was published by the Brothers Grimm in 1816,[23] although Mary Shelley may have heard it much earlier.

The Godwin dwelling at Skinner Street was unhealthy, even considering the standards of the time. It had, in fact, been condemned. Various members of the Godwin household had complained of the dampness and of a musty atmosphere. The ground floor, with its large display window, was reserved for business, and the counter was built low enough for young children to be able to peer over and glance at the latest titles of fairy tales. To reach the living quarters where the Godwins entertained, one had to climb a narrow stairway that led to the parlour or drawing room. Square-shaped, with a vaulted ceiling and a central fireplace, the room was dark and dusty because of the lack of windows and the innumerable rows of shelves where Godwin's precious books were stored. The cheap, soiled furniture only served to reinforce the faded and gloomy atmosphere.

The area around Skinner Street was equally decayed. About one hundred yards from the door on Newgate Street was Old Bailey, where public executions were legion. Whenever a criminal was hanged, the bell on nearby St Sepulchre's Church tolled, and crowds gathered. The street itself was filled with coffee dealers, oil shops, food warehouses, cheap cloth manufacturers, and tailors. Life at Skinner Street was not entirely gloomy, however; the house was continually filled with distinguished visitors (among them Wordsworth) who came to discuss the latest gossip or the great topics of the day. For the children there were also many family excursions – out to dinner or to the theatre.

Mary Wollstonecraft Shelley

What kind of a girl was Mary, the daughter of Mary Wollstonecraft, a celebrated woman of the eighteenth century, who was one of the founders of the women's emancipation movement, and William Godwin, the well-known philosopher and novelist? Dowden describes Mary's first encounter with Shelley after Mary had returned from a long visit to the Baxters, friends of Godwin's, in Scotland.[24]

[A] girl in her seventeenth year, with shapely golden head, a face very pale and pure, great forehead, earnest hazel eyes, and an expression at once of sensibility and firmness about her delicately curved lips. It is possible that Shelley may once have seen her as a child in 1812; in the following summer when he was in London, Mary was away at Dundee. Whether he saw her or not on previous occasions, certainly now for the first time he felt her rare attraction. The daughter of Godwin and Mary Wollstonecraft had gifts of heart and mind such as Shelley had never hitherto known in woman. 'She is singularly bold, somewhat imperious, and active in mind' – so Godwin described Mary at the age of fifteen; 'her desire of knowledge is great, and her perseverance in everything she undertakes almost invincible.' From her father she had inherited clearness

and precision of intellect, firmness of will, and a certain quie-
tude of manner, which sometimes gave way before an outbreak of strong feeling; for under this quiet bearing lay her
mother's sensibility and ardour, with an imaginative power
which quickened and widened her sympathies. Though of a
temper naturally more conservative than that of Godwin or
her mother, Mary had breathed during her entire life an atmosphere of free thought; she could not live in Godwin's house
and meet Godwin's friends without insensibly learning to consider the facts of life from the rationalist or critical point of
view.

If the watercolour of Mary painted at Geneva in 1816 is
accurate, her long, fine, golden hair had tinges of red. She
wore it tightly combed with braids on the crown of her head,
adding to the severity of her countenance. Later she let her
locks fall to her shoulders, making her face appear even
tinier. Her swan-like neck and elegant sloping shoulders were
particularly pleasing to the eye. By modern standards Mary
can be described as petite, only five feet four inches tall, but
she had a good figure, carried herself well, and moved grace-
fully. Most observers were also struck by the winning expres-
siveness and sparkle of her eyes, the vivacity of her face when
animated in conversation, and by her general look of intelligence. They also noted the conventionality of her dress.

Mary's character has often been described by her father,
Percy Bysshe, and her biographers. One passage – often
quoted – written by her father when he sent the fifteen-year-
old girl to live with the Baxters, is a subtler character analysis
than is immediately apparent: 'I am not, therefore, a perfect
judge of Mary's character. I believe that she has nothing of
what is commonly called vices, and that she has considerable
talent ... I am anxious that she should be brought up ... like a
philosopher, even like a cynic. It will greatly add to the
strength and worth of her character. ... I wish, too, that she
should be *excited* to industry. She has occasionally great perseverance, but occasionally, too, she stands in great need to
be roused' [author's italics].[25] This character was largely hewn
by the adverse circumstances of her youth, which somewhat

paralleled that of her mother. Her stepmother tended to favour her own children, and Mary's reluctance to perform household chores, combined with her intellectual predilections, did not endear her to Mary Jane Godwin. Her father, sensing her unhappiness in the household, sent her away, at first to a pension on the Kentish coast, then to Dundee, 'the Geneva of Scotland', on the estuary of the river Tay, where Mary spent two relatively happy years from 1812 to 1814 with the Baxters.

Mary's escape from life on Skinner Street was to create her own world, where she might take refuge, inhabited by people she admired or read about. Such daydreaming is obviously what Mary meant when she alluded to the formation of castles in the air, which gave her such intense pleasure. Inevitably she jotted down her thoughts, but always as an imitation, 'doing as others have done' rather than 'putting down suggestions of my own mind'.

Her place of refuge was her mother's grave. Her frequent visits may have been prompted by little more than a desire to escape from the noise and chores of Skinner Street – or perhaps by a desire to be closer to the mother she had never known. 'When Mary was 17,' writes Samuel Rosenberg, 'she began taking her books and writing materials to the nearby Old St Pancras Church, where her parents had been married and where her mother was buried. There, seated in the graveyard behind the church, the haunted girl read and read and wrote and wrote under the willow tree that drooped mournfully over her mother's grave.'[26]

There is still another striking passage: this one in Mary's novel *Falkner*, generally autobiographical in nature, that may be an allusion to these cemetery visitations:[27]

A little girl, unnoticed and alone, was wont, each evening, to trip over the sands – to scale, with light steps, the cliff, which was of no gigantic height, and then, unlatching the low, white gate of the church-yard, to repair to one corner, where the boughs of the near trees shadowed over two graves ... This tomb was inscribed to the memory of Edwin Raby, but the neighbouring and less honoured grave claimed more of the child's attention – for her mother lay beneath the unrecorded turf.

Beside this grassy hillock she would sit and talk to herself, and play, till, warned home by the twilight, she knelt and said her little prayer, and, with a 'Good night, mamma,' took leave of a spot with which was associated the being whose caresses and love she called to mind, hoping that *one day* she might again enjoy them.

In these moments of solitude Mary may have developed the beginnings of an adulation for her mother. She may also have felt guilty for her mother's death; her birth had brought a premature end to this extraordinarily gifted woman's career. In time, she learned to emulate her, referring to her as, 'One of those beings who appear once perhaps in a generation, to gild humanity with a ray which no difference of opinion nor chance of circumstances can cloud. Her genius was undeniable ... Her sound understanding, her intrepidity, her sensibility and eager sympathy, stamped all her writings with force and truth, and endowed them with a tender charm that enchants while it enlightens. She was one whom all loved who had ever seen her ... no one who has ever seen her speaks of her without enthusiastic veneration.'[28] After due reflection Mary's act of atonement was to pursue Mary Wollstonecraft's work. She early began to map out her career as a writer, seeking the kind of immortality that would crown her mother's accomplishments.

Mary Shelley presented two faces to the world: one was a polite, silent, placid, gentle, and melancholic young girl, who kept things very much to herself. To some she seemed conventional, and some of the artifice may have moulded itself upon her character to the end of her life. For instance, she could not bring herself to read at the British Museum Library in London because it was 'not respectable' for a woman to do so. When *Frankenstein* was first published in 1818, it was not proper for a member of her sex to append her name, particularly to a book of this nature ... hence it was printed anonymously. She liked to make a good impression and took great pains to satisfy the standards of the people she met.

Her other face was hidden behind this phlegmatic, reserved young lady, and occasionally surfaced to break the façade. Depending upon the circumstances, she could suddenly become an extrovert, be flighty, giddy, wild, even flirtatious in the presence of male company; at other times she could be impatient, expressive, bad-tempered, and irritable, qualities which made her a difficult person to live with.

There can be no question of Mary's deep need for love and affection, and 'her reserve was also a cloak for strong feelings not always perfectly controlled',[29] though she was not so passionate as her mother. Although Mary believed in free love, it would be fair to presume that with few exceptions most of her male relationships were 'communications of spirit' in the Godwinian sense. Sensually she was not easily aroused and Shelley, on one occasion, noted that her serenity in the end seemed even to him like the light of the cold chaste moon.[30]

What of her intellect? It would have been difficult for the daughter of Mary Wollstonecraft and William Godwin not to have been intelligent and well read. By the standards of eighteenth-century England, Mary, like her famous mother, possessed and exhibited exceptional intelligence. Yet, in spite of her enormous reading list – of which she kept only a partial record in her journal – there was little consistency or direction in Mary's schooling. With some guidance from her father and the Baxters, and later, a great deal more from Shelley, Mary was essentially self-taught. At idle moments she would steal into her father's study and pick books at random from the shelves or listen to occasional conversations in the drawing room that as a child she could half understand. Study of the 'greats' was relatively easy reading, but with science, which interested her, things had to be made easy, and one wonders to what extent she understood discussions of the laws of electricity or those of the circulation of the blood. Her reluctance to embark upon medical or scientific explanations were as much due to delicacy as to simple ignorance of fact and naivety. In essence, Mary had read voraciously and indiscriminately, had been taught innumerable half-assimilated lessons, but she was hardly cultured in the fullest sense – even her English at times was deficient.

Mary's biographers and critics have alluded to her lack of originality. Her admirer Trelawny noted that Mary was a most conventional slave, and was devoid of imagination. Elizabeth Nitchie notes that: 'Writing autobiography as she always did, no matter how it was disguised, she [Mary] incorporated in all her work not only the persons and situations which she knew from personal experience, but also the places she visited, the people whose nature and customs and costumes she observed and the social and political conditions under which she lived.'[31]

These comments by her biographers suggest that the models and settings for Mary Shelley's *Frankenstein* probably emerged from Mary's environment and travels, rather than appearing 'ready-made' in a nightmare. For the complex personality of Victor Frankenstein, the scientist, there must have been a flesh-and-blood model.

Percy Bysshe Shelley

Percy Bysshe was a tall and large-boned, but fragile-looking young man, who perhaps appeared smaller than he was because he stooped. He had flowing, rich brown hair, large, luminous blue eyes, and a pink complexion. His gestures were abrupt, sometimes even violent, and his voice excruciatingly shrill. His temperament was kind and gentle, but highly excitable. His dress was generally careless but his presence was, according to his closest friend, Thomas Jefferson Hogg, 'extremely powerful'. His features 'breathed an animation, a fire, an enthusiasm, a vivid and preternatural intelligence, that I have never met in any other countenance'.[32]

Shelley was born in August, 1792, of an established family at Field Place in Sussex, the oldest among four sisters and one brother. His prestigious schooling was consistent with his breeding: Sion House Academy, Eton, and University College, Oxford.

The tenor of Shelley's years at Oxford was generally unconventional and radical; his convictions were strong and his arguments impetuous. As an atheist, he was expelled from Oxford along with Hogg for refusing to disavow a pamphlet Shelley had published entitled *The Necessity of Atheism*. Shelley was also a pacifist, favoured liberation of women, and, like Mary, evidently believed in free love. Hogg attests to the fact that he maintained a largely vegetarian diet, and drank much tea. Shelley was continually espousing good causes, many of them revolutionary for his time, and in Ireland at a later point in his life he promoted Irish nationalism.

At the early age of twenty-two, he was already a poet and author, as well as a brilliant conversationalist, who held his audiences enthralled. He was a voracious reader and could converse on the most extraordinary range of topics: the aesthetic values of Ancient Greece, the virtues of the Roman Republic, the humanism of the Renaissance, the Enlightenment and the Age of Reason, the libertarianism and egalitarianism of Rousseau's *Social Contract* recast into the Godwinian mould, the poetry of Wordsworth and Coleridge. Hogg maintains of Shelley that he read sixteen hours a day out of twenty-four.

In spite of his many accomplishments, Shelley protested that he was ostracized by everyone, and disinherited by his conventional, narrow-minded family (hardly likely to endear him to Godwin, who was banking upon Shelley's inheritance).

Besides poetry and dialectic, Shelley's other fascination was science – a fascination that he shared with Godwin. Like Godwin, he had studied the works of the famous Paracelsus, who later taught medicine at Ingolstadt. As a boy, recalls Dowden, 'science transformed the world into a place of enchantment'.[33] He borrowed forbidden books on chemistry constantly. At Sion House, Shelley had been exposed to androids, or mechanical toys that functioned like humans – a product of the scientific genius of Adam Walker, who had lectured there. Later, at Eton, his room must have resembled an alchemist's laboratory, with strange-coloured powders, vials, and odd smells and fumes issuing from his room. He reportedly would return to Field Place for the holidays 'with face and hands smudged and stained by explosive powders and virulent acids'.[34] Once, he 'half-poisoned himself with some arsenical mixture'. Shelley was equally overawed by the new-found powers of electricity and had, in fact, purchased a small galvanic battery from an attendant of Walker while at Eton. There follows a tale in which his tutor, Mr Bethell, 'suspecting from strange noises overheard that his pupil was engaged in nefarious scientific pursuits', appeared without notice in Shelley's room to find the poet half-enveloped in a blue flame.[35]

'What on earth are you doing, Shelley?'
    'Please, sir,' came the answer in the quietest tone, 'I am raising the devil.' 'And what in the world is this?' resumed the pedagogue, seizing hold of some mysterious-looking apparatus on the table. In an instant the intruder was thrown back ... against the wall, having undesignedly exhibited a very pretty electrical experiment, and received an unstinted discharge.

At Oxford Hogg describes Shelley's room as even more elaborate: containing, among other things, an electrical machine, an air pump, the galvanic trough, a solar microscope, and large glass jars and receivers.[36] After his expulsion from Oxford, Shelley had also given some thought to becoming a physician; he had begun seriously to study anatomy at St Bartholomew's Hospital in London.

Shortly after his expulsion from Oxford, Shelley married Harriet Westbrook, the youngest daughter of a coffee-house owner. (Harriet had carried money to Shelley from his sisters while he was penniless in London, just after his expulsion – his father had disowned him.) Described by Hogg as 'Lovely ... bright, blooming, radiant with youth, health and beauty,'[37] Harriet was but a mere schoolgirl when they married – mostly out of obligation, Harriet entrusting herself to the poet's protection rather than be forced to return to school where she had been taunted for being the friend of an 'atheist'. Although Harriet was uncultured and naive, the marriage was initially blissful (there were two children, Eliza Ianthe, b. 1813, and Charles Bysshe, b. 1814). Harriet also proved to be a gentle and faithful wife (she, after all, refused the advances of Hogg while Shelley was away). After the birth of Ianthe, the marriage began to disintegrate, however, probably because of the overbearing and constant attendance of Harriet's older sister, also called Eliza, whom Shelley grew to despise, and Harriet's increasingly extravagant material demands.

Certainly by the time Shelley met Mary Godwin, the marriage was beyond repair. Yet, Shelley made continual bids to Harriet for reconciliation, and even, in a desperate effort, remarried Harriet according to the rites of the English Church. But by July, Harriet had removed to Bath, and remained completely alienated from him. Shelley by this time had begun to doubt that she had ever loved him, and suspected that Charles was not his legitimate son. Shelley was at that time suffering physically from sharp spasms of nervous pain, seeking relief in excessive doses of laudanum, and Peacock writes of him that:[38]

> [H]e showed in his looks, in his gestures, in his speech, the state of a mind 'suffering, like a little kingdom, the nature of an insurrection'. His eyes were bloodshot, his hair and dress disordered. He caught up a bottle of laudanum, and said, 'I never part from this.' He added, 'I am always repeating to myself your lines from Sophocles –
>
> > 'Man's happiest lot is not to be;
> > And when we tread life's thorny steep,
> > Most blest are they who earliest free
> > Descend to death's eternal sleep.'

On 3 January 1812, William Godwin, whose affairs were going from bad to worse, had received a 'fan letter' from a certain Percy Bysshe Shelley, then at Keswick, and the author of *Queen Mab*. The letter was somewhat unflattering, since the author had only just discovered that Godwin was alive: 'I had enrolled your name in the list of the honourable dead,'[39] he noted. Shelley followed this letter by another, in which he

gave certain autobiographical details mentioning the problems he had had with his father, and including the fact that
Shelley was 'the son of a man of fortune in Sussex' and 'heir
by entail to an estate of £6000 per annum'.[40] Godwin obviously saw some advantage in pursuing this friendship, and
answered with a few words of parental advice (warning him
against offending his father excessively). Further correspondence followed and finally an invitation for Shelley and his
attractive young wife Harriet to visit with Godwin at his
home on 4 October 1812. The meeting was followed by
others and the financial commitment of Shelley to his mentor was deepened. By 1814 Shelley made almost daily visits to
Skinner Street, now rarely accompanied by Harriet, and was a
constant dinner guest. It was certainly during one of these
visits to Skinner Street that Shelley met Mary Godwin. By
June of that year, they seem to have become very involved:
Hogg describes the poet's visit to Skinner Street on the evening of 8 June. Godwin was apparently not there, and Shelley
seemed displeased at not finding the author of *Political
Justice* at home:[41]

> 'Where is Godwin?' he asked me several times, as if I knew. I
> did not know, and, to say the truth, I did not care. He contin-
> ued his uneasy promenade; and I stood reading the names of
> old English authors on the backs of the venerable volumes,
> when the door was partially and softly opened. A thrilling
> voice called, 'Shelley!' A thrilling voice answered, 'Mary!' And
> he darted out of the room, like an arrow from the bow of the
> far-shooting king. A very young female, fair and fair-haired,
> pale indeed, and with a piercing look, wearing a frock of tar-
> tan, an unusual dress in London at that time, had called him
> out of the room.

We can judge the depth of feeling from a few words which
Mary scribbled at the end of *Queen Mab*, which the poet had
presented to her, and which bears the inscription:[42]

> 'You see, Mary, I have not forgotten you.' The flyleaf at the
> end of the same volume has an inscription in Mary's hand-

writing, which is dated July 1814: 'This book is sacred to me and as no other creature shall ever look into it I may write in it what I please – yet what shall I write – that I love the author beyond all powers of expression and that I am parted from him dearest and only love – by that love we have promised to each other although I may not be yours I can never be another's. But I am thine exclusively thine

'By the kiss of love, the glance none saw beside,
  The smile none else might understand,
The whispered thought of hearts allied,
  The pressure of the thrilling hand

'I have pledged myself to thee and sacred is the gift. I remember your words – you are now Mary going to mix with many and for a moment I shall depart but in the solitude of your chamber I shall be with you – yes you are ever with me sacred vision –'

It seems that Godwin – who remained close to both Harriet and Shelley, and who had tried many times to reconcile them – disapproved of the relationship. Earlier he had had a serious talk with Mary, after which he wrote to Shelley. (Mary probably promised her father to break off the romance, for Shelley now ceased to dine at Godwin's house.) Shelley banned from Skinner Street, the two lovers continued to meet at the tomb of Mary Wollstonecraft in St Pancras Cemetery.

Judging from old prints, St Pancras – now a public park – must have been a peaceful and bucolic place in the early nineteenth century. Situated on the outskirts of London, it sat in the middle of a pasture, with the Fleet river at the foot of a hill – at that time not yet surrounded by the sprawling suburbs of Somers Town and Camden Town, or the railroads and gas works which have since been constructed close by. In those days Mary Wollstonecraft's grave was shaded by a flourishing willow tree. Of course, Godwin, Harriet, and Claire Clairmont (who occasionally accompanied them) were well aware that the two were meeting at St Pancras. Here Mary confided her ambitions to Shelley. Shelley, for his part, had learned to share in Mary's idealization of her mother. As the dramatic story of Mary Wollstonecraft unfolded, Shelley's admiration for the dead mother expressed itself in greater love for the daughter.

Compelled by the trying circumstances of Harriet's alienation, and Shelley's new passion for Mary, the two made plans for an elopement – a journey that would have many parallels with the travels of their spirited and spiritual mentor, Mary Wollstonecraft. They sought happiness on the European Continent, even at the risk of alienating society and parents.

It is interesting to speculate on conversations of a different nature that may have been pursued well after twilight in the darkened cemetery. As a boy, Shelley had 'devoured tales of haunted castles, necromancers, bandits and murderers'.[43] Even at Eton, Dowden claims that, 'He had faith in apparitions and the evocation of the dead; his sleep was afflicted by frightful dreams.'[44] Although he later became an atheist, Shelley believed in a great variety of spirits; he sought spirits, devils, vampires, all sorts of ghosts wherever he could find them – in abandoned alleys, woods, caves and, naturally, in cemeteries. His own words in 'Hymn to Intellectual Beauty' confess his fondness for dabbling in the occult.[45]

> While yet a boy I sought for ghosts, and sped
>   Through many a listening chamber, cave, and ruin,
>   And starlight wood, with fearful steps pursuing
> Hopes of high talk with the departed dead.
> I called on poisonous names with which our youth is fed.
>   I was not heard, I saw them not;
>   When, musing deeply on the lot
> Of life, at that sweet time when winds are wooing
>   All vital things that wake to bring
>   News of birds and blossoming,
>   Sudden thy shadow fell on me: –
> I shrieked and clasped my hands in ecstasy!

I vowed that I would dedicate my powers
To thee and thine: have I not kept the vow?

Since neither Mary nor Shelley believed in a formal marriage, on a certain unrecorded daybreak in early summer of 1814, Mary Wollstonecraft Godwin and Percy Bysshe Shelley, with tears in their eyes, may have pledged each other eternal love at the tombstone of Mary Wollstonecraft in Old Camden Town. Mary Wollstonecraft was not only their sole witness; symbolically, the spirit of the mother had also performed the marriage rites.

The escape had all the suspense of a Brontë novel: Mary had spent the night of 27 July without sleep, packing the bare essentials in a trunk (she later lost it in Paris); she had stuffed into it as many of Mary Wollstonecraft's books as it would hold (including Godwin's biography of Mary Wollstonecraft), and Mary Wollstonecraft's *Letters Written during a Short Residence in Sweden, Norway, and Denmark*.

Shelley, for his part 'ordered a chaise to be ready by 4 o'clock,' and then 'watched until the lightning and the stars became pale. At length it was 4. I believed it not possible that we should succeed; still there appeared to lurk some danger even in certainty.' Finally, at daybreak, waiting in the chaise, Shelley exclaimed, 'I saw her, she came to me. Yet one quarter of an hour remained. Still some arrangement must be made and she left me for a short time. How dreadful did this time appear; it seemed that we trifled with life and hope; a few minutes passed, she was in my arms – we were safe; we were on our road to Dover.'[46]

3

The Elopement to the Continent: 1814

The account of the Shelley elopement to the Continent in 1814 is based upon several journals: *The History of a Six Weeks' Tour through a Part of France, Switzerland, Germany, and Holland*,[1] jointly written by Mary and Shelley, and printed in a slightly altered form in 1817, *Mary Shelley's Journal*,[2] and *The Journals of Claire Clairmont*.[3] Of the last two, Claire's journal is more detailed and supplements the scanty information given by Mary and Shelley, who sometimes would let days pass without an entry, only to group the events of several days under one date.

Neither diary can be considered completely accurate, however. Given her volatile temperament, Claire was hardly a trustworthy or impartial witness: she tended at times to be secretive and intense. Since she completed the manuscript years later from her notes, her memory sometimes failed. Nevertheless, in some ways she could be irritatingly precise: for instance, the mysterious crosses that appear with some regularity in her journal, according to at least one expert, merely recorded her menstrual periods, during which time she may have suffered 'her horrors', often alluded to by Shelley. On the other hand, there is abundant evidence that whole passages in her journal were crossed out, written over, or even torn to pieces – such was the case with the crucial year 1816, which, as we have noted, is missing.

We were at first inclined to give greater weight to Mary's testimony on account of her more placid temperament and disposition. However, the discrepancy in the following passage startled us: 'we were passing through the Rhine celebrated in the Third Canto of *Childe Harold's Pilgrimage*, and read these verses with delight, as they conjured before us the lovely scenes with the truth and vividness of a painting'[4] – Byron did not write his celebrated 'Third Canto' until the famous summer of 1816, two years after Mary's journey down the Rhine! Mary was evidently citing this passage with dramatic intent. We reasoned, therefore, that if Mary was guilty of adding material, she might be equally guilty – if it suited her story – of not revealing certain points. In fact, we do know that, like her stepsister Claire, Mary had also a tendency to hide unpleasant facts and to blot out indiscretions, or any circumstances that were not likely to enhance what we shall refer to as 'The Shelley Legend'. We are not alluding here to the innumerable errors of fact, spelling, or chronology, which have been noted by André Koszul.[5] Mary can be accused as well of misspelling the names of obscure French villages: she wrote Mort for Morre and Noè for Nodz. A far more serious problem for scholars, however, is the mysterious disappearance of her travel notes for the months of June, and part of July, 1816, during which time *Frankenstein* was being written. Is it mere coincidence that the diaries of both half-sisters are missing for that crucial period?

Travelling with Mary and Percy Bysshe was Mary's stepsister, Claire Clairmont. Claire, whose peculiar relationship with Shelley will be discussed later, had known of the romance between Mary and Percy, and had even occasionally accompanied the lovers to St Pancras; she had also acted as a helpful 'buffer' at home.

Claire claims that when she left the Skinner Street house with Mary, she thought they were only going for a walk. It is possible that Mary may not have taken Claire into her confidence. When they met Shelley in the chaise, it seems they persuaded her to accompany them because of her skill with French. (Mary's knowledge of French was slight: she wrote bat*a*lier for bat*e*lier, and av*e*lenche for av*a*lanche.)

Even as he watched the white cliffs of Dover recede into the distance while crossing the stormy channel, Shelley 'was still worried 'lest our pursuers should arrive'. (Mary was seasick throughout the journey and Shelley commented: 'She lay in my arms through the night; the little strength which remained to my own exhausted frame was all expended in keeping her head in rest on my bosom.') He was not disappointed: Shelley comments in the journal that, in Calais, Captain Davison informed the fugitives that 'a fat lady had arrived, who had said that I had run away with her daughter.' Convinced as she was that her stepdaughter had masterminded the entire plot, Mary Jane Godwin had pursued the trio across the Channel. There followed a stormy interview with Claire, during which Mrs Godwin used every argument to persuade her daughter to return with her. Should Claire refuse her offer, she would denounce the fugitives to the municipality of Paris. All entreaties were unavailing, however, and Shelley accidentally met the woman in the streets of Calais, preparing to embark after the failure of her mission.

A few of the statistics concerning the Shelleys' elopement to the Continent are impressive enough: approximately 800 miles by foot, mule, horse and carriage, canoe, and boat – 48 days in all (from 28 July to 13 September), with hardly a moment's rest; crossing six different customs: France, Switzerland, Baden, Hesse, Prussia, and Holland; visiting famous cities of Europe: Paris, Lucerne, Basel, Strasbourg, Mannheim, Mainz, Cologne, Rotterdam – all of this on less than £30 pounds – no mean achievement for novices. Their journey even rivals the voyages of Mary Wollstonecraft, a seasoned traveller.

It is important at this time to recall the situation on the Continent of Europe in the summer of 1814. The Shelleys were among the first English tourists in twenty-one years to indulge in the 'Grand Tour' (since 1793 to be exact, when Britain joined the coalition against France). Europe was devastated in the wake of Napoleon's exile and terrorized by Cossacks, bandits, and retired soldiers who raped, pillaged, and burned what they could not consume on the spot. Supporters of Bonaparte battled the Bourbon supporters of Louis XVIII on the soil of France, the Germanies, Holland, even traditionally neutral Switzerland. There was in addition a climate of resentment against those 'perfidious' English, who had led other nations to fight their own wars. Communications were badly disrupted: bridges had been blown up, provisioning had broken down, and there was a scarcity of bread, clean linen, and accommodation.

To make matters worse, the Shelley party had no money. By the time they reached Paris, little was left of the original sum that Shelley had scraped together for the journey. They spent days as 'prisoners in Paris', wrote Shelley, awaiting certain sums that they had been led to expect. Finally, after some effort they found a French money-lender, Tavernier, who procured them the glorious sum of £60 pounds, which hardly sufficed, and Shelley was forced to sell his gold watch and chain which brought exactly '8 napoleons and 5 francs'.

The objective of the travellers was to settle in Switzerland – the paradise of Mary Wollstonecraft, who, as we have noted, had a fantasy about settling there, and had planned to travel there on at least two occasions: she was thwarted once in 1793, when she had to abandon the idea because of problems in obtaining a passport from Paris. After the breakup of the Imlay affair in 1796, she had thought of abandoning England for Switzerland, but marriage to Godwin halted her plans.

The French portion of the journey, although entertaining, is only of marginal interest to us. One thing was certain: they had to see Paris – the Paris of Mary Wollstonecraft that they had read about in her autobiography – this was their guidebook. From the shabby Hôtel de Vienne in the heart of the city, they visited the obvious sites: the Louvre, the Church of Notre Dame, Place Vendôme and of course, the Tuileries, where Mary Wollstonecraft had witnessed the last days of the French Monarchy in the summer of 1792, when the palace was stormed by the people. The fugitives' attempt to re-live the adventures of Mary Wollstonecraft was carried to the point of trying to locate some of the intimate friends who had belonged to her 'circle', such as Helen Maria Williams, who could not be found.

Beyond Paris, their itinerary to the Swiss border intrigued us sufficiently to follow it ourselves: Charenton, Guignes, Provins, Nogent-sur-Seine, St Aubin, Trois-Maisons, Pavillon, Echemine, Troyes, Vendeuvre-sur-Barse, the valley of the Aube, Clairmont, Langres, Champlitte, Prelot, Gray, Besançon, Morre, Nodz, and Pontarlier. This route is definitely not the shortest way to Switzerland; nor does it always follow any main roads or scenic routes. From the point of view of culture and history, our trip was not as rewarding as some alternative routes that we could have taken. Our sole consolation was a visit to de Gaulle's tomb at Colombey-les-Deux-Eglises, near the river Aube. The only explanation for Shelley's choice of the route is that he was avoiding the main thoroughfares and heeding the advice of their Paris innkeeper who warned them that the 'ladies would be kidnapped', presumably by Cossacks. It is also possible that they thought supplies would be easier to obtain in small villages. They were, in any event, looking for seclusion and they had always had a preference for the quiet pleasures of the countryside. The following passage from Mary's *Journal* is an indication:

> From the summit of one of the hills we see the whole expanse of the valley filled with a white undulating mist, over which the piny hills pierced like islands. The sun had just risen, and a ray of the red light lay on the waves of this fluctuating vapour. To the west, opposite the sun, it seemed driven by the light against the rock in immense masses of foaming cloud until it becomes lost in the distance, mixing its tints with the fleecy sky. At Noè, whilst our postilion waited, we walked into the forest of pines; it was a scene of enchantment, where every sound and sight contributed to charm.
>
> Our mossy seat in the deepest recesses of the wood was inclosed from the world by an impenetrable veil.

Both journals are, of course, filled with amusing anecdotes too precious not to be mentioned. While in Paris, Shelley had used a substantial portion of his small capital to buy an ass from an 'ass merchant'. The animal was evidently underfed, as the journal for the same day notes that they set out for Charenton in the evening, 'carrying the ass ... who was weak and unfit for labour'. At Charenton Shelley traded the ass for a mule – another unprofitable transaction. Mary was generally unwell, and Shelley often led her on the mule. After Shelley sprained his leg in a fall at Trois-Maisons, imagine Claire leading the animal, Shelley riding it, and a sick and dejected Mary trailing behind in a black silk dress! At Troyes, Shelley sold the mule for 40 francs, and the saddle for 16 francs, and purchased a carriage and hired a coachman, who more often than not complained of the impracticality of the road chosen by his masters and occasionally abandoned the travellers. At Nodz, while they were walking in the forest of pines, the coachman departed without them, leaving word that he would meet them on tile road. The journal continues:

> We proceeded thereupon on foot to Maison Neuve, an auberge a league distant. At Maison Neuve he had left a message importing that he should proceed to Pontarlier, six leagues distant, and that unless he found us there should return. We dispatched a boy on horseback for him; he promised to wait for us at the next village; we walked two leagues in the expectation of finding him there. ... At Savrine we found, according to our expectation, that M. le Voiturier had pursued his journey with the utmost speed.

To compound the hazards and fatigue of their journey, Mary's and Claire's journals both attest to the horrible condition of the inns in which they stayed, as well as the quality of the food. Indeed, Claire's journal seems preoccupied with the word *dirt*: 'perhaps never was dirt equal to the dirt we saw,' they stayed at a 'most terrificly dirty inn', 'the town is narrow and very dirty,' etc. When they finally found a room with an old lady at Guignes, the beds were detestable. At Trois-Maisons, where they stayed in a kind of inn, Claire was unable to sleep all night 'for the rats, who put their cold paws upon her face'. Seeking refuge, Claire climbed on to Mary and Shelley's connubial bed 'which her four-footed enemies dared not invade'. On another occasion, Claire records that Shelley was much '[di]sturbed by the creaking door, the screams [of] a poor smothered child, and the *fille* who washed the glasses'. Quite a Gothic atmosphere! Is it any wonder that Claire often experienced her famous 'horrors' – probably no more than shrieking nightmares? (Shelley had quite a way of soothing her.) Shelley himself suffered from 'spasms', and, with his hypochondria, began to believe that he was consumptive.[6]

Yet love has a way of hardening the human frame to physical discomfort and hardship. Since the Cossacks had taken most of the sheep and poultry – at St Aubin they had not left a cow in the village – Percy, Mary, and Claire often dined 'on milk and sour bread', though Shelley, being a vegetarian, was accustomed to such a diet. Yet in spite of the Cossacks, the dirty inns, rats, sprained ankles and other tribulations, the group displayed sublime fortitude, and seemed insensible to all evils. 'Mary,' wrote Shelley, 'feels as if our love would alone suffice to resist the invasions of calamity.' Claire, always in love with adventure, was indefatigable; her enthusiasm was infectious.

With his superb idealism, Shelley, though financially destitute, was ready to adopt a 'lovely child', Marguerite Pascal, from Champlitte, if only her father would have allowed him to do so. (He was still at this point suggesting to his wife, Harriet, that she join them in Geneva.)

On Friday, 19 August, the trio reached the Swiss border just beyond the town of Pontarlier, where they caught their first glimpse of the Alps. Exclaims Claire: 'oh, then come the terrific Alp[s]. I thought they were white flaky cloud[s] what was my surprise when after a long & steady examination I found them really to be the snowy Alps.' Switzerland and its Alpine setting had the effect of an uplifting tonic upon all of them, but particularly on Claire, who was of Swiss ancestry. She remarks of Switzerland that it is a land 'which I love [to] consider my own country'.

The travellers also were impressed by how, as if by magic,

everything changed as they crossed the border into Switzerland. 'The Cottages & people ([as] if by magic) became almost instantaneously clean & hospitable – The [c]hildren were rosy & ⟨&⟩ interesting, no [s]allow care worn looks ...' At Neuchâtel they put up at the Falcon's Inn, where they spent their first restful night and experienced their first clean bed since leaving England.

Neuchâtel and the surrounding villages are famous even today for their watchmaking, which they have perfected to an art. By watching these craftsmen assemble the marvellously intricate and precise machinery of a clock, some unnamed eighteenth-century person in the area was inspired to create a mechanical man – he must have been struck by the analogies between the mechanism of the human body and the intricacies of a clock. There thus developed between 1710 and 1773 a veritable industry in the Neuchâtel area dealing with this unusual speciality, well known in Europe at the time and ever since – this is the centre for the manufacture of androids. To this day thousands of visitors each year admire the versatility of these robots, and the extraordinary skill and inventiveness displayed in these complicated human machines, that can write, draw, play music, and perform other chores. Indeed, some of these androids, looking increasingly human, are on view at the History Museum of Neuchâtel, and in the tiny village of L'Auberson, only a few miles from the French border. Certainly Shelley with his fascination for mechanical and electrical devices, would have made an effort to view these androids, and may have shown them to Mary and Claire when the group stayed at Neuchâtel.

After many false starts, and some indecision, the party proceeded from Neuchâtel to Lucerne and established their headquarters just outside Brunnen, not far away from the site at which, according to tradition, William Tell had built a small chapel on the shores of the lake. They had taken two rooms of Spartan simplicity in a delapidated mansion that was euphemistically labelled a 'château', for which they paid one louis a month. They rented the place for a period of six months. While the visit of a chaplain and a doctor in residence

gave the illusion of grandeur, the location, with the view of
Lake Lucerne and the mountains of the Valais in the background, provided the kind of romantic, nostalgic setting that
they were seeking; it augured well for a lengthy stay.

Within twenty-four hours of their arrival, they had decided
to return to England. Claire did not know the real reason for
this sudden change of plans and naively believed that they
left because the stove didn't suit and because there were too
many cottages in the neighbourhood. A more probable reason
for the sudden return was the fact that Mary and Shelley
realized their money would run out well before the end of a
six months' stay. They decided to return to England, of necessity by the cheapest and least tiring method of travel – by
water down the Rhine, from its source in Switzerland to its
mouth in Holland. (They did take a diligence from Cologne
onwards but still travelled along the banks of the river.)

Journeying down the Rhine – that extraordinary frontier
that divides France and Germany – was part of the classic
itinerary of the well-rounded and cultured traveller on the
Grand Tour. The beauty and grandeur of the Rhine Valley, its
combination of dark forests, gloomy castles, and cheerful
vineyards has often been sung by poets and painted by artists.
For the Shelley party, however, touring was not the original
intent, and the notes on the numerous cities on the Rhine
they visited are of marginal interest.

The initial stops on the Rhine journey – Basel, Mettingen,
Laufenburg, Mumpf, Rheinfelden (in Switzerland), Thauphane
(probably Shauphane), Strasbourg, and Mannheim in various
Rhenish states will not detain us much; we are equally unin-
terested in the last portion of the journey from Mainz to
Rotterdam (Holland). Rather, we are most interested in the
details of their stay between Mannheim and Mainz – for
between these two cities, at a site not far from the river, is
located Castle Frankenstein. That the Rhine Valley made a
profound impact on the travellers is evident not only from
the journals, but also from the novel *Frankenstein*.

Mary's *Journal* states that: 'The banks of the Rhine are very
fine – rocks and mountains, crowned with lonely castles; but,

alas! at their feet are only still towns for ever; yet did the hills half compensate, as in Switzerland the cottages did not pierce into their very recesses, but left something to fancy and solitude.' Mary continues, 'A ruined tower, with its desolated windows, stood on the summit of another hill that jutted into the river; beyond, the sunset was illumining the mountains and the clouds, and casting the reflection of its hues on the agitated river. The brilliance and colourings in the circling whirlpools of the stream was an appearance entirely new, and most beautiful.'

We have referred to Mary's dependence on her geographic surroundings for the settings of her novels; these few short journal entries pertain to an entire segment of *Frankenstein*, when Victor Frankenstein and his friend Clerval, like Mary Shelley herself, had journeyed by boat down the Rhine from Strasbourg to Rotterdam.

> We had agreed to descend the Rhine in a boat from Strasburgh to Rotterdam, whence we might take shipping for London. During this voyage, we passed by many willowy islands, and saw several beautiful towns. We staid a day at Manheim, and, on the fifth from our departure from Strasburgh, arrived at Mayence. The course of the Rhine below Mayence becomes much more picturesque. The river descends rapidly, and winds between hills, not high, but steep, and of beautiful forms. We saw many ruined castles standing on the edges of precipices, surrounded by black woods, high and inaccessible. This part of the Rhine, indeed, presents a singularly variegated landscape. In one spot you view rugged hills, ruined castles overlooking tremendous precipices, with the dark Rhine rushing beneath; and, on the sudden turn of a promontory, flourishing vineyards, with green sloping banks, and a meandering river, and populous towns, occupy the scene.

Clerval then compares the scenery with Switzerland:

> The mountains of Switzerland are more majestic and strange; but there is a charm in the banks of this divine river, that I never before saw equalled. Look at that castle which overhangs

yon precipice; and that also on the island, almost concealed
amongst the foliage of those lovely trees; and now that group
of labourers coming from among their vines; and that village
half-hid in the recess of the mountain.

Shelley, as usual, passed the time by reading aloud. During
the journey he repeatedly cited passages from Mary Wollstone-
craft's *Letters Written during a Short Residence in Sweden,
Norway, and Denmark*. 'One of my very favourite Books,'
states Claire. 'The language is so very flowing & Eloquent &
it is altogether a beautiful Poem.'
It is quite evident from the entries in both journals that
Mary, Percy, and Claire did not care very much for their
German travelling companions – three students from the
University of Strasbourg, named Hoff, Schwitz, and Schneider.
On this point, Claire's journal is the most descriptive: 'One of
our Passengers of the name of Hoff very odious – The Second
was neither one thing or the other – he was called Schriwtz –
the third was an ideot of the name of Schneider. A woman &
her child made up the number of our Companions.' In her *Six
Weeks' Tour*, Mary describes the three Strasbourg University
students as follows: Schwitz, 'a rather handsome, good tempered young man'; Hoff, 'a kind of shapeless animal, with a
heavy, ugly, German face'; and the idiot Schneider, 'on whom
his companions were always playing a thousand tricks'.
The trio reached the crucial stage of the Rhine journey –
the course of the Rhine lying between Mannheim and Mainz
– between Friday 2 and Saturday 3rd September; for it is along
that segment of the river, at a distance of no more than eight
or nine miles directly east, that Castle Frankenstein is
located atop Magnet mountain. Both Mary's and Claire's
diaries contain summaries for these two days, though there
are substantial differences between the two entries. Let us
cite completely both journals and interpret them, trying to
account for the discrepancies. Of course, it is important in
our search to prove that Mary and Shelley either visited the
castle or became acquainted with its history and folklore during their journey down the Rhine. Also, we shall have to

speculate on the reasons for the extraordinary 'conspiracy of silence' in both diaries concerning this possible visit. (We have already mentioned the mysterious disappearance of the journal entries for the months of June, and early July, 1816.) Short of written documents, the literary sleuth has at least the right to make use of circumstantial evidence and that quality which, for lack of a better term, can best be referred to as 'historical insight'. Let us first cite Mary's *Journal* (*The History of a Six Weeks' Tour* is not essentially different on this point).

Friday, Sept. 2. – We arrive at Manheim early in the morning; breakfast there; the town is clean and good. We proceeded towards Mayence with an unfavourable wind; towards evening the batelier rests just as the wind changes in our favour. *Mary and Shelley walk for three hours; they are alone.* At 11 we depart. We sleep in the boat.

Saturday, Sept. 3. – In the morning, when we wake, we find that we have been tied all night to an island in the Rhine; the wind changed against us immediately on our departure the night before. With much difficulty we reach Mayence at 12. *Mary and Shelley are alone.* Shelley takes a place in the diligence *par eau* to Cologne. We sleep at Mayence. [Author's italics.]

Claire's *Journal* does not coincide with Mary's:

Friday Sept. 2nd. – About five in the Morning we arrive at Manheim situated on the Banks of the Rhine – We were obliged to wait here till seven as the Gentlemen of the Custom-House did not rise till then – We went into the three Boys I have already mentioned and breakfast – Afterwards walk over the town which i[s] the most noble I have ever seen – The Buildings are immensely large ⟨&⟩ regular & clean – The Streets are wide & we now & then found some that were paved – a comfort we had never met with since we left England – Very near the Entrance of the town is a large Chateau ⟨with⟩ surrounded by Pleasure Grounds [bo]th of which are ⟨made⟩ very much [i]n the English Style – The outside of the Cathedral is very fine – it is very old & the iron

gates are ⟨ver⟩ worked in a very curious manner. The Walk
from Mannheim down to the River (about a mile) is very
pretty – It is a long Avenue – with trees on each side princi-
pally ⟨Accaccia⟩ Acaccia's which is a very peculiar & beautiful
tree – Set off about six Continue till about eleven – Re[st] in a
most lovely & woody Wildern[ess.] From thence to a
⟨W⟩ Village where Shelley & I seek Provisions – *It was rather a*
Town & was called Gernsheum [Gernsheim] – The Batelier
insists upon staying till the Moon rises – When the Moon had
risen then he would stay till he then set off & after proceeding
half a league tied the Boat to an Island & there staid till
Morning. [Author's italics.]
Saturday 3rd. – [T]he Wind was strong against us so [th]at
Schriwtz & his companion Hoff & the Boatman dragged us
along the shore to Mayntz which we reached at one.

The contradictions between the two accounts should be
obvious to the reader: according to Mary, at an unnamed
place between Mannheim and Mainz, she and Shelley walked
alone for three hours. Claire, on the other hand, is much
more specific: She went shopping with Shelley on 2
September at a place called Gernsheim; then, because of
adverse winds, the pilots decided to anchor the boat off an
island in the Rhine half a league beyond Gernsheim until
morning.

Travelling to the area with both journals in hand, the accuracy of Claire's geographic description is readily continued:
Gernsheim is indeed a bustling port, and just a little to the
north of the town, as the Rhine forms a bend, a large island
partially obstructs the view of the eastern bank (see map on
pages 68–9).

As we travelled to the outskirts of Gernsheim, and looked
to the east towards the forested Magnet mountain we could
easily discern, even with the naked eye, the sinister silhouette
of the two chief towers of Castle Frankenstein, profiled
against the horizon and dominating the hill. (The bend in the
Rhine can also be seen from the castle.) The silhouette of the
castle must have been far more visible in the early nineteenth
century, given the much smaller size of the town of

Gernsheim and the lesser damage to towers and battlements, as well as the smaller growth of the trees, which literally engulf the castle today.

If Claire's account of the voyage is correct, Mary and Percy had ample time to visit the castle, since, according to both journals, the boat was anchored until morning.

If they could *see* Castle Frankenstein from Gernsheim, Mary and Shelley had every incentive to visit the castle. We have speculated already that Mary may have heard the tale of Knight Georg and the dragon-monster at Castle Frankenstein through the juvenile bookshop on Skinner Street or her step-mother's translations of German and Swiss children's tales. Or Mary may have heard the saga of Castle Frankenstein or that of the treasure hunters at the castle from some peasants at Nieder-Beerbach, or at Traisa, in much the same manner as the Brothers Grimm, who transcribed these tales for the first time in a volume entitled *Deutsche Sagen*.[7] As cultured travellers, certainly Mary and Shelley would have been acquainted with the travel guides of the period. One guidebook suggests, in fact, that 'No traveller will repent … the effort of climbing the 1160-foot high mountain on which the castle is located.'[8]

Shelley's penchant for the macabre is well documented at this point. Mary's journal attests to the fact that Shelley was a 'night' person, often spending the entire night without sleep, reading. The journals note also that the trio spent much time walking, sometimes great distances; surely a short carriage-ride to the castle would not have been a deterrent to the adventurous Shelley. We are left to entertain the notion therefore that, given their motivation and proximity, Mary and Shelley could have visited Castle Frankenstein on the night of 2 September 1814.

We can, however, establish a stronger case for a possible visit to the castle. Imagine a conversation (probably in bad French), on board ship between Mary and Shelley and their German travelling companions Hoff, Schwitz, and Schneider. Let us recall that they were students at the University of Strasbourg (a city which Mary and Percy visited). Claire mentions that on the boat much time was spent by the students drinking, smoking, singing, and cracking jokes. At one such time they may have related the story of Dippel, the alchemist, necromancer, and theologian who thought he had discovered 'the principle of life'. It was in essence because of this unorthodoxy that this brilliant young alchemist was expelled from the University of Strasbourg. Johan Konrad Dippel was born, coincidentally enough, *at Castle Franken-stein*. Indeed, Dippel had signed his doctoral dissertation: 'Franckensteina,' meaning the Frankensteiner from the mountain road, in memory of the castle on the Rhine where he was born. The German students were also intrigued by the travel notes of Mary Wollstonecraft, which Shelley read aloud daily. They could point out the added coincidence that Mary Wollstonecraft, like Dippel, was fascinated by the Promethean fire stolen from heaven, 'to give life, not animation to the inert clay.'[9] After his expulsion from the University of Strasbourg, Dippel, like Mary Wollstonecraft, had had a series of misadventures in the Scandinavian countries, attempting to sell his peculiar alchemical craft.

Even admitting that our party consisted of the most oblivious travellers in the world, the fact that they were passing through 'Frankenstein country' imposed itself in yet another way. Although by 1814 the castle itself had been sold to the Landgraves of Hesse, much of the surrounding countryside was still owned by the Frankensteins in 1814. Whether they looked towards Nierstein, or Oppenheim, both on the western banks of the Rhine, they would see extensive Frankenstein vineyards and, it being September, peasants in the vineyards during harvest. These peasants may have sung the very ballads adapted by the Brothers Grimm. (In the novel, Frankenstein states, 'We travelled at the time of the vintage, and heard the song of the labourers as we glided down the stream.') In addition, several distinguished members of the Frankenstein family were buried in the cathedrals of Mannheim and Mainz, both stopping points on the Rhine journey. Finally, when the party passed through the customs at Mannheim, they entered the estates of the Grand Duchy of Hesse, a house that, during the eighteenth century, had acquired an international reputation for dabbling in and encouraging the study of alchemy. They had subsidized a dozen alchemical laboratories throughout the state, one of which was located at the castle.

Why was there no mention of a visit to the castle, or of its 'secret' in either Mary's or Claire's journals?

We have already mentioned the predisposition of both sisters to distort facts when they did not tend to enhance 'the Shelley Legend'. Mary also had her unaccountable way of skipping certain places. When Mary's *The History of a Six Weeks' Tour* was first published, she had in essence already composed *Frankenstein*. Her explanation in the Introduction to the 1831 edition attributes the origins of the plot of the novel to the suggestion by Byron that they each write a ghost story, and relates her nightmare that night. For sheer dramatic effect, it would have been difficult to find a better introduction.

We do not intend to belabour further our earlier point about Mary's 'uncreativity', and her tendency to rely on 'raw materials' directly encountered or experienced. But perhaps that very lack of originality was offensive to her ego; particularly as she had vowed to follow in the footsteps of her mother's distinguished career. How could Mary become immortal unless she proved her creativity? Perhaps she wanted to destroy any evidence attesting plagiarism in this, her first story. The name of 'Frankenstein' and the plot inherent in the story of the alchemist were all her own. Any evidence purporting to show otherwise must be destroyed and a good story covering the origins of her novel must be 'manufactured'. It would seem that Claire, who completed her travel notes much later, was involved in the conspiracy of silence.

It matters little whether Mary and Shelley spent the night at the castle or in some village in the vicinity, like Nieder-Beerbach, perhaps at an inn called Dippelshof (presently a club in the village of Traisa) as some local stories would have it. Whether they first heard the history of the alchemist at Castle Frankenstein from the German students of Strasbourg

University, or from the ballads of the Frankenstein grape har-
vesters, it would have been difficult for Mary to have missed
that ominous name of 'Frankenstein' or the legend of the
castle.

Whether the model for the scientist Victor Frankenstein
was provided by Shelley, or by Konrad Dippel – or a combination of both – assuredly the name 'Frankenstein', and the
theme of the scientist seeking to find 'the principle of life'
were germinating in Mary's mind from the time of her visit
to the Rhine in 1814, even though she developed the plot in
Geneva two years later. The Frankenstein story was certainly
not born as suddenly or as dramatically as Mary would have
us believe. The insemination of *Frankenstein* is far more
complex, but the journey down the Rhine had its role to play
– more than merely in scenic descriptions.

Later in her life, after Shelley's death, Mary developed a fondness for revisiting old haunts connected with moments in her
youthful writings. Undoubtedly, these were her motives for
revisiting Geneva, where she was deeply immersed in
memories of *Frankenstein*. Another 'pilgrimage', however, is
far less well known. When, in 1842, she accepted her son's
offer to revisit the Continent, it is worth noting that, after
crossing France, the first place in Germany she visited was
the Valley of the Rhine.

Wielding her pen with far more judicious choice of words,
style, and maturity than she had displayed in her 1817
Journal, Mary wrote her *Rambles* – representing some of her
best writing, and in some ways reminiscent of Mary
Wollstonecraft's travelogue.[10]

> Years had elapsed since I passed down this river, before steamers
> were in use – in an ungainly boat, managed in a still more
> ungainly manner. Memory had painted the Rhine as a scene of
> enchantment; and the reality came up to what I remembered.
> The inferior beauty of the banks of the Moselle enhanced still
> more the prouder and more romantic glories of the Rhine. The
> promontories stood in bolder relief – the ruined castles and
> their ramparts were more extensive and more majestic – the

antique spires and Gothic abbeys spoke of a princely clergy – and the extent of mouldering walls marked cities belonging to a more powerful population. Each tower-crowned hill – each picturesque ruin – each shadowy ravine and beetling precipice – was passed and gazed upon with eager curiosity and delight. The very names are the titles of volumes of romance; all the spirits of Old Germany haunt the place.

Even more revealing is the segment of the Rhine that she chose to visit first – not the more scenic upper and lower valleys with their far more splendid and better-known castles and cathedrals. She followed the German border between Mannheim and Mainz, and among the first German cities she visited was Darmstadt – only a few miles away from Castle Frankenstein. As any present-day tourist in Darmstadt knows, a visit to the neighbouring hills where Castle Frankenstein is located is one of the most popular excursions out of the city; hardly to be missed by the visitor.

With *Frankenstein* then a success in prose and on the stage, Mary was returning to the site of her initial inspiration. Among the records of many distinguished visitors to the castle, there is still a local legend in several villages near the castle, that a young English lady and a man visited the castle at the beginning of the nineteenth century – a story that has been related to us by the Mayor of the town of Nieder-Beerbach, Eric Naut, whom we visited during the summer of 1973.

Some villagers believed that the mysterious couple spent the better part of the night at Dippelshof in Traisa, drinking schnapps and hock wine and listening to the peasants' tales about Castle Frankenstein unfold until dawn. Since the peasants could not otherwise account for the visit of those strangers, rumour had it that the young lady was in some way related to the Frankensteins.

It seems, then, that the impact of the castle, with its strange legend and mysterious alchemist, were brooding in Mary's receptive mind from her journey down the Rhine in 1814, awaiting the shock of a Genevan thunderstorm to launch the most powerful horror story of all times.

4

Castle Frankenstein and the Alchemist Dippel

'More than by the romantic remnants of a bygone age of chivalry, I was surprised by the most marvellous view in the world. Like the curtain in an opera, a door opened in the walls, and there before me lay, like in a milky haze, the plains of the Rhine. The Rhine itself glittered like silver. Many villages were recognizable by their steeples. The Bergstrasse, marked by the trees, was creeping along at the foot of the Odenwald mountains: the Donnersberg [thunder mountain] was the last one could see in the distance.'[1]

This passage describes the truly extraordinary view from Castle Frankenstein – it extends to a radius of forty miles on a clear day – written by a Prussian army chaplain who visited the castle several years before the Shelleys, while he was campaigning against the young armies of the new French Republic.

From the village of Nieder-Beerbach at the foot of the mountain, we ascended the 1160 ft climb to the castle by a meandering, asphalted mountain road. Above a certain height, we became surrounded by the mysterious shroud of a dense coniferous forest. At a turn in the road, the badly worn outer defences of the castle emerged on our right.

Perched on the northern edge of the summit of Magnet mountain, the medieval fortress known as Castle Frankenstein proved an awesome sight in the evening light, looming in the distance. Its walls were disintegrating and it was covered with moss and mountain overgrowth. The impact of the castle with its two command towers and smaller rounded donjons appeared much more extensive and far more 'Gothic' in character than Dracula's diminutive Byzantine fortress that we had scaled just a few years earlier. In contrast to the skeletal remains of Dracula's fortress, Castle Frankenstein exhibited all the characteristics of a traditional medieval castle. Outside the formidable walls, and anchored to the mountain rock, were the outer defensive ramparts, consisting of round towers for storing gunpowder. Inside the gate, with its porticos and observation posts, is a moat and a drawbridge with end stones built into the castle wall, pulleys, and palisades. Beyond the inner walls, the castle seems to have been designed for two separate feudal masters. The older section, dominated by the Kern tower to the north-east, is a self-contained unit with living quarters (stables, kitchens, wine cellars, etc.) for one Lord. Another inner court, with buildings built into the wall, is a fortress unto itself. Like all fortifications in the Age of Faith, there was a chapel – clearly built upon an older foundation – containing the graves and effigies of a few prominent Frankensteins of the older line of the family.

A nineteenth-century travel guidebook describing the castle recommended an inn located on the top of the Magnet mountain at the edge of the castle walls.[2] That hostelry has long since ceased to exist; however, in 1970, the State of Hesse built a small hotel, which also no longer exists, and a large restaurant with a beautiful terrace now occupies the site of that ancient inn. One summer evening in 1974, we invited a number of local historians from Nieder-Beerbach, Pfungstadt, Eberstadt, and Traisa for a schnapps on the veranda of the inn, with the intention of soliciting the extraordinary tale of the castle that had been passed down through generations. As we listened to their story, looking at the distant lights of Gernsheim from the veranda, it was not too difficult to envisage a boat, anchored on a Rhine island several miles to the

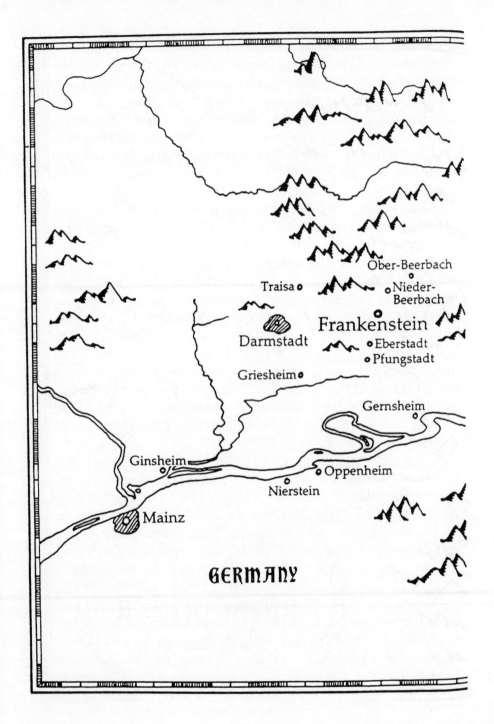

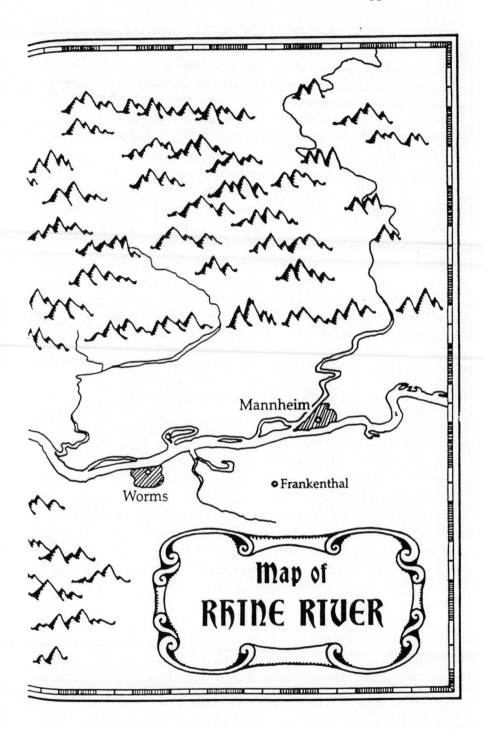

Mannheim

Worms

● Frankenthal

Map of
RHINE RIVER

west, carrying the Shelley party; we could even pretend to hear the distant sound of horses galloping up the dusty mountain road to the castle, 160 years earlier.

Although we had planned to stay at the castle and had actually reserved a room at the inn, as the saga of the castle unfolded, we heeded the local witch's warning to depart before the chapel chimes struck midnight, even though it was not Ash Wednesday, when, according to local superstition, hobgoblins, ghosts, and other wicked spirits are supposed to play havoc. With migraine headaches, undoubtedly caused by emotion rather than by any psychic or other phenomena, we descended quickly the winding Bergstrasse. As we left the castle site, many unanswered questions remained, among them this paradox: given the peace and serenity that seems to reign at this spot, and that had in fact lured us there, what could explain the odd fact, related to us by the management of the inn, that they had difficulty in hiring local people to serve at the castle? And, why, we had to ask ourselves, did *we* leave so suddenly?

The history and myth of the Barons Frankenstein

Legend has it that the Frankenstein family has a thousand-year-old history – one of the oldest in Germany. The family can be traced back to one Arbogast von Frankenstein (the name Arbogast is still current in the family), a victorious jouster in a tournament of knights at Cologne in AD 948. The first recorded history of the family begins with the construction of the castle bearing the Frankenstein name, originally built on a small scale in the middle of the thirteenth century, around 1250. The territory was acquired by the Lutzelbachs of Odenwald (the ancestors of the Frankensteins), through their marriage with the Weisterstadt family, who owned some of the villages surrounding the castle. In German the name *Frankenstein* means castle or rock of the *Franks*, and is originally derived from that powerful German tribe which has also given its name to France and the Duchy of Franconia. On a more intimate scale, memory of the Franks survives on both banks of the Rhine: *Frankenhausen* is the house of the Franks; *Frankenthal*, the valley of the Franks; and *Frankenwald*, the forest of the Franks. The Frankish origin of the family is also reflected in their coat of arms, which can be seen above the gate leading to the castle, as well as on some of the tombs in the chapel. It bears a red double war hatchet, without a handle, pointed upwards to the left. Over the axe is a helmet with the wings of a swan and clover leaves, set against a golden background.

The domain of the Frankensteins has not changed substantially through the ages; originally it included seven villages in the vicinity of Darmstadt and three parishes: Eberstadt, Nieder- and Ober-Beerbach, which they ruled with little interference from their feudal overlord from Katzenelnbogen. Within the family, however, there developed marriage disputes and feuds over inheritances, etc., that caused the Frankenstein family to split into two separate lines, although both sides continued to live at the castle for another 250 years – this feud accounts for the partitioning of the castle into an inner and outer fortress.[3] It also explains why the older line of the family is buried in the chapel at the castle, while the younger line is buried in Nieder-Beerbach.

A number of the Frankensteins achieved international prominence, beyond their principality. One was a pilgrim who sojourned to Jerusalem, travelling through Hungary and Transylvania at the time of Dracula's birth (1431–1433). Another joined the Teutonic order, a semi-military, semi-monastic organization of German knights with the avowed mission of Christianizing heathens and other unorthodox sects in Eastern Europe at the point of the sword. The order built a number of imposing fortifications during the thirteenth century, extending from the Baltic to the Transylvanian plateau, many of which, such as Castle Bran in Transylvania, survive to this day. Since Dracula was, in essence, an opponent of the German political and economic penetration of Eastern Europe – he impaled the Germans of Transylvania in large numbers – the spoof played up by recent horror movies and cartoons entitled *Dracula vs. Frankenstein* (see

Filmography) has a genuine historical background. It is by no means impossible that the *historical* Dracula may have met a *real* Frankenstein in battle at Bran or any other Teutonic fortress of Transylvania (a Frankenstein may even have ended his career impaled on Dracula's stake!).

Highlighting this Dracula–Frankenstein antagonism, it should also be remembered that the Frankensteins had obtained the support of one of Dracula's most bitter enemies in 1442 – the Holy Roman Emperor, Frederick III. Was it a Frankenstein who persuaded the Holy Roman Emperor, residing during the winter of 1463 in Wiener-Neustadt, to engage the court singer Michel Beheim to compose his Dracula poem, which in essence launched the anti-Dracula paper crusade, with ominous consequences for the Wallachian prince's reputation?[4]

When the Katzenelnbogens, the immediate suzerains of the Frankensteins, died out in 1479, the Landgraves of Hesse took over the Frankenstein principality, and power relations with the vassals changed drastically in that part of the Rhine. What particularly embittered relationships was the onset of the Reformation, since the Landgraves of Hesse converted to Lutheranism, while their vassals remained loyal to Catholicism. The ruling Landgrave of Hesse at the time of the Reformation was Philip 'the Magnanimous' (1504–1567), a fiery Lutheran convert and friend of Melanchthon, the theologian of the newly found church. When the Prince, like Henry VIII, fell passionately in love with one of his attractive ladies in waiting, Margaret von der Saal, he appealed to Luther to resolve the conflict. Citing the example of Abraham, Luther felt his authority sufficient to allow the prince to keep his paramour without the formality of divorce, in effect sanctioning bigamy. Although Philip of Hesse finally came to terms with the Catholic Emperor Charles V (by which time he had had no less than seven children by Margaret), his unorthodoxy shocked the Catholic conscience of the Frankensteins. We found still in existence on one of the castle walls a little plaque, attributed to Ludwig von Frankenstein, which bore the following inscription: 'In the year of Our Lord 1528 with God I place my faith,' reaffirming the family's loyalty to the Roman Church.

The Catholic–Protestant feud following Luther's condem-nation, and the continued religious defiance of their feudal overlords by the Frankensteins, brought reprisals from the Landgraves of Hesse, who pronounced a curse on his insubor-dinate vassals. In the eyes of the superstitious peasantry, the anathema worked only too well – for within a few years, one Frankenstein after another was unaccountably felled by mysterious maladies or untoward accidents during a period which might be looked upon as 'the great Frankenstein curse', In the early decades of the sixteenth century, several Frankensteins died in the full vigour of their youth, beginning with the deaths of the sister and the wife of Philipp Frankenstein in 1525. Their deaths were followed by the vio-lent deaths of Philipp's two sons: Georg (1531), Hans von Frankenstein (1566), and his wife Irmel von Cleen (1553).[5] These untoward events were referred to by the local minister, Wolfgang Weissberger, as *'das grosse Sterben der Franken-steiner'*, or 'the unprecedented Frankenstein death'.

In the village church at Nieder-Beerbach the visitor can still admire a tomb with the effigy of knight Georg in full armour, battle-axe in hand, having slain a snake-like creature, the *Scheusslicher Lindwurm*, curled around his leg, which succeeded, just before it died, in piercing the armour below the left knee and inserting its poisonous dart in the wound. The inscription on the tomb is still visible: 'In the year of our Lord 1531 upon the day of St Lucia the noble and honourable Georg von Frankenstein passed away; God have mercy upon him.' According to the legend, exploited by the Brothers Grimm, in the Katzenborn, a little brook that wells up not far from Nieder-Beerbach, there lived a hideous dragon, terroriz-ing the entire vicinity. Only by sacrificing the fairest maiden in the valley could the dragon be persuaded to return to the Katzenborn. Annemarie, a ranger's beautiful daughter, the 'Rose of the Valley', was picked to be the victim. Sir Georg, just having returned from a war, went out at dawn to face the monster, well-armed to rescue his secret love. After a long, hard fight he finally rendered the furious dragon a deadly blow. The monster, however, grappled the knight's left leg with its tail and in a last dying effort injected poison through the open armour into the bend of his knee, thus mortally wounding him. Ever since, the little brook has been darkened by the monster's blood.

As in all folkloric sagas, fact and fiction are hopelessly intertwined. No matter what the 'creature' may have been in fact (possibly a poisonous snake), in the eyes of the peasants, it assumed the shape of the Dragon – symbol of the devil because of the popular identification of Knight Georg with St George the dragon-slayer. That there may have been a factual basis for the legend is further attested to by a stone engraving of a beautiful woman who could not be identified as any of Knight Georg's official wives, at the entrance of the chapel. If there was a curse, it continued to strike descendants of the family indiscriminately so long as they continued to live at the castle. Some of that brutal history is inscribed within the castle chapel. Seventy-one years after the death of Georg, another member of the Frankenstein family, Philipp Ludwig, was killed in an accident near the castle (1602), barely aged twenty. Philipp was the last male descendant of the younger Frankenstein line, which died out. He is not to be confused with Ludwig von Frankenstein (d. 1606) whose likeness, as well as that of his wife, Katharina von Rodenstein, has been beautifully sculpted under a niche in the castle chapel, under the heavy Frankenstein crest; they belonged to the older line. Both sculptures are in a prayerful and submissive attitude, with two angels watching over them.

Although we do not know the precise circumstances that motivated the sale of the castle, given the family's loyalty to Rome during the Thirty Years War (1618–1648), surrounded as it was by Protestant territory, and the unique record of personal misfortunes, it is not entirely surprising that the castle was sold to the Landgraves of Hesse in two successive transactions for the total sum of 109,000 guilders. The family then moved to new estates at Franken in the city of Ulstadt, where their present descendants still reside. A letter written to us recently by the present descendant of the older line, Baron Georg von Frankenstein, was clearly intended to dissociate the newly found fortunes of the family and the fortress that bears the family name. Georg states in his letter that 'our family sold our ancestral home, Castle Frankenstein, near Darmstadt, in the year 1662; since that time we have had no further connection with it. Ulstadt, where we presently reside, has no connection with Mary Shelley.' In point of fact, the Baron was not quite correct; at the time of Mary Shelley's passage in 1814, the family still owned extensive vineyards and properties in the area of Oppenheim and Nierstein on the Rhine, and were still making Frankenstein wines there.

The title of 'Baron of the Empire' (Freiherr), which Hollywood has adopted for its movie caricature of Frankenstein, must be traced back to the year 1670, *after* the sale of the castle, when Emperor Leopold I of Germany (1658–1705) raised Frankenstein's namesake, the leader of the German Saxons of Transylvania, to the title of Baron, perhaps because of the loyalty of the family to the Roman Church. It was this same Emperor who freed Hungary and Transylvania from the Turks.

Reputations die hard; so do relationships: when we visited the unusual tomb and ghastly effigy of Baron Frank von Frankenstein (1647–1693) in the Protestant church of Sibiu, not far from the place where Dracula's only surviving son, Mihnea the Bad, is interred, one of the church attendants, having heard of our interest in Dracula, took us aside and whispered in our ear: 'Do you know that this is the tomb of the famous alchemist who thought of creating an artificial man?'

In fact, as we delved into Baron Frank von Frankenstein's distinguished career we found he was a cultured man who dabbled in most things. He wrote a fascinating history of the origins of the Germans of Transylvania, refuting the legend, implicit in Browning's *Pied Piper of Hamelin* (exploited by a few scholars), according to which the children led by the piper through a hole in the mountain at Hamelin, emerged on the Transylvanian plateau, to become the ancestors of the Germans in that area. Sadly, however, we discovered that alchemy was not one of Baron Frank von Frankenstein's avocations.

The history of the Frankenstein family after they sold the castle is of no further interest to us in our search, since it does not form part of the castle saga. The family served Germany with distinction, as soldiers, politicians, diplomats, jurists, bishops, abbots, artists, and writers. The main branch stayed in Franken: another moved to Munich, Bavaria, where the University of Ingolstadt is located. As in the case of Dracula, there is an English branch of the family – Baron George Frankenstein served as Austrian ambassador to London and stayed on after Hitler's *anschluss*; there is a Turkish branch living in Istanbul, and genuine American descendants in Minnesota, Connecticut, and California. Finally, another family from the castle area took the name Frankenstein, became famous nineteenth-century artists, and linked the name to a site in the White Mountains in New Hampshire.

The alchemist Dippel

As the armies of Louis XIV of France once again ravaged the empire, a son was born on 10 August 1673 to Anna Eleonora Munchmeyer and Johann Philipp Dippel, a Lutheran minister. At the time both were refugees at Castle Frankenstein, which had been turned into a hospital for the injured of the war. (Later the castle served as a military jail.) The son was named Johann Konrad Dippel (Konrad was a name frequently used by the Frankensteins). He was a most unusual boy, and was to become a fascinating scholarly figure of the late seventeenth century. Although there is some literature on Dippel in German, most of the works are outdated (and centre almost exclusively upon his theological career). In spite of his international reputation as a theologian, natural philosopher, physician, alchemist, and chemist, except for the interest of a few specialists, Dippel has been relegated to the status of yet another forgotten man of science. This is partially due to the fact that many of the primary sources were permanently destroyed during allied bombings of the archives of Darmstadt and Giessen (where he studied) – even his original doctoral dissertation has been lost. With the help of the seventy-odd books he composed on a great variety of subjects, contained in the two volumes of his *Eröffneter Weg*, which includes his *Autobiography* (vol. 2),[6] as well as in the biography of Dippel by Karl Voss and others,[7] there is sufficient material for a biographical sketch of this alchemist's extraordinary career.

Playing truant among the disfigured and amputated soldiers at the castle, Dippel was a loner from his early childhood. He was nicknamed 'the owl' by his playmates – a sobriquet alluding to his tastes for solitude and to his habit of reading by candlelight in the main castle tower at night. Even while attending secondary school at Darmstadt, Dippel considered himself 'a superior' individual animated by a 'higher spirit' which endowed him with exceptional powers and perspicacity, by means of which he could penetrate the mysteries of the universe; he also felt that there were no limitations to his intelligence. The peasants thought he had, like Faust, sold his soul to the devil in return for material advantages. Dippel enrolled at the University of Giessen, an ancient citadel of learning some sixty miles to the north of Castle Frankenstein. He registered as 'Franckensteina', from the mountain road of Frankenstein. The name of the castle thus stuck to his name to the end of his life. Within three years, Dippel had completed his dissertation and shocked many of his masters. His thesis, entitled *De Nihilo (On Nothing)*, implied that he had learned very little from his mentors and was a confession of scepticism.

We are not here concerned with Dippel's career as a theologian, or with his philosophy, however. From his theological writings one gathers that he was more interested in winning a point in debate than in seeking fundamental truth. On the whole, he adopted the Lutheran pietist point of view, writing under the pseudonym 'Christianus Democritus' (the Christian Democritus), the name of the fifth-century BC Greek 'laughing philosopher', sometimes labelled the father of Epicurianism and of the atomic theory.

It is as an alchemist, chemist, and physician that the career of this unusual man assumes a remarkable parallel with that of Mary's Victor Frankenstein. He shocked his colleagues at the University of Giessen on a great variety of counts, but in essence because he questioned the authority of his masters and the theological and scientific truths they propounded. It is undoubtedly for that reason that he failed in his bid for a professorship at Giessen. Rejected by his peers, he temporarily left his native Germany.

Dippel settled at the prestigious Imperial University of Strasbourg in 1694 – this university earlier had granted the great Paracelsus an honorary degree. Within its more tolerant atmosphere Dippel soon gained a local reputation for lecturing wherever he could get an audience – in the more refined salons of the avant-garde, in local taverns, churches, even in the streets. He spoke on a great variety of subjects but his more popular courses included astrology and chiromancy, greatly in vogue at the time. He was considered a visionary who had the power of divination and prophecy by some of his students. Chronicles of the period also allude to 'scandalous behaviour' on the part of Dippel. And, after two years of residence, Dippel was compelled to flee unexpectedly from Strasbourg at night, owing to a 'serious incident'. Although little is known of the scabrous affair, local gossip implicated Dippel in bodysnatching episodes at a neighbourhood cemetery.

Hiding from the authorities and virtually destitute, our 'visionary' returned to his homestead near Darmstadt, and more seriously turned to the study of alchemy. He lived with his parents near Castle Frankenstein and attempted to interest the Landgrave of Hesse in his nefarious pursuits. Count Ernst Ludwig of Hesse (1667–1739) was one of those petty princes who entertained a dream of transforming his drab court at Darmstadt into a small-scale imitation of Louis XIV's Versailles, with all the pomp and ostentation of the French court. In the process of achieving his goal the Prince had all but bankrupted the treasury – which ran a huge deficit. Since alchemy was fashionable at that time, the Landgrave decided to recoup his losses and create the necessary revenues by hiring alchemists to manufacture gold. Thus, all through his estates at Seeheim near the Rhine, Dornberg, Arheilgen, Giessen, at Castle Frankenstein and villages within the former Frankenstein domain, laboratories were established where alchemists worked day and night, using vast quantities of mercury, sulphur, and other materials to find the secret formula – the philosopher's stone. The most promising experiments took place at Seeheim, only fifteen miles from Castle Frankenstein, in what was known as the Red Lion Inn, where five alchemists were permanently engaged. In most instances, in spite of euphoric reports from a few, vast sums were squandered to no purpose. In each instance of failure the wily alchemist gave a specific reason for the lack of success of his particular experiment. The pleas to the Landgrave are really quite pitiful and worth reproducing in full.[8] With 'their million pardons for not having kept their promise', they blamed the failures on the fact that the mercury, the silver, the lead, or the copper were not pure enough, that the laboratories were inadequate, or even offered such a flimsy excuse as lack of adequate food provisioning.

In the course of an excursion near Giessen, Dippel met a Lutheran minister who showed him a number of works from his small personal library. Dippel relates of the Lutheran minister that he showed him two of the tiny folios in his possession, whose authors he thought Dippel would be able to penetrate. One was the famous treatise of Guillaume Postel, entitled 'Veil Raised on the Mysteries of the Beginning of the World'.[9] The other was a collection of various authors on chemistry, including the *Experiments* of Raymond Lull (1235–1315), the great Catalonian intellectual and inventor of red tincture; the *Prophecies and Practices* of the Italian Count Treviso; the *Dicta* of Alain de Lille (1128–1202), a Cistercian monk who became bishop of Auxerre, and the *Twelve Keys (to Knowledge)*, of the so-called Brother Basil Valentinus, the French mystic, prophet, and linguist who tried unsuccessfully to become a Jesuit and who was finally condemned to fifty years' imprisonment for indulging in magic and witchcraft. (He finally escaped from jail and retired to a monastery.) Dippel relates that having read the latter, he abandoned them laughing, since he did not believe in the assertions of the alchemists; the minister, however, finally convinced him with appropriate arguments that he should take the book with him and read it, since he believed that Dippel would be more capable than anyone else of understanding the mysteries of nature. Dippel also consulted the works of Paracelsus, Agrippa, and von Helmont, who are often cited in his works.

When Dippel completed his theoretical preparation, he approached the Landgrave of Hesse for funds to build a laboratory. There is evidence to suggest that Dippel would have liked to secure Castle Frankenstein, the ideal location for secret alchemical operations, although it seems that purchase of the castle was beyond his means. Instead he purchased property in the vicinity on credit (we have not been able to locate the actual place) for 50,000 guilders and planned to pay for it by producing his own gold. After three months of intensive work, in 1701 to be precise, and following a secret formula, Dippel claimed to have succeeded where others had failed. By mixing fifty parts of silver and mercury with the philosopher's stone, he was able to produce a very pure gold, to the delight of his master, the Landgrave.

According to an ancient tradition, however, the alchemist must never exploit the gold he manufactures for personal gain – and, according to legend, Dippel broke that rule by using the gold for the purchase of his large estate, and he had to be punished. By accident, the jar containing the philosopher's stone broke, and the secret formula that had taken him years to achieve was lost. After three years of fruitless effort to rediscover the 'secret', Dippel admitted defeat and left the Darmstadt area shortly after his father's death – on 25 June 1704 – to begin his peregrinations through other German and foreign lands that were to keep him away from home for some twenty-five years (1704–1729).

At first he settled at Berlin, the capital of the newly established Kingdom of Prussia under the rule of Frederick I. He came under the protection of Count August von Wittgenstein, general administrator of the royal domains, who had taken

Dippel under his wing; the Count persuaded King Frederick I to place a mansion and sufficient resources at Dippel's disposal to promote scientific research in other fields. Associating his efforts with those of J C Rosenbach, Dippel turned his attention to the discovery of an unusual elixir, one that would provide a panacea for a wide variety of ailments. Since 'Blood is the life', why not distil blood – we are not told whether animal or human – to obtain a heavy, viscous, odorous brown solution, which when re-distilled, became limpid and colourless? He later experimented with bones, boiling them in water to retain the fatty matter, then distilling them in iron retorts. The product was conducted through iron condensing tubes and fed into receivers where the crude bone oil collected. The product, named Dippel's oil, was a universal panacea and was used in medical practice for curing a number of diseases (when taken internally, it was said to act as an anti-spasmodic and stimulate the nervous system).

Another discovery is associated with Dippel's stay in Berlin. By heating bones, dried blood, refuse hair, and other unnamed ingredients to a high temperature, and by mixing the product with scrap iron and crude potash, Dippel obtained a chemical called potassium ferrocyanide, which, when mixed with air, assumed a striking blue coloration – the substance was widely used by artists and became known as Prussian or Berlin blue. (The discovery was made public only in 1724.) Further experimenting with Dippel's accidental discovery, the German chemist Scheele produced yet another liquid solution by diluting Dippel's chemical with sulphuric acid, yielding hydrocyanic or Prussic acid, one of the most potent poisons which, even taken in small doses, causes instant paralysis of the heart and the spinal cord. Prussic acid – one of the most effective methods of suicide – was known to John Polidori, who committed suicide in August 1821, by using this powerful poison – in circumstances to be related in Chapter 6.

Given his notoriety and the protection he enjoyed from King Frederick and Count Wittgenstein, one might have expected that Dippel would be richly rewarded. Unfortunately, the jealousy he had incurred from fellow scientists and famous quacks (such as Count Don Dominico Manuel Cajetano) and the continued hostility of theologians, caused him to become the victim of an intrigue. Accused of being a Swedish spy – some secret correspondence with Charles XII (1682–1718) of Sweden, to whom Dippel bore an uncanny resemblance, was discovered – he was briefly flung in jail in Berlin in 1707. Released upon the intervention of his powerful patron, Count Wittgenstein, he left for Holland, a country that traditionally gave asylum to those seeking relief from the oppression of enemy lands. He settled at Maarsen, between Utrecht and Amsterdam, assumed Dutch nationality, and dedicated himself to medical studies. His medical thesis at Leyden University (1711) did in fact centre upon his earlier chemical and animal experiments at Berlin (*Vitae Animalis Morbo et Medicina, suae vindicata origini disquisitione Physico-Medica*, Leyden 1711).

Dippel was also fascinated by the mechanism and functioning of limbs, particularly by the way limbs, sinews, and muscles were attached to the main body. He freely experimented on animals, practising vivisection. At least one of Dippel's biographers[10] suggests that the alchemist-turned-physician used his experiments on animals to research (with the help of the philosopher's stone) the chemical or other processes that engender life itself. Dippel's philosophy concerning the relationship between body and spirit was by no means original: he felt that the body was an inert substance animated by an errant spirit that could leave it any time to infuse life into another. According to Dippel's premise, the creation of the life impulse simply meant facilitating the passage of one spirit into the inanimate corpse of another. Dippel did not answer the question as to the manner in which this operation was to be performed. Judging from his philosophy, however, the life-giving process could be performed through magical rites, rather than the science in which Mary Shelley's Victor Frankenstein allegedly believed.

Like Mary Shelley's Victor Frankenstein, Dippel seemed condemned to the life of a wanderer. After spending seven fruitful years of research in Holland (from 1707 to 1714), during which time he assembled all of the writings he had written heretofore – and acquired his medical skills – Dippel once again felt compelled to flee, leaving Holland for Denmark in the summer of 1714. The circumstances that motivated Dippel's successive 'flights' are very involved and have never really been satisfactorily explained. For example, why was he forced to leave Holland, essentially a tolerant state? Was the *real* cause due to yet other subversive activities in which he might have engaged? We shall probably never know the real truth.

Dippel was initially well received in Denmark at the city of Altona (a city also visited by Mary Wollstonecraft in 1795), and was given the title of 'Royal Councillor'. Having written several pamphlets offensive to the local political rulers, he incurred the wrath of his former patron, a Count Reventlow, and in 1725 found himself behind prison bars. The sentence was now far more severe than his prison sentence at Berlin. He was condemned to life imprisonment; his works were burned by the public hangman before his very eyes; he was bound hand and foot and flung into a dark, damp cell in the castle of Hammarshus on the Island of Bornholm in the Baltic. He was to stay in prison only until 1726, however, for his extraordinary medical reputation resulted in the personal intervention of the Danish queen (the wife of Frederick IV), who wanted Dippel to become her personal physician. By that time, Dippel had established a reputation as a 'miracle worker' and his fame had spread far and wide – even to the court of Catherine I (1725–1727), who wanted him summoned to St Petersburg. Dippel, however, finally accepted service in 1727 at the Court of the Swedish king, Frederick I, who was suffering from an indisposition that none of his physicians were able to cure. Dippel's formula – that disease does not originate in a malfunctioning of the body; rather, the spirit has to be healed first, by psychic or suggestive means, and only then could the body be restored with the aid of chemistry – apparently worked.

Dippel continued to be a most controversial character

during his stay in Sweden, however. One of the Swedish bishops, alluding to his medical talents, called him 'the Messiah of the nobility'. Others suspected him of being a Russian spy (in Berlin, we might recall, he had been accused of spying for Sweden). 'We certainly do not recognize him as a Messiah,' stated a Swedish baron, 'we might even call him the bane of the Bishops, since on his coming to Sweden he made as much noise as if a Russian army of 100,000 had invaded the country.' It was undoubtedly because Dippel continued to be 'suspect' that he was denied the bishopric of Uppsala, and left the country, returning home to Germany in 1729 after an absence of a quarter of a century.

Dippel had always remained extremely loyal to his surviving family of five sisters: Clara, Anna, Maria, Catharina, and Juliana, and two brothers: Heinrich Adam, a fellow physician, and Johann Albert, a teacher, and his numerous nephews (he himself remained a bachelor). He felt, in addition, the hold of the region in which he was born and had spent his formative years, especially the strange attraction of Castle Frankenstein. He determined to complete his 'Grand Design', at or near the site of his birth. Dippel first bought a house in the village of Berleburg, which no longer exists, only a few miles from Castle Frankenstein. He resumed some of his earlier experiments that his life abroad had, in a sense, interrupted. The vast mansion owned by his brother Heinrich Adam, on the edge of the village of Traisa, which today bears the name Dippelshof, or Dippel's inn, provided an excellent location for a scientific laboratory. It looks like a vast gloomy mausoleum, although it now serves as a country club and restaurant, and some villagers can recall stories of the work of the extraordinary alchemist and his physician brother.

Success seems finally to have crowned Dippel's efforts; he found unnamed chemical or alchemical 'secrets', which he then offered to share with the Landgrave of Hesse. We have this evidence from an unusual document that is ignored by most scholars. In return for yielding 'the secret', Dippel demanded Castle Frankenstein and its domains as they originally extended, for himself and his heirs:[11]

The most humble undersigned asks of His Princely Highness to permit him to receive and to buy as a *feudum bonum* for himself and his brothers and sisters along with their offspring of both the masculine and the feminine sex, who are his responsibility in this matter, the free and titled property and the castle Frankenstein situated at the beginning of Bergstrasse, along with all dependents, subjects and judicial rights which belonged to the property before it was sold to the princely house of Hesse-Darmstadt.

For this he promises to cede to His Princely Highness an *Arcanum chymicum* which easily, with little labour and no dangerous work, and with the help of three to four persons, should yield at least as much revenue, all expenses deducted, as the total sum would be if the property were sold according to the ordinary assessment. I am saying that it will bring in at least as much: for the results will show that it can bring in much more.

This secret, it was further stipulated, must remain in the hands of the house of Hesse, and be confided only to the male heirs of that family; only if the last male heir died out, would he be able to reveal the secret to others. Negotiations with the Landgrave of Hesse broke down, however, and nothing ever became of that peculiar transaction.[12]

What was the nature of the 'chemical secret' Dippel was willing to sell to the Landgrave of Hesse in return for Castle Frankenstein? Why was Dippel so intent upon assuming the status of 'Lord of Frankenstein', at that time little more than an abandoned ruin? Was the mere fact that he was born there a sufficient explanation? What use did he intend to make of the castle if the transaction had been consummated? He was, after all, a single man. Was it to have been converted into a sinister scientific laboratory? Unfortunately, the available documents do not provide any answers to these questions. Indeed, the whole 'deal' has an aura of mystery, and is ignored by most of Dippel's biographers.

One possible clue to the nature of his 'secret' comes from a mysterious pamphlet Dippel had printed at Darmstadt one year later (1733), just after the failure of negotiations.[13] While his enemies were circulating rumours of his impending death, Dippel startled his readers by announcing that he had discovered a formula for prolonging his own life until the year 1801, when he would die at the age of 135 years.

Within one year of this prophecy, on the morning of 24 April 1734, Dippel was found dead in a room of the palace of his life-long patron and friend, Count August von Wittgenstein. When his body was found it was cold and rigid. He had foam at the mouth, and the right side of his face was blue. The authorities were afraid to conduct an autopsy in the usual manner, though his head was opened. Although some physicians concluded that Dippel had suffered an attack of apoplexy, others considered his death 'unnatural'. A few in the village of Traisa believed that Dippel had been killed by the Devil, for not keeping his contract. The most logical explanation for his death was that Dippel had been poisoned, or had poisoned himself. He was buried in the chapel of Laasphe, in the vicinity of Castle Wittgenstein, although, like Dracula's remains, Dippel's have since mysteriously disappeared, trailed by the strangest rumours. Only indirect descendants of his numerous sisters survive in the area to the present day.

Having served the Frankenstein family as a feudal fortress and place of refuge, and the Counts of Hesse as an alchemist's laboratory, the castle fell into the hands of the demented wife of a German soldier who had defected to the French, called Euler.[14] Euler began selling the castle's valuables: expensive religious relics, gold and silver chalices, furnishings, and paintings, down to the parquet of the residential quarters, the stone and bricks from the outer walls, the copper and shingles from the roofs – all this to maintain her 'court' of lovers. What she did not sell she consumed as firewood to keep herself and her court warm: on one occasion she almost set fire to the main edifice. Soon it began to rain in the gate tower, window panes were broken by the winds and storms, and the Frankenstein chapel was turned into a stable for horses. Within the castle itself, owls, eagles, and bats were multiplying so fast that they became the terror of visitors. Ruling in the middle of this pandemonium was the insane 'mistress of Frankenstein', with her two male companions who died in quick succession. It all ended abruptly with Euler's death in the 1740s – only the ornithological collection at the parish church of Nieder-Beerbach, one of the richest bird collections in Germany, bears silent testimony to this extraordinary period when the castle was in fact abandoned to birds of prey.

With such a bizarre history it was inevitable that Castle Frankenstein should engender a rich folkloric tradition. Abandoned fortresses with a mysterious past have a way of arousing interest, particularly when they are associated with 'curses' and 'evils'. But it was the hope of finding gold at the castle that attracted the most attention – manufactured or alchemical gold created by Dippel and other alchemists, ill-begotten, and belonging to the Devil.

One of the first authentic Frankenstein alchemy tales dates back to 1763, and is attributed to the minister of Nieder-Beerbach, Philip Moritz Scriba, who inscribed it in the parish records:[15]

In the year 1763, the week before the feast of Pentecost, a band of treasure seekers came here claiming that they had to bring to light a treasure that was in the aforesaid castle above the church, and that they had the permission of His Majesty Ludwig IX. Their chief or 'commissioner', as he called himself, was the chief forester Paul Meister, from Frankenstein Castle. These treasure seekers and their chiefs started talking at great length about what the hillside could well contain. They maintained that vaults were hidden there, and that in one there were considerable sums of gold and silver. They thought they could see all this in crystal balls, mirrors, and 'magic bottles', of which they possessed a large number. The people of the village were so dazzled by these rumours that I felt I had to come forward and express my anger at such stupid and devilish things. Nevertheless, I could not stop some of my parishioners from joining them, such as Johann Heinrich Drott, Christopher Hess, Georg Hess, and Johannes Bender. I tried by all the means in my power, especially as they were acting in a devilish, impious fashion, but their chiefs always made them more and more stubborn and used the name of His Lordship, the Count, shamefully ill; encouraging the men with the hope of receiving half the money, they attracted them even further, since these fellows were the worst and least Christian in the whole parish. I had therefore a great many problems at that time, all the more so because the most important members won over people from the Court and from that quarter I had to listen to many unpleasant things said about His Grace, my dear master, and even listen to threats of having me dismissed. But the Lord had armed me with courage and strength, and I refused to keep quiet and betray his Word. If I were to describe all their foolish and senseless actions it would take up a great deal of time and paper; suffice it to say that they preached things contrary to all the principles of the true Christian religion. They dug into the two hills, they hacked out in various directions the most terrible caves and great caverns, many of which reached a depth of 50 to 60 feet; but after all that, they did not find a single thing in the spots where, according to them, silver should be buried. Even after that, these people were so blinded by the devil that they only gave up, when one of them, Johann Heinrich Drott was killed by a fall of earth.

On this occasion the priest noted in the parish death register:

On August 5th, Johann Heinrich Drott died here in a shameful fashion; he is buried in this very place, for with others, under the order of wicked, godless people, he dug and excavated for 12 weeks under the castle above the church to find silver ... which was said to be hidden in the hillside. The holes they made were indescribable. They would not listen to all my warnings, I, the clergyman of this place; they simply insulted me in a terrible way. On the afternoon of August 5th, at one o'clock, the band went as usual to their wicked work, and this man Drott was working crouched in a deep hole which shortly afterwards fell in on him and killed him. He was so deeply buried by the earth that it was not until the afternoon of August 6th, at three o'clock, that they were able to bring him out with great difficulty, using chains and ropes. The authorities gave orders for the corpse to be buried at nightfall on

August 8th, next to the church wall and without any burial rites. He was 52 years of age.

The excavations were interrupted for a few years, but started again in 1770 as indicated by the following report in the parish register:

In 1770, on St Michael's Day, digging for the treasure was resumed and continued without a break until Pentecost in 1771. The leader was a linen weaver from the Bergstrasse in Hofen. He claimed to have permission from His Highness Ludwig IX, and to be digging at his own expense. At that time between 20 and 30 men were working on it daily, some miners among them, and during this period two or three soldiers from an infantry battalion mounted guard. Despite all the efforts and experience, they found nothing but a section of wall towards the foundation and another alongside the church.

The mirror-soothsayers and those who conjured up spirits were numerous among them, making even more foolish speeches than on the first occasion. In 1787, the treasure-seeker Kaspar Gunther undertook a third attempt. He, too, flashed in front of the people's eyes so much legend about the castle and its treasures that eventually he was able to assemble a group from Nieder-Beerbach and Eberstadt, who, on the pretext of looking for gold, had excavations made at the site of the fountain and a gallery dug out. The latter was fifty feet long, and even after digging another well twenty feet deep, they still had found nothing but a little iron ore.

One year later, on 15 November 1788, Nicolaus Werner was attempting to blow up some rocks, with the same purpose in mind, in the fields surrounding Darmstadt, when an exploding rock wounded him in the head with damage to his skull. After being delirious for some time, he died on 20 November at Nieder-Beerbach as a result of his wound. In that same year the local authorities placed a strict ban on further digging.

The fortunes of Castle Frankenstein revived in the last decades of the eighteenth century, when it became a shrine for a small number of literary pilgrims who loved old ruins, had a penchant for the Gothic, and were sensitive to the beauties of nature. The patroness of this small circle of literati – known as the 'Darmstadt circle'[16] – was the Countess of Hesse, Henrietta Christina Caroline of Pfalz-Zweibrucke, the wife of Ludwig IX. As an Enlightened Sovereign, she had a sustained correspondence with Voltaire, and had admired Frederick the Great. The 'Darmstadt circle' was, for the most part, composed of mediocre writers, strongly influenced by English eighteenth-century literary currents. One member was the beautiful princess Louisa of Mecklenburg-Strelitz, the future queen of Prussia who so captivated Napoleon at Tilsit, and her sister Fredericka. The group spent weekends at Castle Frankenstein and sang their songs under the linden tree in front of the castle, a favourite meeting place. Among the visitors to the Darmstadt circle was the German dramatist Goethe.

Goethe seems to have enjoyed his visits to Darmstadt and Castle Frankenstein. He wrote:[17]

> The Darmstadt society pleased me under all the totality of its aspects for it was composed of a great many men of merit and remarkable women among whom I shall merely mention the fiancée of Herder, as interesting by her personal qualities as by her attachment to so distinguished a man. In this society they liked to hear me read my verse either completed or begun; they encouraged me and scolded me whenever new composition prevented me from completing the old ones. *Faust* was advancing and Goetz von Berlichingen was warming up in my thoughts.

It should be remembered that one of the titles often read by the Darmstadt group was Goethe's *Sorrows of Young Werther*, a work which profoundly impressed Mary Shelley and is mentioned in *Frankenstein*.

Historic, folkloric, and literary fame brought with it an influx of tourists who travelled up the Bergstrasse long before Mary Shelley's time. The castle was painted by Primavesi about 1819.[18] It was mentioned in all the better nineteenth-century guidebooks and in one of the first editions of the *Encyclopaedia Britannica*.[19] Also, given the notoriety achieved by the Darmstadt circle in the pages of the *Edinburgh Review* (read by the Shelleys), Castle Frankenstein could hardly have escaped the attention of English voyagers travelling up and down the Rhine. A visit to the castle would have been a 'must' to any knowledgeable European literati. The list of famous visitors reads like a European *Who's Who*. Among the more distinguished visitors to the castle was Bismarck, who visited it shortly after he had united Germany by 'blood and iron'. During a picnic organized by the Prime Minister of Hesse, Bismarck astounded his colleagues by driving his four-horse carriage up and down the winding castle road at a reckless speed: 'that is the way to drive in Prussia', he said pointedly, 'when I am on board.' To which the somewhat shaken coachman answered: 'Well, those accompanying you must really watch out for their hands and legs.' Replied Bismarck arrogantly, throwing him a gold coin, 'I know how to repay them for their pains.'

It was during the reign of Ludwig II (his father, Ludwig I, had assumed the title of Grand Duke of Hesse in 1806) that serious work of restoring the castle was begun. In a letter dated 7 February 1835, the Grand Duke wrote: 'Since Castle Frankenstein was visited frequently by foreigners, and sometimes even by the highest dignitaries and Princes, one should encourage visits by the construction of a road in the immediate vicinity of the castle.' The most urgent reconstruction was undertaken shortly thereafter by repairing breaks in the walls, shoring up towers, and by completing a room in the southern end of the main tower. The third Grand Duke of Hesse – still another Ludwig III (1806–1877) – was so interested in the castle that he commissioned the local architect to sketch the way he envisaged the castle in its days of splendour. As the visit of King Maximilian II of Bavaria was announced, Ludwig III ordered the main gate, tower and chapel repaired and the tombs of the Frankenstein family brought back to the chapel from Eberstadt and Nieder-Beerbach.

Between 1892 and 1893 further restoration was done on the castle: two towers were capped with pointed, high pitched roofs – totally out of keeping with the original Gothic style of a medieval castle. Further repairs were undertaken just before World War I, between 1912 and 1913.

According to the mayor of Nieder-Beerbach, in recent times since the hotel and restaurant were built, no less than 40,000 to 50,000 people visit Castle Frankenstein each year; this includes many American GIs from the neighbouring bases. One odd footnote, not entirely out of keeping with the 'secretive' nature of the castle's history, was related to us by the mayor of Nieder-Beerbach: 'In the years following World War I, as Germany was denied an air force in accordance with the provisions of the Treaty of Versailles, the castle site was used for secret experiments by the German Air Force. Sheltered by the dense forests surrounding the castle, the Luftwaffe used the mountain site to launch small planes and gliders from the castle. These experiments came to an end in 1933 when Hitler more openly defied the provisions of the Treaty of Versailles and withdrew from the League of Nations.'

Considering the bizarre history of Castle Frankenstein, as well as the international reputation of some of its inhabitants during the eighteenth and early nineteenth centuries, it seems unlikely that the parallels between the castle, Dippel, and Mary Shelley's novel are mere coincidence. We have already mentioned the more-than-coincidental parallels between the life of Konrad Dippel and the main character of Mary's novel, Victor Frankenstein. Both were exceptional minds, far ahead of their times, little understood by their superiors and peers; both scientific 'Hamlets' were condemned to wander from country to country, even to suffer imprisonment because of their work. Both firmly believed in the ability of man to conquer death, and to create life by artificial means, and both worked in secrecy. Mary to the end does not disclose the formula used by Frankenstein to create the monster; neither does Dippel ever reveal his 'secret' to the Landgrave.

5

The Haunted Summer of 1816

A most unusual equipage slowly travelled across the dusty, battle-scarred field of Waterloo in May of 1816. The oversized diligence looked like a copy of Napoleon's famous carriage, equipped with travelling library, couch, plate chest, crockery – in sum, everything needed for rest, meals, and study. Three servants, luggage, and a menagerie of animals of all sizes and description followed. In the larger carriage one could distinguish two men: one was extraordinarily handsome, with a pale complexion, penetrating blue-grey eyes, and dark, curly hair; he was dressed like a dandy, with a tight-fitting olive waistcoat. When he got out of the carriage one noticed his only flaw – a club foot. As a result he always carried a sword-cane at his side. The other man, aged about twenty-three, was also handsome, but had more regular features, a round, doll-like face, and carefully dressed hair. Because of his olive-skinned complexion, he looked distinctly Latin. Given the notoriety of the former and the large 'B' painted on the carriage door, there was no doubt that the identity of at least one of these men, evidently the master, was the great Lord Byron. Byron was leaving his native England for good; travelling in the direction of Geneva with his Italian-born private physician, John William Polidori, and his three servants: Fletcher, Rushton, and the Swiss, Berger. Since the government of

Louis XVIII had refused visas 'to His Satanic Majesty', they were compelled to travel through Flanders and then by road along the Rhine.

Byron was at the height of his literary and personal career at the time; in England he was idealized as a demigod, but also condemned as the worst of men. There could be no question of his poetic genius, but his unconventional lifestyle had, to say the least, raised a few eyebrows. Byron seems to have deliberately aimed at 'shocking' society since his early student pranks at Harrow and Trinity College, Cambridge. Somehow his feats, imaginary or real, compelled attention; he had swum across the Bosporus; killed his unfaithful Turkish mistress by drowning her in a sack; imitated the folkloric 'vampire' by living in a half-ruined abbey that reportedly was haunted by a hooded monk; upon occasion ate nothing but water, vinegar, and rice, or hard biscuits and soda water; he frightened his friends by uttering strident war cries (he called them 'songs' he had learned in Albania, hence his nickname 'Albé'). He separated from his first wife Anabella Milbanke, after one year of marriage and one child; had committed incest with his half-sister, Augusta Leigh, but was enough of a homosexual to persuade Caroline Lamb to disguise herself as a page in order to seduce him. Though he complained of 'being accused of every vice of public rumour and private rancour', it is difficult to shake the impression that he took pernicious pride in deliberately flouting society with his orgies. If it were possible to penetrate the mask of cynicism of the twenty-eight-year-old poet, one might have found a shy, melancholic, sensitive, courageous, even affectionate, and certainly an athletic young man, brilliant and well-read, and far more conventionally minded than he cared to admit. Like Shelley, he was a hypochondriac, living frugally only to live long: in Geneva he lived on tea, bread, and vegetables, with a little wine, and dieted to stay thin. His most reprehensible trait, perhaps, was his lack of generosity; the least accountable, his superstitious mind. Byron believed he was hounded by a curse that would ultimately destroy him and his friends.

Byron's companion, the baby doctor 'Polly-Dolly', was truly droll and doll-like in appearance, a true dandy but with the irascible temperament of a Latin lover and the vanity of a minor poet. His credentials and background were impressive enough for the role of a house doctor: Polidori's father Gaetano had been the secretary to the Italian poet, Alfieri. John had been educated by the Benedictines at Ampleforth and had received his medical diploma at the record age of nineteen from the University of Edinburgh, writing a dissertation on *The Psychosomatic Effects of Sleepwalking and/or Nightmares*.[1] Had Polidori been content to play the role of physician that his solid grasp of medicine, even of psychology warranted, relationships might have been smoother; unfortunately he also imagined he had literary gifts, and was no doubt encouraged to pursue them by the fact that Byron's publisher, John Murray, had advanced him £500 to keep a diary of the journey and another £150 to write two plays. Notwithstanding gaps caused by diverse crises, self-censorship, and the deletion of several passages that his sister Charlotte Lydia Polidori, who had possession of his manuscript right after his death, considered 'improper', it is fortunate that Polidori's *Diary* has been published by his nephew, William Michael Rossetti.[2] Only a careful reading of the *Diary* will reveal the doctor's painful attempts to maintain an exclusive relationship with Byron, and his hurt in being reduced to the status of court jester by the constant quips of Byron, who became irritated at his very presence. Byron describes him as 'exactly the kind of person to whom, if he fell overboard, one would hold out a straw to know if the adage be true that drowning men catch at straws'. Witticisms such as these soon drove Polidori to a state of hysteria, even paranoia, bordering on suicide.

The journey from London (they left on 24 April, according to Polidori) to Geneva (which they reached on 25 May), was almost precisely the route followed by the Shelley party, though Byron travelled in the opposite direction, up, rather than down, the Rhine valley, by land rather than by boat. Our chief interest in Polidori's *Diary* is for the information he lends to the interactions at Diodati. (As travel notes the *Diary* has its peccant passages: we are informed, for instance, that at Ostend, Byron 'fell like a thunderbolt upon the chambermaids'.[3]) Passing the region from Mainz to Mannheim, Polidori notes in his journal: 'Arrived at Mayence at 6½. Saw along the Rhine many fine old castles.'[4]

The party arrived at the village of Sécheron just outside the city of Geneva on May 25 and stopped at Dejean's Hôtel d'Angleterre, one of the best inns in the area, which catered especially to the delicate palates and tastes of true English gentlemen. Although by no means new (it was built in the early 1700s), judging from contemporary prints the inn was spacious, if unpretentious, had a view of Mont Blanc, boasted elaborate gardens extending to the lake, its own harbour, and boats and boatmen at the disposal of its guests. Its greatest advantage for the night revellers was the fact that it was located outside the city gates of Geneva and was exempt from the curfew imposed by the city Elders, who closed the gates nightly at 10 p.m.[5]

Ten days earlier and late at night, a much more modest carriage had pulled up in front of the main portico of the same inn. Five tired travellers emerged, three of whom, Mary, Percy Bysshe, and Claire Clairmont, have already been introduced; they were accompanied by little William – Mary and Percy's son, who was born in January at Windsor – and a Swiss maid called Elize. The Shelleys had spent one of the most trying years of their lives in England, beset by financial and other worries, including requests for support from Harriet for her and their two children, delicate demands from Godwin to keep the publishing house solvent, and more forceful demands for payment from other creditors. All appeals for help to the prosperous Shelley family had failed, and Godwin, notwithstanding the money he was still accepting from the Shelleys, had banned the couple from his house, communicating only through the good-natured Fanny. Given all their trials, the couple had travelled to Geneva in the hope of finding a little peace in the serene surroundings 'of the lovely lake, blue as the heavens which it reflects',[6] and to restore their broken health and spirits. Shelley also realized that he could live more comfortably on his modest income on the Continent than in England.

Certainly the Shelleys' choice of Geneva had been determined by Claire's 'pressing solicitations' to follow Byron to Geneva. Shelley, it seems, after the unfavourable resolution of a lawsuit pertaining to the disposal of the family estate after the death of his grandfather, had planned to escape to Scotland – perhaps even to Italy.

Sometime before he had left for Geneva, Byron had received a letter from an anonymous woman who placed her future happiness in his hands: 'If a woman, whose reputation has yet remained unstained, if without either guardian or husband to control she should throw herself upon your mercy, if with a beating heart she should confess the love she has borne you many years, if she should secure to you secresy and safety, if she should return your kindness with fond affection and unbounded devotion, could you betray her, or would you be silent as the grave?' And in a second missive: 'Lord Byron is requested to state whether seven o'clock this Evening will be convenient to him to receive a lady to communicate with him on business of peculiar importance. She desires to be admitted alone and with the utmost privacy.'[7] There must have been some particular quality in both these notes for Byron (who received many fan fetters of this kind from unknown female admirers) to decide to be 'at home' at the aforementioned hour. The rest is history, and without the affair between Byron and Claire Clairmont, which began in London (where their daughter Allegra was conceived), there would have been no Genevan rendezvous, and probably no *Frankenstein*. 'Think of me in Switzerland: the land of my ancestors,' wrote Claire to Byron. 'Like my native mountain [sic], I am tranquil and [like] as they are tranquil so is my affection ... We shall meet again at Geneva: to me the most beautiful and endearing of words.'[8]

When Byron finally arrived he did not seem anxious to meet Claire, and for two days he avoided her in the large hotel, being unperturbed by Claire's urgent notes. The two parties finally met, perhaps on 25 May certainly on 27 May, as Byron and Polidori were returning from a boat ride on the lake. Polidori notes in an off-hand manner in his *Diary* for 27 May: 'Getting out, L[ord] B[yron] met M[ary] Wollstonecraft Godwin, her sister, and Percy Shelley.'[9] Byron seemed more pleased to meet Shelley than to renew his liaison with Claire. 'Are you Shelley the author of *Queen Mab*?' he inquired, remembering the poet had sent him that work some years earlier. That evening they all dined together on the terrace of Dejean's inn and since the poets had so much in common, they developed an immediate rapport. Notes Dowden, 'both were poets; both were children of the Revolution, the one representing its temper of indignant revolt; the other, its doctrinal evangel and its wild-eyed hopes; both had warred against the laws of society, and were rebels under the ban.'[10] At this point a friendship began that was to make literary history. Sensing danger to the monopoly he had so far exercised over Byron, Polidori was immediately hostile towards Shelley, and comments, in his diary, inaccurately, that Shelley was, 'bashful, shy, consumptive; twenty-six [he was actually twenty-four]; separated from his wife; keeps the two daughters of Godwin, who practise his theories [meaning free love]; one L[ord] B[yron]'s'.[11] Polidori obviously was aware that Claire was Byron's mistress. The affair seems to have resumed shortly thereafter, as Claire was observed nightly stealing between the two villas, Diodati and Chapuis. Of the affair Byron wrote, 'I was not in love,' and continues defensively, 'nor have I any love left for any; but I could not exactly play the Stoic with a woman, who had scrambled eight hundred miles to unphilosophise me. Besides, I had been regaled of late with so many "two courses and a *desert*" (Alas!) of aversion, that I was fain to take a little love (if pressed particularly) by way of novelty' – and she was certainly pressing.[12]

Geneva, a city of some 40,000 inhabitants, strategically located at the confines of three great nations (France, Italy, and Germany), had just been liberated by the allied victory over Napoleon and re-attached to the Swiss Confederacy after some years of French rule. Mary, who found occasion to stroll with Shelley in the narrow cobblestone and badly lit streets of the old city, either to browse in bookstores, admire watch- or lens-makers (she bought Shelley a telescope), shop for balloons or kites – also for Shelley – and perhaps peek into the inner courtyards of the more elaborate mansions of the patricians of the city, describes the places in Geneva which caught her particular attention:[13]

But while I still dwell on the country around Geneva, you will expect me to say something of the town itself; there is nothing, however, in it that can repay you for the trouble of walking over its rough stones. The houses are high, the streets narrow, many of them on the ascent, and no public building of any beauty to attract your eye, or any architecture to gratify your taste. The town is surrounded by a wall, the three gates of which are shut exactly at ten o'clock, when no bribery (as in France) can open them. To the south of the town is the promenade of the Genevese, a grassy plain planted with a few trees, and called *Plainpalais* [from *palus, paludis*, meaning marsh]. Here a small obelisk is erected to the glory of Rousseau, and here (such is the mutability of human life) the magistrates, the successors of those who exiled him from his native country, were shot by the populace during the revolution which his writings mainly contributed to mature, and which, notwithstanding the temporary bloodshed and injustice with which it was polluted, has produced enduring benefits to mankind ... From respect to the memory of their predecessors, none of the present magistrates ever walk in *Plainpalais*. Another Sunday recreation for the citizens is an excursion to the top of Mont Salère [should be Mont Salève]. This hill is within a league of the town, and rises perpendicularly from the cultivated plain. It is ascended on the other side, and I should judge from its situation that your toil is rewarded by a delightful view of the course of the Rhone and Arne [Arve], and of the shores of the lake.

She is far more ecstatic when describing the surrounding countryside:[14]

To what a different scene are we now arrived! To the warm sunshine, and to the humming of sun-loving insects. From the windows of our hotel we see the lovely lake, blue as the heavens which it reflects, and sparkling with golden beams. The opposite shore is sloping and covered with vines, which, however, do not so early in the season add to the beauty of the prospect. Gentlemen's seats are scattered over these banks, behind which rise the various ridges of the black mountains, and towering far above, in the midst of its snowy Alps, the majestic Mont Blanc, highest and queen of all. Such is the view reflected by the lake; it is a bright summer scene without any of the sacred solitude and deep seclusion that delighted us at Luceme.

Mary then turns to her favourite avocation while at Sécheron:[15]

[Y]ou know our attachment to water excursions. We have hired a boat and every evening, at about six o'clock, we sail on the lake, which is delightful, whether we glide over a glassy surface or are speeded along by a strong wind ... the tossing of our boat raises my spirits and inspires me with unusual hilarity. Twilight here is of short duration, but we at present enjoy the benefit of an increasing moon, and seldom return until ten o'clock, when, as we approach the shore, we are saluted by the delightful scent of flowers and new-mown grass, and the chirp of the grasshoppers, and the song of the evening birds ... We read Latin and Italian during the heat of noon, and when the sun declines we walk in the garden of the hotel, looking at the rabbits, relieving fallen cockchafers, and watching the motions of a myriad of lizards, who inhabit a southern wall of the garden. You know that we have just escaped from the gloom of winter and of London; and coming to this delightful spot during this divine weather, I feel as happy as a new-fledged bird.

Mary did not quite share Claire's uncritical adulation for everything Swiss. Her letters indicate she found the inhabitants 'lacking in grace and vivacity', and 'did not enter society', though she extolled the greater 'equality of class', as compared to England, and 'the refinement of manners among the lower orders'. She noted as well their 'Puritanism', and took few pains to acquaint herself with the inhabitants of Geneva.

Byron was less generous in his comments on the Swiss: 'Switzerland is a curst, selfish, swinish country of brutes, placed in the most romantic region of the world. I never could bear the inhabitants, and still less their English visitors ... I know of no other situation except Hell which I should feel inclined to participate with them.'[16]

This negative attitude may have been caused by the fact that the only newspaper in existence, the *Gazette de Lausanne* (25 June 1816) dismissed this egomaniac's presence in one sentence.

A legend has of course grown around Villa Chapuis, the birthplace of *Frankenstein*, and many of the chief actors involved in the summer of 1816, including Mary, are responsible. First, we note the inaccuracy of names dealing with the house that the Shelleys occupied, a fact that has confused many scholars. Mary refers to it by many names and various spellings: Montalègre, Chapuis, Chappuis, Bellerive, Coligny, Cologny, even Diodati. Byron enthusiasts have compounded the confusion by giving Diodati an ancient pedigree, noting that Diodati was the house 'where Milton returning from Italy in 1639, had visited John Diodati, a Genevan professor of theology'.[17] In fact, 'Campagne' *Chapuis* (rented by the Shelleys) and Villa *Diodati* (rented by Byron) were located in the *Montalègre* section of the hill, within the village of *Cologny* – located on the outskirts of the city of *Geneva*.

The Shelleys were the first to leave Sécheron after only a fortnight's stay. They had first rowed across the lake with Polidori and found 'a very pretty little villa in a vineyard', owned by Jacob Chapuis, refurbished a few years earlier for rental purposes. Although, as we noted in the first chapter, very little of the original Chapuis house remains today, we were able to reconstruct Chapuis from a few faded pictures of the house. It was a humble, unpretentious, square-shaped, two-storey dwelling with four windows facing the lake on the western side. Judging by the area of the basement and foundations, it could not have contained more than five or six rooms at best. Nestled in a vineyard and surrounded by trees, the location was bucolic and secluded. The property bordered the lake and contained a small private harbour. As we sat on the edge of the remains of Chapuis, watching the dying sun setting across the not so 'dark' Jura, colour playing on the leaves of summer, one could easily understand why Mary had finally found her Elysium, the little intimate nest for which she had longed. Reading her words aloud gave the scene an indescribably *real* dimension.[18]

> You will perceive from my date [the letter was addressed campagne Chapuis, 1 June] that we have exchanged our residence since my last letter. We now inhabit a little cottage on the opposite shore of the lake, and have exchanged the view of Mont Blanc and her snowy *aiguilles* for the dark frowning Jura, behind whose range we every evening see the sun sink, and darkness approaches our valley from behind the Alps, which are then tinged by that glowing rose-like hew which is observed in England to attend on the clouds of an autumnal sky when daylight is almost gone. The lake is at our feet, and a little harbour contains our boat, in which we still enjoy our evening excursions on the water.

As in Scotland and on the Rhine, Mary still indulged in her favourite pastime – daydreaming, with the sweet background of the vinedressers up Montalègre hill singing monotonous old ballads with their harmonious voices 'in the stillness of evening, while we are enjoying the sight of the setting sun, either from the hill behind our house or from the lake'.[19] She later wrote in the Introduction to the 1831 edition of *Frankenstein*: 'I see them still; the very room, the dark parquet, the closed shutters, with the moonlight struggling through, and the sense I had that the glassy lake and white high Alps were beyond,' and again (on 28 May 1817): 'Do you not remember, Shelley, when you first read it [the Third Canto of *Childe Harold*] to me? One evening after returning from Diodati. It was in our little room at Chapuis. The lake was before us, and the mighty Jura.'[20] Years later, haunted by that scene, Mary came back to see the house where she had composed the first lines of *Frankenstein*. 'There, on the shores of Bellerive, stood Diodati; and our humble dwelling, Maison Chapuis, nestled close to the lake below. There were the terraces, the vineyards, the upward path threading them, the little port where our boat lay moored; I could mark and recognize a thousand slight peculiarities, familiar objects then – forgotten since – now replete with recollections and associations.'[21] To really understand the 'mood' of Mary Shelley and the frame of mind that governed her writing of *Frankenstein*, a visit to the ruins of Chapuis is almost a necessary pilgrimage.

One evening, Mademoiselle Françoise Ramu, whose greatgrandfather Alexandre Ramu had acquired the Montalègre property in 1863, continued the story of that skeleton of a house:[22]

I shall always be grateful to my grandfather for having purchased the old Chapuis property. It was the incomparable vacation 'campagne'; plunging in a fairly sheer incline on the luminous lake and presenting, from top to bottom, a series of glimpses on the lake that many voyagers have declared most beautiful. Montalègre, which forms part of the hill of Cologny, means 'joyous hill', and deserves the name. In Shelley's time the region was covered with vines; the Chapuis property, which was located at about the centre of the hill, was divided in two by the path of Montalègre, which meandered along the lake and lay parallel to it. Close to the wine press and the principal dependencies, surrounded by trees and a garden, it had the exterior of a modest gentleman's house. Between buildings flights of rustic stairs linked the various levels: through the vines led some paths from the lake to the top of the hill. The property extended directly to the shore of the lake though there were no harbours in the strict sense, only deep indentations here and there, serving as private moorings. During the summer of 1816, Byron descended almost daily to visit the Shelleys and the two poets made numerous excursions on the lake. The region seems to attract English artists: some twenty years later the family which had bought the Chapuis property in 1830 had the English painter, Francis Danby, as their tenant.

The nucleus of the property was a small house. Successive owners bore the old names of this region. Moses Viridet (who may have built it), David Bourdillon, Jacques Chapuis, then the brother and sisters Chapalay. Then our grandfather, François Alexandre Ramu, bought Montalègre from the Misses Chapalay, having spent a summer there with his young family. Of all this cluster of ancient homes, only the renovated dependency that we presently inhabit remains ... We have also rented the upper apartment ... to Englishmen quite naturally. The latter, when told of the stay of their illustrious predecessor [for the house was standing when Mary Shelley lived] began to complain that the apartment was haunted by a rather gracious ghost. At night one heard footsteps in the corridor ... without the slightest tumble of chains; the lights suddenly and maliciously extinguished themselves then lit up again. It was certainly a very well brought up ghost.

Comfortable as he was at Sécheron, Byron had been looking for an alternative to the Hôtel d'Angleterre almost from the beginning of his stay and had apparently negotiated for Villa Diodati as early as 26 May, but found the rent excessive – Polidori notes that they were asking five-and-twenty louis a month. Byron's banker friend, Charles Hentsch, seems to have interceded and completed the rental by 6 June, for six months – until 1 November – for 125 louis. By 10 June the noble Lord, Polidori, the three servants, the menageries, books, pictures, crockery, etc. were installed at Diodati for the duration of the summer. Byron seemed as delighted with his find as the Shelleys were with theirs; it 'was the most beautiful house of all around the lake located in a vineyard with the Alps behind and the Mount Jura and the lake before. It is called Diodati from the name of the proprietor who is a descendant of the illustrissimo Diodati.'[23] Since we discovered during our visit to Diodati that it was not built until 1710, it was clear that the villa had not housed either Milton in 1639 (Milton indeed visited John Diodati at his Genevan home near St Peter's Cathedral), nor John Evelyn in 1654, as Byron was led to believe. The property had been acquired by the Diodatis, an ancient Italian family that was ennobled by Charles V and had sought refuge in Geneva after their conversion to Calvinism. Diodati was then built in several stages during the middle of the eighteenth century, finally acquiring the proportions of an elaborate Genevan 'campagne'.

The rich history of Diodati unfolds the moment one crosses the threshold of its heavy and ornate oak door – this was after all the house where Byron composed the Third Canto of *Childe Harold*, and where the novelist Balzac visited with Eveline Hanska, the one great love of his life, in December 1833.[24]

Chapters could be written on the villa that housed more eminent men than any other comparable mansion in the Geneva area, and Mrs Simone Washer, who owned it in 1974, was often besieged by a great variety of literary specialists and antiquarians. Ours was probably the first expedition to Diodati that was searching for clues not for *Childe Harold* or Balzac's loves, but for Polidori's *Vampyre* and particularly for Mary Shelley's *Frankenstein*.

Built with the traditional good taste of the Swiss, it could have been dismissed as a simple edifice were it not for the elegant columns that supported the porch and elaborate railings that surrounded the house and on which were centred the Diodati coat of arms. In the centre of that famous room, the fireplace so often referred to was exactly as we pictured it; a mirror in a heavy gilt frame was mounted over the mantelpiece. With a good deal of concentration and much imagination one could almost see in the mirror the reflections of the famous fivesome sitting around the fireplace, in the glow of the embers – which were burning the day of our visit, lending a reddish tinge to the room.

To the left of the main hallway lay Byron's former bedroom, converted into an elegant study; the chief object of our interest was the main living room, with its heavy Louis XV decor and furnishings virtually unaltered. It faced the lake and the veranda. Diodati was full of Byron memorabilia, including the famous print where the noble Lord is seen pensively standing on the balcony gazing into the lake, the city and port of Geneva at his feet, and the Jura in the distance.

With the help of all the diaries and journals it is not difficult to reconstruct life among the two households of Diodati and Chapuis. At Chapuis the routine was simple and life was frugal. Mary and Percy got up early, often read aloud, played games with William, ate almost nothing, sailed on the lake in any weather from their little harbour (together with Byron they had just purchased the first sailboat with a keel on the lake). Sometimes they launched balloons – one of Shelley's favourite hobbies. Remaining secluded, they only occasionally went into Geneva. Both Mary and Shelley were too distraught to write when they first arrived at Chapuis. In the evening, together with Claire, they would climb up the meandering path among the vines to Diodati. Only at sunset would the day really begin for them. If the weather was inclement they would usually all spend the night there. Claire's routine varied little from theirs ... except that as her pregnancy with Allegra advanced, she spent most of the day resting. Her very presence had begun to irritate Byron, though Claire accepted her altered status with equanimity, declaring that she would ten times rather be his male companion than his mistress.

Byron himself continued in a sullen mood and seemed concentrated on his health. Barring occasional visits from Hentsch or Bonstetten – or an occasional outing at Coppet or Mon Repos (Madame de Staël had returned from Italy only in the middle of June), he would spend the morning indoors, often in bed, the afternoon sailing, walking, or talking with Shelley on a bench in the garden below the apple tree under which, according to local tradition, Byron would always sit. (It has since died.) When inspired, he would write, watching the sun set behind the Jura from the balcony of Diodati. In default of food, the nights at Diodati provided his spiritual sustenance and helped induce an atmosphere of perpetual excitement, which his poetry needed. Polidori was the only member of the household who regularly ventured to Geneva.

*

The weather during that summer played an important role in the creation of *Frankenstein*, and thus deserves to be mentioned. As Mary noted in her journal on her way to Geneva, it had been a late spring and many of the Jura mountain roads were barely passable, being covered with snow. 'Next day, winding in chill air among ravines overhung by pine forests, or climbing amid the snows which still gathered in the tardy spring, they passed the village of Les Rousses, and, with the aid of a team of four horses and ten men to support the carriage, pushed on through pelting snowflakes to the neighbourhood of Geneva.'[25]

A few astronomers and some astrologers, seeing mysterious patches on the sun in their telescopes, had announced the end of the world for the middle of June. Weather forecasters, writing in Swiss almanacs of that period, had predicted a wet, almost unprecedented summer of winds, rainstorms, squalls, and electrical storms of great intensity on the lake. We often witnessed such pyrotechnics above the lake with lightning and thunder: during our stay in the summer of 1974, there were many grandiose spectacles of nature, making the fireworks on 1 August (Switzerland's national holiday) and the sonic boom of jet planes landing at Cointrin airport pale by comparison. Speaking of these storms, Mary Shelley relates, 'We watch them as they approach from the opposite side of the lake, observing the lightning play among the clouds in various parts of the heavens, and dart in jagged figures upon the piny heights of Jura, dark with the shadow of the overhanging clouds.'[26] There was an atmosphere of gloom that accompanied the storms – people were warned to stay indoors. Even Shelley's and Byron's sailboat, which could brave the tempests by virtue of its deep keel, was ordered into port by the Swiss authorities. As the summer wore on, the Arve and the Rhone overflowed their banks, flooding the low sections of the city – bridges were washed away, roads became impassable, the damage to crops was inestimable, and bread was scarce. Dead animals were seen floating on the river and the lake had risen by almost seven feet. It was chilly in the homes, and fires were lit to keep warm. The persistent rain, beating against the windowpanes at Chapuis and Diodati, had caused frayed tempers – but independently of the storm raging outside, problems had developed within both households, which contributed to the stormy atmosphere within.

Too little has been said so far of the complex relationships existing between the various members of the Diodati and Chapuis households, and of the emotional climate that existed within each villa. In essence there were two classes of citizens, the two demigods occupying centre stage, Byron and Shelley, their heads in the clouds, and the lesser mortals, who spent morning to dusk listening, weighing each word, in silent and reverential adulation. It is not our purpose to describe relations between Byron and Shelley, since others have written at great length on that topic. Rather, our interests lie with the lesser personalities; the so-called, secondary literary talents – Mary, Claire, and Polidori: these figures listened rather than talked, and if they talked, were usually ignored or occasioned mirth. Mary states in her Introduction to the 1831 edition, in fact, that, 'Many and long were the conversations between Lord Byron and Shelley, to which I was a devout but nearly silent listener.'

Each of these three suffered from frustration at the *éclat* of the two 'greats': Polidori's trials are better known; jealous over his eroding influence with Byron, in the face of Shelley the ascending star, he made desperate, almost childish attempts to regain it. At times he made his presence at Diodati scarce; he was, after all, the darling of Geneva society. Far from ingratiating him, however, Polidori's pranks merely amused Byron, and he became the object of the famous Byronic 'sneer'. Unperturbed, the resourceful doctor tried new tactics to gain attention – one was to write a play within a record period of time. The play was entitled *Cajetan*, the name of Dippel's contemporary alchemist at Berlin as well as a version of the Italian name Gaetano – the name of Polidori's father. Polidori read his play one night at Diodati, but the lines were so bad that not even Byron could restrain his laughter and within minutes a minor tragedy ensued.

Thoroughly humiliated, Polidori rushed upstairs and shed bitter tears in the privacy of his rooms – Byron lamely attempted to console his doctor saying he had heard worse lines when he was on the literary committee of the Drury Lane Theatre. The terse note in Polidori's diary, however, reveals the doctor's deep sense of bitterness: 'having delivered my play into their hands, I had to hear it laughed at.'[27] There is even more pathos in Polidori's pique, aroused to the point of surly revenge. Earlier in the course of the Rhine journey he had asked Byron: 'What is there you can do that I cannot?' Bryon replied: 'Three things. I can swim across that river, I can snuff out that candle with a pistol shot at the distance of twenty paces, and I have written a poem of which fourteen thousand copies were sold in one day.'[28] Unable to endure his humiliation any longer, Polidori used physical means to vent his anger: on one occasion he hit Lord Byron with an oar on the leg, and expressed joy at the pain he had caused. On another occasion, having lost a sailing match, he challenged Shelley to a duel, which the poet laughed off. Byron responded to the challenge with 'Recollect, that although Shelley has some scruples about duelling, I have none, and shall be, at all times, ready to take his place.'[29] Polidori was further embittered by Byron's decision to leave Diodati for his lake tour from 22 June–1 July,[30] alone with Shelley, leaving Polidori – who was suffering with a bad ankle – behind at Diodati.

In her quiet and undramatic way, Mary also had suffered because of the relationship between Byron and Shelley. Perhaps it had hurt her pride to be so intellectually discounted by Shelley, who exhibited a marked preference for Byron's company. Moreover, she had found the personality of Byron so overwhelming that in his presence she was virtually tongue-tied, unable to express a single thought. Very much in love with Shelley, she was distressed that for lengthy hours he was neglecting her, forever walking with Byron in the surrounding hills, talking with Byron on the veranda, or sailing with Byron on the lake. Even in his idle moments Shelley seemed more interested in Claire's predicament than in Mary.

Mary had always resented her stepsister Claire, 'the bane

of my life', who persisted in cohabiting with Mary and Shelley in spite of all Mary's attempts to get rid of her. Such resentment turned to jealousy when Mary realized that, as Byron was discarding Claire as his mistress, she was transferring her affections to Shelley, who was becoming her chief confidant and friend. (Unfortunately the full story of the Claire–Shelley relationship can never be told, because all documents were deliberately destroyed.) Circumstantial evidence overwhelmingly suggests the depth and durability of their relationship. When the writer William Graham visited Claire Clairmont towards the end of her life, he asked her whether she had ever loved. She answered she had. 'Shelley?' was the innocent query. 'With all my heart and soul' was the impetuous reply. On another occasion, speaking of Allegra, his so-called natural daughter by Claire (later Claire relinquished her daughter to Byron) Byron predicted that Allegra would eventually become his mistress. Upon the shock expressed by the interviewer, Byron went on to explain: 'I can well do it, she is no child of mine. She is Mr Shelley's child.'[31] Among the serious scholars of Shelley, at least one believed that Shelley was in love with Claire and that she later had a child by him, the mysterious Adelaide who was born in Naples in 1818 and died soon afterwards.[32] It is a well-known fact that on her deathbed, Claire 'was seen clutching Shelley's shawl on her breast'.[33]

Mary and Polidori were constantly in each other's company during Byron and Shelley's *Tour du Lac*; Mary came to label him 'her brother' (a very meaningful term for Mary). At first, while they were both staying at Sécheron, Polidori gave Mary lessons in Italian. Reading Dante and Tasso, they were seen wandering through the isolated footpaths leading to the hills behind the hotel, or rowing on the peaceful lake by moonlight. Polidori says just enough in his *Diary* to entice the literary detective to read between the lines. His entry for 31 May reads: 'read Italian with Mrs S[helley] dined; went into a boat with Mrs. S[helley], and rowed all night till 9; tea'd together; chatted, etc.'[34] Polidori also played the role of doctor and baby-sitter to little William, inoculating him for smallpox, for which the doctor received a golden chain and a seal as a fee. In Byron's absence, Polidori had found Mary a fascinating substitute – she was, after all, the daughter of the famous Mary Wollstonecraft and the 'immortal' Godwin. For one who liked to hear himself talk, Mary was a good listener. In her he could safely confide, find solace, and relate the story of Eliza, the love he had left behind in England, or his latest romantic escapades in Geneva, without incurring the risk of ridicule. On her part, Mary needed someone in whom to entrust herself, and when the two parties moved to Cologny, their intimacy increased.

According to a local legend, one of the English ladies on the hill often visited the village cemetery in the company of a man at night, stopping in front of the grave of a little girl, a relative of the Diodatis, who had died in mysterious circumstances at a tender age in 1813. The old cemetery of Cologny no longer exists (by accident the tombstone of that child with its pitiful inscription was dug up by some workman and encased in a stone wall in front of the village church, where it can still be seen). Knowing of Mary's pilgrimages to St Pancras, and her fondness for the sombre and morbid atmosphere of a cemetery, there could be no shadow of a doubt concerning the identity of the young lady.

On the night of 15 June, after a rain shower, as Polidori and Byron were watching Mary and Shelley climb Diodati hill from the veranda, with some prompting from Byron to offer his arm, Polidori jumped over the railing of the balcony – a ten-foot drop – to help Mary negotiate the slippery grass. The reward for this act of gallantry was a painfully sprained ankle, which the doctor was to nurse for the next few weeks, virtually confining him to the villa and preventing him from participating in the famous *Tour du Lac*. The sprained ankle has its role to play in the history of the *Frankenstein* plot, however. With the poets away, and pregnant Claire sulking, the ailing Polidori was Mary's constant companion, as his diary confirms.[35]

June 23. – Went to town; apologized to Rossi. Called on Dr Slaney etc. Walked to Mrs Shelley. Pictet, Odier, Slaney, dined with me. Went down to Mrs S[helley?] for the evening. . . .

June 24. – Up at 12. Dined down with Mrs S[helley] and Miss C[lare] C[lairmont].

June 26. – Up. Mounted on horseback: went to town. Saw Mrs Shelley: dined. To Dr Rossi's party of physicians: after at Mrs S[helley's?].

June 27. – Up at Mrs Shelley's: dined. No calèche arrived: walked to G[eneva]. No horses: ordered saddle-horse. Walked to Rossi's – gone. Went to the gate: found him. Obliged to break off the appointment. Went to Odier's. Met with Mr—, a friend of Lord Byron's father. Invited me to his house: been a long time on the Continent. Music, ranz des vaches, beautiful. Rode two hours; went to Mrs S[helley]; Miss C[lairmont] talked of a soliloquy.

June 28. – All day at Mrs S[helley's].

June 29. – Up at 1; studied; down at Mrs S[helley's].

June 30. – Same.

July 1. – Went in calèche to town with Mrs S[helley] and C[laire] for a ride, and to mass ... Found Lord Byron and Shelley returned.

July 2. – Rain all day. In the evening to Mrs S[helley].

The next entry after 2 July in Polidori's diary is 5 September – well after the Shelleys' departure. Was Polidori's explanation that he failed to keep up his diary 'through neglect and dissipation', merely a facile excuse? Or, was he more upset by the arrival of the poets than he cared to admit? There is in existence a curious note in Polidori's diary that has mystified scholars, in which Polidori 'threatened to shoot S[helley] one day on the water'. Is it not likely that if Mary and Polidori had an affair, it took place during this crucial week from 22 June–1 July, when Byron and Shelley were making literary history by visiting Clarens, Meillerie, Chillon and Ouchy in search of Rousseau, and the historian Gibbon?

The legend of the few days (from 15 June to 22 June) which precede the *Tour du lac* can hardly be equalled for sheer dramatic impact. We will, for convenience' sake, and as some other commentators like Samuel Rosenberg[36] have in fact done, corn-press the explanation of the forces that inspired the writing of *Frankenstein* into a single night.

Let us imagine the evening of 16 June:[37] outside the rain and wind are pounding against the tall windows overlooking the veranda, lightning is marching over the lake, and thunder echoes in the mountains. At Diodati, everyone huddles in the main living room, around the fireplace – waiting for a cue. Byron has just selected a book from the shelves that he or Polidori has purchased from a Genevan bookdealer. The volume is entitled *Fantasmagoriana, or Collection of the Histories of Apparitions, Spectres, Ghosts, etc.*[38] With the appropriate intonation, Byron reads the story of a husband who kisses his new bride on their wedding night, only to find, to his horror, that she has been transformed into the corpse of the woman he once loved. The group, numbed into silence, waits. Byron, with even greater dramatic emphasis, intones the following lines from Coleridge's 'Christabel':[39]

> Then drawing in her breath aloud
> Like one that shuddered, she unbound
> The cincture from beneath her breast:
> Her silken robe and inner vest
> Dropt to her feet, and full in view
> Behold! her bosom and half her side,
> Hideous, deformed and pale of hue,
> A sight to dream of, not to tell!
> And she is to sleep by Christabel.

Outside, the storm rages unabated, and the conversation not unnaturally turns to the mysterious powers of electricity, as Byron relates how he had seen a tree spun into life by lightning. Discussions then centre upon galvanism, the experiments of Dr Erasmus Darwin (the grandfather of the great scientist) who, according to Mary, preserved a piece of vermicelli in glass until 'by some extraordinary means' it began to move. Perhaps a corpse could be thus re-animated; perhaps the token parts of a creature might be manufactured, brought together, and shocked into vital warmth? When silence followed, according to Polidori's *Diary* – for 18 June – 'Shelley, suddenly shrieking and putting his hands to his head, ran out of the room with a candle. Threw water in his face, and after gave him ether. He was looking at Mrs S[helley] and suddenly thought of a woman he had heard of who had eyes instead of nipples, which, when taking hold of his mind, horrified him.'[40] When Shelley's hallucination was over, Byron proposed, 'We will each write a ghost story.' It being dawn, and the storm having subsided, they departed for the night.

Mary explains her 'nightmare' that night in the introduction to the 1831 edition of *Frankenstein*:

> When I placed my head on my pillow, I did not sleep, nor could I be said to think. My imagination, unbidden, possessed and guided me, gifting the successive images that arose in my mind with a vividness far beyond the usual bounds of reverie. I saw – with shut eyes, but acute mental vision – *the pale student of unhallowed arts kneeling beside the thing he had put together. I saw the hideous phantasm of a man stretched out, and then, on the working of some powerful engine, show signs of life, and stir with an uneasy, half vital motion.* Frightful must it be; for supremely frightful would be the effect of any human endeavour to mock the stupendous mechanism of the Creator of the world. His success would terrify the artist; he would rush away from his odious handywork, horror-stricken. He would hope that, left to itself, the slight spark of life which he had communicated would fade; that this thing, which had received such imperfect animation, would subside into dead matter; and he might sleep in the belief that the silence of the grave would quench for ever the transient existence of the hideous corpse which he had looked upon as the cradle of life. He sleeps; but he is awakened; he opens his eyes; behold the horrid thing stands at his bedside, opening his curtains, and looking on him with yellow, watery, but speculative eyes.

That the reading of *Fantasmagoriana*, 'Christabel', and a discussion of the principles of life did not all occur during one night's seance is true. That, combined, they created sufficient impact on Mary's consciousness to occasion her nightmare is certain. It is important at this point, to reconstruct, with the aid of the diaries and journals, as well as with the assistance of scholars like Dowden and Rieger, the probable chronology of events. The reading of the *Fantasmagoriana* and the proposal by Byron that they each write a ghost story, probably occurred on the night of 16 June, when Polidori was laid up with a sprained ankle and the Shelley party spent the night at Diodati. (It is a pity that so few scholars have bothered to read these rather lengthy two volumes of *Fantasmagoriana* in full, for they serve to focus attention on the Germanic atmosphere, which both parties had already encountered in their journey on the Rhine.) Polidori's entry for 17 June notes that 'the ghost-stories are begun by all but me.' Certainly the reading of Coleridge's 'Christabel' and Shelley's subsequent hallucination occurred on 18 June. According to Polidori's *Diary* the discussion 'about principles, – whether man was to be thought merely an instrument', occurred on 15 June.[41]

> *June 15.* – Up late; began my letters. Went to Shelley's. After dinner, jumping a wall my foot slipped and I strained my left ankle. Shelley etc. came in the evening; talked of my play etc., which all agreed was worth nothing. Afterwards Shelley and I had a conversation about principles, – whether man was to be thought merely an instrument.

As we have noted in Chapter One, the result of Byron's proposal was that the two literary underdogs – Mary and Polidori – wrote the most enduring horror stories of their time; creating monsters and vampires that were to inhabit the world thereafter. Polidori, according to Mary, wrote a story about a skull-headed lady who was punished for peeping through a key-hole. Shelley, contrary to what is commonly supposed, also wrote his *Fragment of a Ghost Story* (a grandmother sees a ghost made of ashes) probably intended for the benefit of his son William.[42] Byron composed his famous fragment 'The Vampyre', which was later appended to the poem *Mazeppa* dedicated to the Cossack leader Mazeppa.

Although improvising a 'nightmare' to account for her inspiration was a sound literary device, it was quite possible that the three nights of reading and discussions (15 June, 16 June, and 18 June) that centred on both Gothic literature and science had awakened thoughts and speculations that had germinated in Mary's mind since her visit to the Rhineland. If added scientific explanations were needed in the composition of her 'scientist' or 'monster', it is more than likely that Mary obtained these from Polidori – the only one in the group who was a scientist in the strict sense – during the days that followed, when the two poets were on their *Tour du Lac*.

Referring to the composition of *Frankenstein*, Mary wrote – again in her Introduction to the 1831 edition: 'I certainly did not owe the suggestion of one incident, nor scarcely of one train of feeling, to my husband.' The statement is not altogether true, for Shelley contributed far more to the story than Mary cares to admit. When Shelley finally returned to Cologny on 1 July there was an attempt on both sides to rekindle the affectionate, spiritual, and intellectual rapport of 1814. Leaving little William behind with the maid Elize, Mary and Shelley decided, in the company of the inevitable Claire, to seek loftier air in the shadow of the great Mont Blanc, only dimly perceptible in the clouds that constantly shrouded this snow-capped giant. After a period of almost total silence during the months preceding – Mary's *Journal* begins on 21 July 1816 – it is refreshing to read almost superabundant trivia for that particular excursion.[43] The journal indicates that the relationship between Mary and Shelley had improved.

Given Mary's close literary dependence on her immediate location, apart from rekindling their love, one of the chief purposes of the six-day trip (21 July–27 July), from Mary's point of view, was to find a new, dramatic, Alpine setting for the confrontation between the monster and his creator – a setting with the kind of overwhelming and desolate background needed to heighten the pathos of such a critical scene.

We followed Mary on her journey along the valley of the Arve, to Bonneville, passing by Cluses, Sallanches, Servoz, and finally to Chamonix (a small village in those days with only three respectable inns), which they reached on the evening of 22 July. They stayed at the Hôtel de la Ville de Londres, owned by J Tairras, where Shelley registered as an 'atheist', in classical but sloppy Greek:

Ειμι φιλανθρωπος δεμωχρατιχος [*sic*] ταθεος τε

Some time later, a God-fearing English tourist, evidently better versed in classics than Shelley, corrected the poet's poor Greek spelling.[44]

When Byron, Polidori, and his Cambridge friend, Hobhouse, finally checked the register of Shelley's hotel at Chamonix on 30 August, Byron thought he was rendering a service to posterity by blotting out the words 'atheist' and 'fool'. The blotted-out but corrected Greek could still be seen by tourists a few decades later. The whole episode had in fact become a *cause célèbre*, related by English newspapers. 'Mr Shelley is understood to be the person,' stated the *London Chronicle*, 'who, after gazing on the Mont Blanc, registered himself in the album as P B Shelley, the atheist, with gross and cheap bravado which the natural taste of the new school took for a display of philosophic courage.'[45]

Fortunately neither Mary nor Shelley were mad enough to try to climb Mont Blanc – no one had successfully climbed the summit since 1802. Instead they contented themselves with the grandeur and desolation of the *Mer de Glace* and Montanvert.[46]

Tuesday, July 23. – Chamounix. – In the morning, after breakfast, we mount our mules, to see the source of the Arveiron. When we had gone about three parts of the way, we descended and continued our route on foot, over loose stones, many of which were of an enormous size. We came to the source, which lies like a [stage?] surrounded on the three sides by mountains and glaciers. We sat on a rock, which formed the fourth, gazing on the scene before us. An immense glacier was on our left, which continually rolled stones to its foot. It is very dangerous to go directly under this. ... We see several avalanches, some very small, others of great magnitude, which roared and smoked, overwhelming everything as it passed along, and precipitating great pieces of ice into the valley below. This glacier is increasing every day a foot, closing up the valley.

On 24 July, as the weather cleared, Shelley and Mary began the ascent of Montanvert, and Mary comments:[47]

Nothing can be more desolate than the ascent of this mountain; the trees in many places have been torn away by avalanches, and some half leaning over others, intermingled with stones, present the appearance of vast and dreadful desolation. It began to rain almost as soon as we left our inn. When we had mounted considerably, we turned to look on the scene. A dense white mist covered the vale, and tops of scattered pines peeping above were the only objects that presented themselves.

But they succeeded in climbing only half way, as the rain began in torrents. During the descent, Shelley tripped and fell on his knees, fainted, and was incapacitated for some minutes.

On Thursday, 25 July, they set out again for Montanvert with *beaucoup de monde*; they gained the top at 12, and beheld *la Mer de Glace*:[48]

This is the most desolate place in the world; iced mountains surround it; no sign of vegetation appears except on the place from which [we] view the scene. We went on the ice; it is traversed by irregular crevices, whose sides of ice appear blue, while the surface is of a dirty white. We dine on the mountain.

Shelley could hardly restrain his enthusiasm: 'I never knew. I never imagined, what mountains were before. The immensity of these aerial summits excited, when they suddenly burst upon the sight, a sentiment of ecstatic wonder, not unallied to madness.'[49]

Mary was equally inspired by the setting; within sight of Mont Blanc and with memories of her excursion to Montanvert, while it rained outside, she began composing some of the best lines in *Frankenstein* – the confrontation between the scientist and the monster – on Monday, 29 July, writing an almost literal description of what she had just seen.

The rain was pouring in torrents, and thick mists hid the summits of the mountains, so that I even saw not the faces of those mighty friends. Still I would penetrate their misty veil, and seek them in their cloudy retreats. What were rain and storm to me? My mule was brought to the door, and I resolved to ascend to the summit of Montanvert. I remembered the effect that the view of the tremendous and ever-moving glacier had produced upon my mind when I first saw it. It had then filled me with a sublime ecstasy, that gave wings to the soul, and allowed it to soar from the obscure world to light and joy. The sight of the awful and majestic in nature had indeed always the effect of solemnising my mind, and causing me to forget the passing cares of life. I determined to go alone, for I was well acquainted with the path, and the presence of another would destroy the solitary grandeur of the scene.

The ascent is precipitous, but the path is cut into continual and short windings, which enable you to surmount the perpendicularity of the mountain. It is a scene terrifically desolate. In a thousand spots the traces of the winter avalanche may be perceived, where trees lie broken and strewed on the ground; some entirely destroyed, others bent, leaning upon the jutting rocks of the mountain, or transversely upon other trees. The path, as you ascend higher, is intersected by ravines of snow, down which stones continually roll from above; one of them is particularly dangerous, as the slightest sound, such as even speaking in a loud voice, produces a concussion of air sufficient to draw destruction upon the head of the speaker. The pines are not tall or luxuriant, but they are sombre, and add an air of severity to the scene. I looked on the valley beneath; vast mists were rising from the rivers which ran through it, and curling in thick wreaths around the opposite mountains, whose summits were hid in the uniform clouds, while rain poured from the dark sky, and added to the melancholy impression I received from the objects around me . . .

It was nearly noon when I arrived at the top of the ascent. For some time I sat upon the rock that overlooks the sea of ice.

A mist covered both that and the surrounding mountains. Presently a breeze dissipated the cloud, and I descended upon the glacier. The surface is very uneven, rising like the waves of a troubled sea, descending low, and interspersed by rifts that sink deep. The field of ice is almost a league in width, but I spent nearly two hours in crossing it. The opposite mountain is a bare perpendicular rock. From the side where I now stood Montanvert was exactly opposite, at the distance of a league; and above it rose Mont Blanc, in awful majesty. I remained in a recess of the rock, gazing on this wonderful and stupendous scene. The sea, or rather the vast river of ice, wound among its dependent mountains, whose aërial summits hung over its recesses. Their icy and glittering peaks shone in the sunlight over the clouds.

The party returned to Diodati on Saturday, 27 July. The entry in Mary's journal reads: 'and alight at Diodati ... then go down to Chapuis'. The entry for 28 July adds: 'Montalègre'. Tired from the arduous journey, but pleased to see their 'pretty babe' after a week's absence. During the month of August, there was a lull in the storms and the sun once again shone upon Lake Léman. At Diodati the period of nocturnal seances and discussions had passed and with it the atmosphere of evil that had engendered *Frankenstein*.

The month of August really provides a quiet epilogue to our story. On the surface, things had normalized. There could be no question of reconciling Claire to Byron – but the discarded and disconsolate mistress contented herself with the role of secretary, transcribing the verses of *Childe Harold* and *Prisoner of Chillon*.

After a tearful reconciliation upon Byron's return from the *Tour du Lac*, Polidori once again resumed his duties as house doctor, this time taking them very seriously, for his diary notes that he had a long explanation with Shelley and Byron about his conduct to Lord Byron. There is an incident on 10 August when a Genevan apothecary caused Byron some physical discomfort by badly mixing his formula of magnesium. The irascible doctor struck the apothecary in the face and trampled his glasses underfoot: the event landed Polidori in court. (The case was dismissed.)

Once again, as at the beginning of the summer, Polidori launched himself into a social whirl. He now had his entrée with Madame de Staël at Coppet, and even had a discussion with the awesome daughter of Necker on somnambulism. The doctor had also made the acquaintance of a lady of lower intellectual calibre and perhaps of even lesser virtue, the Countess of Breuss, who lived in the village of Genthoud. It was with her help and encouragement that Polidori found time to recast Byron's old notes and to compose his *The Vampyre* which finally appeared in *The New Monthly* magazine on 1 April 1819. Thus in three days the vampire in literature, the true precursor to Bram Stoker's *Dracula*, was born on the shores of Lake Léman, as an act of belated revenge against Lord Byron. Possibly Byron served as a model for the vampire figure – a brooding, sullen nobleman with whom all women fell in love, only to be preyed upon.

Shelley, too, had become somewhat disillusioned with Byron, having discovered some of those negative traits that were to weaken their intimacy. He was once again more often in the company of Mary, guiding her more thoroughly with her story, and encouraging her to develop it beyond the scope initially imagined by Mary. The days of August 1816, are filled with entries in Mary's journal such as, 'Shelley and I talk about my story'; 'Write my story'. Neither Mary nor Shelley frequented Diodati as often as they had in June; perhaps they were not as welcome. One revival of the lost atmosphere was the occasion of the visits of Byron's friend, Matthew Gregory 'Monk' Lewis. The 'Monk' and his army of liberated Jamaican domestics (he was a large landowner in the West Indies) reached Diodati on 14 August, and stayed for a week. Mary's journal – which so sparsely records conversations – relates the ghost stories told by the ebullient raconteur in such detail that one had the impression that they made a great impact on Mary. Although the 'seances' of the earlier period could not be renewed, the atmosphere in the Diodati salon was again visited with ghosts, demons, and a tale set in Germany of several cats and a coffin.[50] Mary, in fact, published one of Monk's stories many years later, in 1824, at the end of her essay 'On Ghosts'.[51]

Rather like the 'sensitive souls' of the Darmstadt circle, the attention of the group also turned to Goethe's *Faust*, which Monk Lewis greatly admired, and they discussed among other works *The Sorrows of Young Werther*, which was reason enough for Mary's inclusion of this work in *Frankenstein*, and which creates such an impression on the monster. In *The Sorrows of Young Werther*, states the monster, 'besides the interest of its simple and affecting story, so many opinions are canvassed, and so many lights thrown upon what had hitherto been to me obscure subjects that I found in it a never ending source of speculation and astonishment ... I thought Werteer himself a more divine being than I had ever beheld or imagined.'

The Swiss police, who are known to record carefully the presence of foreigners in their state, did not live up to their reputation for accuracy in the case of the Shelleys. In the archives of the city the date marked for Mary and Percy's departure is 17 August (permit no. 571), though in actual fact, judging from Mary's latest entry, they left Geneva on Thursday 29 August at '9 in the morning', with *Frankenstein* incomplete.

The summer of 1816 was one of the most productive summers in the history of English literature. Byron had completed his Third Canto of *Childe Harold* and had romanticized the life of the Swiss hero Bonnivard in the *Prisoner of Chillon*. He had sung the praises of Lake Léman and, in a sombre mood, presaged the end of the world in his poem 'Darkness'. Shelley, though less prolific, had been far more deeply influenced by the unspoiled beauties of nature and particularly by the majesty of the Alps. His 'Hymn to Intellectual Beauty' is a monument to Rousseau. The poem 'Mont Blanc' was obviously inspired by his visit to Chamonix. In the case of both poets, the impact of that haunted summer goes beyond the works that were actually completed during that span of time, for the period provided future inspiration. Byron had already begun composing *Manfred*, dedicated to his half-sister Augusta Leigh. Shelley was to make the subtitle of Mary's novel *or the Modern Prometheus* the title for his greatest work, *Prometheus Unbound*. Because of the impact of the two poets' stay, Geneva has also become a spot for literary pilgrimages, attracting poets and artists who seek inspiration by the lake.

In the last analysis, however, Mary and Polidori may have won. Although the spokesmen of the *grande littérature* had monuments erected in their honour and *Childe Harold* is still savoured by the specialist, *Frankenstein* has been a lasting commercial success, and to this day is a household word. Although Mary did not witness the total success of her story during her lifetime, only a few years after the 1818 publication, when plays based on her theme were beginning to be produced on the London stage, she perhaps had the consolation of knowing that, rather belatedly, she had kept the pledge she had made at her mother's grave.

6

A Summer's End

With the shrill winds of autumn, the summer of 1816 faded into a sense of foreboding; Shelley's dreams and hallucinations were haunted by premonitions; Byron had apocalyptically prophesied that tragedy would befall all those with whom he had been intimately involved. The succeeding years were punctuated by the untimely and violent deaths or suicides of all the male (and many of the peripheral) members of the Diodati group.

Barely six weeks after Mary's return to England from Geneva – on the night of 9 October 1816 to be precise – the Swansea police authorities in Wales discovered the cold body of a young woman lying on a bed in the dreary Mackworth Arms Inn, with a little Genevan watch, a gift of Mary and Shelley, a necklace, two coins, and a half-empty bottle of laudanum by her side. There was also a suicide note which helped the police to identify the unfortunate victim, Fanny Imlay, Mary Wollstonecraft's child of love, the taciturn, selfless peacemaker in the Godwin household, who had quietly sacrificed her life for the sake of others. The note read: 'I have long determined that the best thing I could do was to put an end to the existence of a being whose birth was unfortunate, and whose life has only been a series of pain to those persons who have hurt their health in endeavouring to promote her welfare. Perhaps to hear of my death will give you pain, but you will soon have the blessing of forgetting that such a creature ever existed as ...[1] 'Poor dear Fanny,' wrote Mary in self-reproach, 'if she had lived until this moment, she would have been saved, for my house would then have been a proper asylum for her.'[2] Consoling Fanny may not have been as simple as Mary would have us believe. Rumour had it that Fanny's despondency was at least in part the result of finally being told that she was born at Le Havre out of wedlock, the illegitimate daughter of an American adventurer. The extent to which Shelley was affected by Fanny's suicide is expressed in the following mournful lines:[3]

> Her voice did quiver as we parted;
>> Yet knew I not that heart was broken
> From whence it came, and I departed
>> Heeding not the words then spoken.
> Misery – 0 Misery,
> This world is all too wide for thee!

Only two months after the death of Fanny another tragedy struck the Shelleys – this time the circumstances were even more macabre. Early in the morning on 10 December 1816, the bloated body of a woman was pulled out of the Serpentine in Kensington, London. Judging by the partial decomposition, the corpse had been immersed in the water for at least one week. A notice in the London *Times* mentioned the bizarre tragedy without identifying the victim by noting that on Tuesday, 10 December, a respectable female, far advanced in pregnancy, was taken out of the Serpentine river and brought home to her residence in Queen Street, Brompton, on having been missed for nearly six weeks. She had a valuable ring on her finger. Want of honour in her conduct was supposed to have led to this fatal catastrophe, her husband having been abroad. The 'husband lately abroad' was none other than Percy Bysshe Shelley, who was compelled to identify the body of his legal wife Harriet, the pretty child bride with whom he had eloped after being expelled from Oxford scarcely five years before, and mother of his two children, Eliza Ianthe, and Charles Bysshe. Harriet's mournful note must have deeply wounded both Mary and Shelley with its intimations.[4]

> My dear Bysshe, let me conjure you by the remembrance of our days of happiness to grant my last wish. Do not take your innocent child from Eliza [Harriet's sister] who has been more than I have, who has watched over her with such unceasing care. Do not refuse my last request, I never could refuse you and if you had never left me I might have lived, but as it is I freely forgive you and may you enjoy that happiness which you have deprived me of. There is your beautiful boy, oh! be careful of him, and his love may prove one day a rich reward. As you form his infant mind so will you reap the fruits hereafter. Now comes the sad task of saying farewell. Oh! I must be quick God bless and watch over you all. You dear Bysshe and you dear Eliza. May all happiness attend ye both is the last wish of her who loved ye more than all others.

It appears that Harriet was still in love with Shelley when she died in spite of the fact that she may have committed adultery with one of several men – either a groom called Smith, or perhaps an Irishman called Ryan or Murray.

Harriet was buried at St Mildred's Church in London, and Shelley hastened to claim custody of his two children. A letter of Mary to Shelley on 17 December states, 'How very happy shall I be to possess those darling treasures that are yours!' Although Shelley was denied custody of Charles and Ianthe by the courts because of his radical views and 'immoral' conduct, his resolve at the time to obtain possession of his children probably counselled Mary and Shelley's decision to marry. The ceremony took place at St Mildred's on 30 December.

At last Percy and Mary were legally man and wife, and Godwin could welcome his benefactor formally into his home. In fact, the notation in Godwin's *Diary* of the marriage was obscured under the year 1814, and was the *fait accompli* of the marriage – an odd gesture of a man who professed to believe in free love for those who were not immediate members of his own family; the entry read, 'Percy Bysshe Shelley, married to Mary Wollstonecraft Godwin at St Mildred's Church, Bread Street, 30 December 1816. Haydon, Curate, Spire, Clerk Present, William Godwin, Mary Jane Godwin.'[5]

The suicide of Fanny particularly affected Mary and Shelley, although that of Harriet probably wounded Mary's conscience more. These deaths were, however, the first in a sequence of tragedies that circumscribed and decimated the charmed Diodati circle during the next few years.

Since the beginning of her liaison with Shelley, Mary had become accustomed to the idea of birth – and death. Already pregnant at the age of sixteen, she remained pregnant constantly during the following five years, and seemed destined to lose all her children. Percy Florence, born 12 November 1819, was the only child of Mary and Shelley to survive. The pain of losing a baby girl born prematurely on 22 February, 1815, and who died one month later, lying cold, curled up against Mary's breast on the morning of 6 March, was surely poignant enough. At the time she made a comment quite appropriate for the future author of *Frankenstein*: 'Dream that my little baby came to life again; that it had only been cold, and that we rubbed it before the fire, and it lived. Awake and find no baby. I think about the little thing all day.'[6]

A greater blow was the death of her second daughter, Clara Everina, in September of 1818, the first victim after the publication of *Frankenstein*. The little girl had been taken ill at Este, falling prey to an Italian fever. Noted Mary in her journal for 24 September, 'Poor Clara [the baby] is dangerously ill. Shelley is very unwell, from taking poison in Italian cakes. He writes his Drama "Prometheus" [*Prometheus Unbound*].'[7] They then hastened to Venice to consult a reliable physician, but Mary felt the little body stiffen in her arms almost the moment they arrived at the inn. By seven in the evening, as the sun was setting on the Lido, at the age of one year and three weeks, little Clara Everina was dead. She was buried the next day in the Lido. Later Mary wrote with an embittered heart of her loss in a poem entitled 'The Choice'.[8]

A happy Mother first I saw this sun,
Beneath this sky my race of joy was run,
Fiat, my sweet girl, whose face resembled *his*,
Slept on bleak Lido, near Venetian seas.

The children's gravedigger unrelentingly pursued his work; there seemed to be no respite to the tragedy of the young ones as the years wore on. One year later, it was the turn of little William, Mary's pretty, blue-eyed babe, nicknamed Willmouse, whose beauty both Mary and Shelley so proudly extolled, and who is so vividly described in the person of William, Victor Frankenstein's brother. Mary must have had a premonition of her own William's ultimate fate when she had the fictional William killed by the monster on the field of Plainpalais. In a strict sense William was the first member of the Diodati circle to perish. He too fell ill of the dreaded Roman fever at the Baths of Lucca on 2 June 1819, and lingered between life and death until noontime on 7 June, when he died in his mother's arms. Shelley roused himself from those hours of agony to send a mournful note to his friend Peacock in a letter dated 8 June 1819. 'Yesterday, after an illness of only a few days, my little William died. There was no hope from the moment of the attack. You will be kind enough to tell all my friends, so that I need not write to them. It is a great exertion to me to write this, and it seems to me as if, hunted by calamity as I have been, that I should never recover any cheerfulness again.'9 The loss of William struck Mary far more deeply, more deeply in fact than any loss she had hitherto suffered. At first, it seemed that William's death signified the end of everything. Intending to put a finish to the *Journal* she had begun during her Genevan stay in 1816, she simply noted: 'Begun July 21(1816), ... ended with my happiness June 7, 1819.'10 At that point it seemed to Mary that she had tasted the cup of adversity to the dregs and had exceeded even her mother's sufferings. She was saved from the danger of abandoning herself to her grief by Godwin's harsh paternal and stoic words of advice. Mary remembered the stern words written to her by her father in a letter dated 27 October 1818, on the occasion of Clara's death: 'I sincerely sympathize with you in the affliction which forms the subject of your letter, and which I may consider as the first severe trial of your constancy and the firmness of your temper that had occurred to you in the course of your life. You should, however, recollect that it is only persons of a very ordinary sort, and of a pusilanimous [*sic*] disposition, that sink long under a calamity of this nature. ... We seldom indulge long in depression and mourning, except when we think secretly that there is something very refined in it, and that it does us honour.'[11]

Some two years after the death of William, in August 1821, John William Polidori committed suicide. Polidori had often threatened to take his life during the summer when snubbed and ridiculed by Byron. Yet his more than three months' stay in Geneva evidently represented an apotheosis in the doctor's career. Byron summarily dismissed him with a mere recommendation shortly after the Shelleys left Geneva, and Polidori and Lord Byron parted company on 16 September. The doctor first went to Milan, where he was expelled for quarrelling with a guard; he then went on to Florence, and finally settled at Pisa where, largely because of Byron's recommendation, he became private physician to three prominent English expatriates (Francis Horner, Francis North, and Lord Guilford) all of whom died in rapid succession in spite of, or perhaps because of, Polidori's medical care. Polidori later returned to England to practise medicine in Norwich, where for some unknown reason he gave up medicine and pursued the life of a recluse in a small apartment at Great Pulteney Street in London. On 27 August 1821, he was discovered dead in his apartment in circumstances strangely reminiscent of those attending Dippel's death or suicide, at Castle Wittgenstein. He had apparently taken his own life by swallowing a lethal dose of Prussic acid – a discovery indirectly linked with Dippel's 'Prussian blue'. The motives for the suicide are unknown: they could have been linked to a disappointed love affair, or gambling debt that the doctor had incurred and was unable to discharge. *The New Times* (11 September 1821) printed the following explanation of the circumstances attending Polidori's death, clearly unwilling to divulge the truth.[12]

Coroner's Inquest on John Polidori, Esquire. – An Inquisition has been taken before T Higgs, Esquire, Deputy Coroner, at the residence of the father of the above unfortunate gentleman, in Great Pulteney Street, Golden Square, who was discovered lying on his bed in a state nearly approaching to death, and soon afterwards expired.

Charlotte Reed, the servant to Mr Gaetano Polidori, the father of the deceased, said her master's son lived in the house, and for some time had been indisposed. On Monday the 20th of August last he returned from Brighton, since which his conduct manifested strong symptoms of incoherence, and he gave his order for dinner in a very strange manner. On the Thursday following the deceased dined with a gentleman residing in the same house, and on that occasion he appeared very much depressed in his spirits. About nine o'clock the same evening he ordered witness to leave a glass (tumbler) in his room; this was unusual, but one was placed as he desired. Deceased told her he was unwell; if therefore he did not get up by twelve o'clock the next day, not to disturb him. Witness, however. a few minutes before twelve, went into his room to open the shutters, and on her return saw the deceased lying in bed; he was not in any unusual position, but seemed extremely ill. Witness immediately left the room, went upstairs, and communicated what she had observed to a gentleman, who instantly came down. Witness then went for medical assistance. The deceased was about twenty-six years of age. – Mr John Deagostini, the gentleman alluded to by the last witness, corroborated her statement on his giving him the invitation to dine, which he accepted in a way quite different from his usual conduct. Witness also observed that, some time since, the deceased had met with an accident – was thrown out of his gig, and seriously hurt in the head. On Thursday at dinner he spoke in half sentences; the conversation was on politics and a future state. The deceased observed rather harshly that witness would see more than him; he appeared to be deranged in his mind, and his countenance was haggard. At dinner he ate very little: soon after left the room, but joined again at tea; hardly spoke a word, and retired at nine o'clock. After breakfast next morning, witness inquired of the servant whether Mr Polidori had gone out. She replied no, and that he had desired her not to disturb him. About twelve o'clock the servant came to him very much alarmed. Witness went immediately to the apartment of the deceased, and observed a tumbler on the chair, which contained nothing but water, and did not perceive any deleterious substance that the deceased might have taken; he was senseless, and apparently in a dying state. – Mr Thomas Copeland, a surgeon residing in Golden Square, was sent for suddenly to attend the deceased, and attempted to discharge the contents of the stomach without effect. He lingered for about ten minutes, and expired. Another medical gentleman soon after arrived, but his assistance was also unavailing. – There being no further evidence adduced to prove how the deceased came to his death, the jury, under these circumstances, returned a verdict of – Died by the visitation of God.

Lord Byron, it seems, had a premonition of the doctor's death which was recorded by Medwin: 'I was convinced', said Byron, 'something very unpleasant hung over me last night: I expected to hear that somebody I knew was dead. So it turns out – poor Polidori is gone. When he was my physician he was always talking of prussic acid, oil of amber, blowing into veins, suffocating by charcoal and compounding poisons; but for a different purpose to what the Pontic monarch did, for he has prescribed a dose for himself that would have killed fifty Mithridates – a dose whose effect, Murray says, was so instantaneous that he went off without a spasm or struggle. It seems that disappointment was the cause of this rash act.'[13]

Mary, in spite of the closeness of her association with Polidori, was conspicuously silent on the subject of his suicide. In fact, throughout her correspondence after the summer at Diodati, she alluded to Polidori only twice – a very unaccountable omission: once, when she was informed by her friend Maria Gisborne of the publication of Polidori's *Vampyre*, in *The New Monthly Magazine* (April 1819). Mary accepted Byron's presumed authorship, although she was probably aware of the true author.[14] The second mention was when Mary, in 1835, wrote to Polidori's nephew, Gabriel

Rossetti, for information on the life of the poet Alfieri, about whom she was preparing a sketch for *Dr Lardner's Cyclopaedia*.[15]

Returning from Geneva to England on 8 September 1816, Shelley and Mary settled for the winter at Marlow, and Claire, to keep her pregnancy a secret from the Godwins, at Bath. Here Allegra (first named Alba, or Dawn by Claire), the illegitimate daughter of Claire and Lord Byron, was born on 12 January 1817.

The Shelleys' stay at Marlow was a period of immense literary productivity both for Shelley and for Mary, and marked a temporary reprieve from the unrelenting course of tragedy. Here Mary completed the last pages of *Frankenstein*, and Shelley negotiated the sale of the manuscript; she worked also on her *History of a Six Weeks' Tour*, published in December. Claire joined them at Marlow with Allegra later that year, and even assembled a book, for which Shelley tried unsuccessfully to find a publisher.

The English winter bore hard on Shelley's failing health, and, at the recommendation of a physician that Shelley seek a warmer and more hospitable climate the party set sail for Italy on 11 March 1817. Their Italian peregrinations took them to Milan, Lake Como, Leghorn, Lucca, Venice, briefly to Lord Byron's residence Villa d'Este, Bologna, Rome, Naples, Villa Valsovano near Leghorn, Florence, Pisa, Ravenna, and finally that fateful little house on the Gulf of Genoa, Casa Magni at Lerici.

In spite of Shelley's prodigious literary output during these peregrinations, theirs was not a happy life, and the continuing losses of their dear ones provides one explanation. Worse, the climate of Italy suited them as little as the climate of England, and they were both intermittently ill; there were strains in their marriage as Shelley found new poetic and platonic relationships, developing a passion for attractive young ladies such as Emilia Viviani and Jane Williams; there were the usual financial problems; the increasing hostility towards Godwin, always prone to exploit Shelley financially; to compound their problems there were intrigues and blackmail by servants and above all Shelley's growing schism with Lord Byron.

Byron, it seems, had demanded as early as 1816 that he be given custody of Allegra. Claire, in spite of her apprehensions over Byron's temperament and lifestyle, consented, determined that Allegra's future would be far more brilliant as the daughter of the illustrious English lord and poet. On 28 April 1816, Allegra, accompanied by the trusted maid Elize, was sent to Venice. Claire's notes for that period reveal her torment over parting with her daughter. 'She was the only thing I had to love, the only object in the world I could call my very own ... I will say nothing as to what the parting cost me; but I felt that I ought not for the sake of gratifying my own affections deprive her of a brilliant position in life.'[16] The intensity of Claire's suffering at being separated from her child are made pathetically clear in her journal. She writes for 21 April 1821, 'I dreamt this night that Tatty [Mr Tighe] had been to Bagnacavallo and had returned [with] bringing Allegra to me.'[17] Allegra's death, at the age of five years and three months, came all too soon, and once again it was presaged by a dream of Claire's: 'Towards Wednesday morning I had a most distressing dream that I received a letter which said that Allegra was ill and not likely to live. The dreadful grief I felt made awakening appear to me the most delightful sensation of ease in the world.' And again, she wrote to Byron: 'I can assure you I can no longer resist the internal, inexplicable feeling which haunts me that I shall never see her [Allegra] any more. '[18]

Allegra died on 19 April 1822, attended by the cares and prayers of the Catholic nuns at Bagna Cavallo to whom Byron had entrusted her. Mary wrote that she died of typhus fever which had been raging in the Romagna, but no one wrote to say it was there. 'She had no friends, except the nuns in the convent, who were kind to her, I believe. But you know Italians; if half of the convent had died of the plague, they would never have written to have had them removed, and so the poor child fell a sacrifice.'[19] Allegra's death was a harsher blow to Claire than William's was to Mary, and she never forgave Byron, holding him personally responsible for her death.

Even Byron's grief for a moment seemed genuine enough. Insofar as Mary was concerned, the death of yet another child simply served to sharpen memories 'of that deathbed at Rome by which she was always haunted'.[20] Little Allegra's remains were eventually buried in the churchyard at Harrow, but in an unmarked grave outside the Anglican cemetery because Allegra had been baptized a Catholic. Two weeks after Allegra's death, while walking with his new friend, Edward Williams, on the terrace of Casa Magni, which the Shelleys were sharing with the Williamses, Shelley had a vision of the figure of a child, rising out of the waves in the Gulf of Genoa. Then, clutching his friend's arms, he murmured: 'There it is again – there!' He later explained that in his hallucination Allegra was coming towards him, naked in the moonlight, clapping her hands as in joy, and smiling at him.[21]

On 16 June, Mary suffered a dangerous miscarriage. 'I was so ill,' Mary wrote 'that for seven hours I lay nearly lifeless – kept from fainting by brandy, vinegar, eau-de-Cologne, etc. At length, ice was brought to our solitude; it came before the doctor, so Claire and Jane were afraid of using it; but Shelley overruled them, and by an unsparing application of it I was restored. They all thought, and so did I at one time, that I was about to die.'[22]

At Casa Magni, the frayed nerves of two households were further shocked by a prophetic dream of Shelley which he later related to Mary.[23]

'I think it was on the Saturday after my illness [June 22],' wrote Mary, 'while yet unable to walk, 1 was confined to my bed, in the middle of the night I was awoke by hearing him scream and come rushing into my room; I was sure that he was asleep, and tried to waken him by calling on him, but he continued to scream, which inspired me with such a panic that I jumped out of bed and ran across the hall to Mrs Williams's room, where I fell through weakness, though I was so frightened that I got up again immediately; she let me in, and Williams went to Shelley, who had been wakened by my getting out of bed. He said that he had not been asleep, and that it was a vision that he saw that had frightened him. But as he declared that he had not screamed, it was certainly a dream and no waking vision. What had frightened him was this. He dreamt that, lying as he did in bed, Edward and Jane came in to him; they were in the most horrible condition – their bodies lacerated, their bones starting through their skin, the faces pale yet stained with blood; they could hardly walk, but Edward was the weakest and Jane was supporting him. Edward said, "Get up, Shelley; the sea is flooding the house, and it is all coming down." Shelley got up, he thought, and went to his window that looked on the terrace and the sea, and thought he saw the sea rushing in. Suddenly his vision changed, and he saw the figure of himself strangling me, that had made him rush into my room; yet, fearful of frightening me, he dared not approach the bed, when my jumping out awoke him, or, as he phrased it, caused his vision to vanish. All this was frightful enough, and talking it over the next morning, he told me that he had had many visions lately. He had seen the figure of himself, which met him as he walked on the terrace, and said to him, "How long do you mean to be content?"'

About this same time, Jane Williams, ordinarily a stable and practical woman, had a vision of Shelley.[24]

[Jane] was standing one day at a window that looked on the terrace with Trelawny; it was day; she saw, as she thought, Shelley pass by the window, as he often was then, without a coat or jacket; he passed again. Now, as he passed both times the same way, and as from the side towards which he went each time there was no way to get back except past the window again (except over a wall twenty feet from the ground), she was struck at seeing him pass twice thus, and looked out and seeing him no more she cried, 'Good God! can Shelley have leapt from the wall? Where can he be gone?' 'Shelley?' said Trelawny; 'no Shelley has past. What do you mean?' Trelawny says that she trembled exceedingly when she heard this; and it proved, indeed, that Shelley had never been on the terrace, and was far off at the time she saw him.

At the time of his vision, Shelley was less than a month away from his death. It is interesting to note that, like

Polidori, Shelley had often thought of suicide and particularly during the month of June had said:[25]

> 'Should you meet with any scientific person, capable of preparing the *Prussic Acid, or essential oil of bitter almonds*, I should regard it as a great kindness if you could procure me a small quantity. It requires the greatest caution in preparation, and ought to be highly concentrated; I would give any price for this medicine. You remember we talked of it the other night, and we both expressed a wish to possess it; my wish was serious, and sprung from the desire of avoiding needless suffering. I need not tell you I have no intention of suicide at present, but I confess it would be a comfort to me to hold in my possession that golden key to the chamber of perpetual rest.'

Shelley as we have seen contained a deep love for the sea, and felt a peculiar exhilaration being on the water in a boat; this may have satisfied his physical well-being and temporarily cured his hypochondria. He was in love with boats, boats of all kinds, but particularly sailboats, like the one he sailed with Lord Byron on Lake Léman. He was always designing boats, tinkering with various propelling devices, interested in the application of steam and often investing money he could not readily afford in such projects. Yet notwithstanding this love of the sea he suffered from one overwhelming handicap, about which Byron often chided him, since he was in effect tempting fate – Shelley did not know how to swim. During their famous lakeside tour (at the end of June, 1816) in search of Rousseau, both poets had courted death during a sudden squall just beyond Evian (where the monster had killed Frankenstein's bride). As the boat was approaching the rocky coast of St Gingoux, and perhaps because the inexperienced boatman did not clew up the sail in time, they lost control; the hull was taking water, and they risked being dashed on the rocks. Byron took off his coat and Shelley did likewise, though not knowing how to swim the latter simply sat at the bottom of the boat, folding his arms and waiting for the inevitable. Byron thought he could save Shelley, but the latter had no notion of being saved and added: 'I knew my companion would have attempted to save me, and I was overcome with humiliation when I thought that his life might have been risked to preserve mine.'[26] Shelley's reactions in the face of death are worth quoting in full for in essence they must have reflected his attitude in the final unrecorded hours of his life, where the circumstances were not in essence dissimilar. He wrote to his friend Peacock later: 'I felt in this near prospect of death a mixture of sensations among which terror entered, though but subordinately. My feelings would have been less painful had I been alone.'[27]

To pass the summer, Shelley and Williams decided to purchase a boat: this one a far more ambitious rig than the humble sailboat that was now rotting away in the harbour at Mon Repos. Designed largely by Williams on the model of an English schooner without deck and with excessively ample sails, the ship was built at Genoa and measured 28 ft long by 8 ft wide, though it looked much bigger. All in all, the boat was rather sturdy. Costs were to have been shared by Shelley, Trelawny, and Williams, but in the end it became Shelley's sole property and contrary to Byron's desire to have it christened 'Don Juan', it was baptized by Shelley the *Ariel*.

On 1 July 1822 despite Mary's tearful pleas, Shelley, Edward Williams, and a sailor boy called Charles Vivian,[28] left Casa Magni for Leghorn to greet their friends, the Hunts, who had travelled to see the Shelleys and Byron on various business matters. They reached Leghorn, and anchored at the back of Byron's yacht, the *Bolivar*. Shelley visited Hunt, but when, on the morning of 8 July, a slight breeze came up, he and Williams were anxious to return to Lerici. A brief thunderstorm passed and, ignoring the warning of Captain Roberts that a tempest was brewing, the friends set sail. Captain Roberts, who had kept the boat in view, ascended a tower and could see them about ten miles out at sea off Via Reggio when a storm hit the small boat. He saw them no more. The night was reminiscent of the evenings at Diodati; driving rain and lightning flashed along the Italian coast. The *Ariel* did not return to port in the morning.

Mary pathetically relates the events of the following days in a letter to Maria Gisborne, dated from Pisa, 15 August 1822.[29]

This was Monday, the fatal Monday, but with us it was stormy all day, and we did not at all suppose that they could put to sea. At twelve at night we had a thunderstorm. Tuesday it rained all day and was calm – the sky wept on their graves. On Wednesday, the wind was fair from Leghorn, and in the evening several feluccas arrived thence. One brought word they had sailed Monday, but we did not believe them. Thursday was another day of fair wind, and when twelve at night came, and we did not see the tall sails of the little boat double the promontory before us, we began to fear, not the truth, but some illness, some disagreeable news for their detention.

Jane got so uneasy that she determined to proceed the next day to Leghorn in a boat to see what was the matter. Friday came, and with it a heavy sea and bad wind. Jane, however, resolved to be rowed to Leghorn since no boat could sail, and busied herself in preparations. I wished her to wait for letters, since Friday was letter-day. She would not, but the sea detained her; the swell rose so that no boat would venture out. At twelve at noon our letters came; there was one from Hunt to Shelley; it said, 'Pray write to tell us how you got home, for they say that you had bad weather after you sailed on Monday, and we are anxious.' The paper fell from me. I trembled all over. Jane read it. 'Then it is all over!' she said. 'No, my dear Jane,' I cried, 'it is not all over, but this suspense is dreadful. Come with me – we will go to Leghorn; we will post, to be swift and learn our fate.'

We crossed to Lerici, despair in our hearts; they raised our spirits there by telling us that no accident had been heard of, and that it must have been known, etc. But still our fear was great, and without resting we posted to Pisa. It must have been fearful to see us – two poor, wild, aghast creatures, driving (like Matilda) towards the sea to learn if we were to be for ever doomed to misery. I knew that Hunt was at Pisa, at Lord Byron's house, but I thought that Lord Byron was at Leghorn. . . .

Both Lord Byron and the lady have told me since that on that terrific evening I looked more like a ghost than a woman;

light seemed to emanate from my features, my face was very white, I looked like marble. Alas, I had risen almost from a bed of sickness for this journey. I had travelled all day; it was now twelve at night, and we, refusing to rest, proceeded to Leghorn – not in despair – no, for then we must have died, but with sufficient hope to keep up the agitation of the spirits which was all my life. It was past two in the morning when we arrived. ... We found [Captain] Roberts at the Globe. He came down to us with a face which seemed to tell us that the worst was true, and here we learned all that had occurred during the week they had been absent from us, and under what circumstances they had departed on their return.

Yet all hope was not extinct. The boat might have been blown to Corsica or Elba, and, not knowing the coast, they might have sailed still further. ... We resolved to return, with all possible speed; we sent a courier to go from tower to tower along the coast to know if anything had been seen or found; and at nine a.m. we quitted Leghorn, stopped but one moment at Pisa, and proceeded towards Lerici. When at two miles from Via Reggio we rode down to that town to know if they knew anything. Here our calamity first began to break on us. A little boat and a water-cask had been found five miles off. They had manufactured a *piccolissima lancia* of thin planks stitched by a shoemaker, just to let them run on shore without wetting themselves, as our boat drew four feet of water. The description of that found tallied with this; but then this boat was very cumbersome, and in bad weather they might have been easily led to throw it overboard. The cask frightened me most; but the same reason might in some sort be given for that. I must tell you that Jane and I were not now alone. Trelawny accompanied us back to our home. We journeyed on, and reached the Magra about half-past ten p.m. I cannot describe to you what I felt in the first moment when, fording this river, I felt the water splash about our wheels. I was suffocated. I gasped for breath. I thought I should have gone into convulsions, and I struggled violently that Jane might not perceive it. Looking down the river I saw two great lights burning at the *foce*; a voice from within me seemed to cry aloud, 'That is his grave.'

Two bodies were discovered on the beach off Via Reggio the 16 or 17 July, and had been buried in the sand by the peasants, as was the custom with drowned victims. Even though bloated and badly mutilated by the water, there could be little doubt concerning the identity of the 'tall figure, green jacket, the volume of Sophocles in one pocket and Keats's poems in the other, doubled back as if the reader, in the act of reading, had hastily thrust it away'. Trelawny, who had to identify Shelley's remains, found them all too familiar to leave any doubt that the corpse was any other but Shelley's.[30] The precise circumstances of the sinking of Shelley's boat are totally unknown. Years later, a Genoese sailor, Sarsanna, allegedly confessed, shortly before his death, that, seeing Shelley's ship in difficulty, he ran it down during the storm, thinking Byron was on board and that they would find gold.

The moving cremation ceremony, which took place on 16 August, indirectly resulted from the Italian quarantine regulations which forbade bodies cast on shore and buried in sand to be disinterred. If they were burned, however, there could be no objections to reburying the ashes. Although there are many versions of the final scene of the burning of Shelley's body on a beach in the Gulf of Genoa, the brush of the French artist, Louis-Edward Fournier, gives us on canvas as accurate a reconstruction as any. There were the usual crowds of the curious. Trelawny presided over the macabre scene with Hunt and Byron watching. Hunt later wrote:[31]

> The sea, with the islands of Gorgona, Capraja, and Elba, was before us; old battlemented watch-towers stretched along the coast, backed by the marble-crested Apennines glistening in the sun, picturesque from their diversified outlines; and not a human dwelling was in sight. Three white wands stuck in the yellow sand from low-water to high-water mark indicated, but not with precision, the place of burial. An hour of silent toil went past before they had discovered the lime in which the body lay concealed; suddenly a mattock with a dull hollow sound struck the skull, causing a general shudder, while the men drew back. The furnace being placed and surrounded by wood, the remains were removed from their shallow resting-place. It was Byron's wish that the skull, which was of unusual beauty, should be preserved; but it almost instantly fell to

pieces. Of the volume of Keats's poems which had been buried with Shelley's body, only the binding remained, and this was cast upon the pyre. Although the fire was greater than that of the preceding day [when Williams' body was burned], the body was but slowly consumed. Three hours elapsed before it separated; it then fell open across the breast; the heart, which was unusually large, seemed impregnable to the fire. Trelawny plunged his hand into the flames and snatched this relic from the burning.

Although Trelawny gave Shelley's heart to Hunt, the latter, after some prodding, gave it to Mary who kept it enveloped in a fine linen and treasured it in a leather-bound copy of Shelley's poem, *Adonais*, to the end of her life. The ashes were then transported to Rome and buried on 21 January 1823 in the Protestant cemetery of that city near the grave of little William (whose remains could not be found). In March of that year, Trelawny purchased another plot, and relocated the box containing Shelley's ashes to that grave.

For Mary, Shelley's death marked the end of one part of her life. She was now alone, penniless, and with a son, Percy Florence, to bring up. But in her later years the strength of character inherited from her father, and the practical side of her personality emerged triumphant, and were somewhat cushioned by her firm belief that the spirit of Shelley, her 'Ariel', remained by her side. She addressed him in her letters, 'O, my beloved Shelley', 'My own Shelley', as if he was still alive. She still considered herself 'his', and for that reason refused to entertain the possibility of remarriage. In a sense the presence of Shelley's heart and a few other token remains aided her in her fantasy.

Lord Byron prolonged his life for another two years of brilliant writing, aimless existence, orgies, and diverse mistresses. Finally, in the summer of 1823, in the quest of an ideal, he sailed for Greece to help the Greek patriots in their struggle for independence from the Turks. After having been associated with so much evil, Byron perhaps wished the world to see him die for a genuine 'good' cause – the glory that was Greece. Instead of dying heroically in battle, however, he fell seriously ill in Greece – hypochondriac to the end.

In a sense the rumours concerning Byron's death proved correct. He died at Missolonghi Bay of an internal disorder, worsened by careless treatment, while a harried body of unruly Greek irregulars were being besieged by the Turks outside his house. The first symptoms of disease occurred on the evening of 15 February 1824, when he fainted.[32]

> [F]rom the rapid changes of his countenance it was manifest that he was suffering under some nervous agitation. He then complained of being thirsty, and, calling for some cider, drank of it; upon which, a still greater change being observable over his features, he rose from his seat, but was unable to walk, and, after staggering forward a step or two, fell into Mr Parry's arms. In another minute his teeth were closed, his speech and senses gone, and he was in strong convulsions. So violent, indeed, were his struggles, that it required all the strength both of Mr Parry and his servant Tita to hold him during the fit. His face, too, was much distorted, and, as he told Count Gamba afterwards, 'so intense were his sufferings during the convulsion, that, had it lasted but a minute longer, he believed he must have died.' The fit was, however, as short as it was violent; in a few minutes his speech and senses returned; his features, though still pale and haggard, resumed their natural shape, and no effect remained from the attack but excessive weakness. 'As soon as he could speak,' says Count Gamba, 'he showed himself perfectly free from all alarm; but he very coolly asked whether his attack was likely to prove fatal. "Let me know," he said: "do you think I am afraid to die – I am not."'

The following day he was better but still weak and pale and complained of a feeling of weight in his head. His doctors applied leeches to his temples, but could not stop the bleeding when the leeches were removed, and from weakness, Byron fainted again. Though Byron recovered from this attack and renewed his activities in the next few weeks he complained of vertigo and of being indisposed. On 7 April, Byron, returning from a ride in the rain, was seized with a shudder-

ing and complained of fever and rheumatic pain and loss of
appetite. On 11 April, he was once again feverish and the following day stayed in bed. It was only on 14 April that Dr
Bruno was summoned, and advised bleeding which Byron at
first refused. At the time, he did not think that death was
imminent, and even professed to be elated at his fever, which
would, he said, cure his tendency to epilepsy. Only his faithful servant, Fletcher, who had been with him since the
Genevan days, had the sense of impending doom. It was
impossible to get real expert advice because a gale was raging
outside, blowing high winds into port and preventing ships
from coming in. Rain was descending in torrents as it had
been at Diodati and the scirocco winds (which had also blown
at Genoa) was blowing from the sea. For all practical purposes, Missolonghi was completely isolated from the outside
world. Still Byron refused bleeding, insisting that his mother
had made him promise on her deathbed never to consent to
being bled. However, in the end, he gave in to his doctors.
Barely recognizing Dr Bruno, he allegedly said, 'there – you
are, I see, a damned set of butchers – Take away as much
blood as you like, but have done with it.'[33] About 20 ounces
of blood were drained during the night but the fever persisted
and Byron's derangement increased; he had become incoher-
ent. On 17 April, bleeding was repeated but appearances of
inflammation of the brain gave concern. Blisters were then
applied to the soles of his feet. The faithful Fletcher realized
only too well that the end was near and asked his master
whether he should bring pen and paper to him. 'Oh no,' was
the reply, 'there is no time – it is now nearly over. Go to my
sister – tell her – go to Lady Byron – you will see her, and say –'
His voice then faltered and became indistinct but for another
twenty minutes he muttered to himself, though the words
were barely distinguishable: 'Augusta, Ada, Hobhouse,
Kinnaird', 'My Lord,' replied Fletcher, 'I have not understood
a word your Lordship has been saying.' 'Not understand me?'
replied a distressed Byron. 'What a pity! – then it is too late,
all is over.' 'I hope not,' answered Fletcher, 'but the Lord's
will be done.' 'Yes, not mine,' replied Byron. He then tried to

utter a few words, none of which were intelligible except, 'my sister, my child'.[34] The doctors gave him a strong anti-spasmodic medicine that incited him to talk wildly about. 'Poor Greece! – poor town! – my poor servants! ... Why was I not aware of this sooner?. .. My hour is come! – I do not care for death – but why did I not go home before I came here?' Later he muttered, 'There are things which make the world dear to me: for the rest, I am content to die.'[35]

Byron was barely thirty-six years old when he died. His embalmed remains were conveyed to England on the schooner *Florida*. Byron's body lay in state in an uncovered bier at Westminster Abbey for two days; later the funeral cortege, bearing his body, proceeded through the streets of London to the village of Hucknall Torkard, not far from Nottingham, where it was to be buried in the family burial ground. As the procession passed a humble house on Highgate Hill, Mary and Claire stood watching in silence at the window, in a last tribute to a man, who, in spite of their differences, Mary had always admired from afar. She had first learned of Byron's death while still in Italy, and had collapsed with shock. In her journal she later noted:[36]

> Byron had become one of the people of the grave – that miserable conclave to which the beings I best loved belong. I knew him in the bright days of youth, when neither care nor fear had visited me – before death had made me feel my mortality, and the earth was the scene of my hopes. Can I forget our evening visits to Diodati? our excursions on the lake, when he sang the Tyrolese Hymn, and his voice was harmonized with winds and waves. Can I forget his attentions and consolations to me during my deepest misery? Never.
>
> Beauty sat on his countenance and power beamed from his eye. His faults being, for the most part, weaknesses, induced one readily to pardon them.

Mary added, 'Albé – the dear, capricious, fascinating Albé – has left this desert world! God grant I may die young! A new race is springing about me. At the age of twenty-six, I am in the condition of an aged person. All my old friends are gone. I

Above, an old print of Villa Diodati – the figures in the foreground are probably Shelley, Mary and little William. Below, the villa as it is today (*both Borel Boissonnas*).

Above, the former stable at Montalègre. Below, the view of Geneva, overlooking Villa Diodati and Lake Léman, from Montalègre (*Borel Boissonnas*).

Above, William Godwin and Mary Wollstonecraft Godwin (*both National Portrait Gallery*). Below left, the alchemist Konrad Dippel (*Union Theological College*) and, below right, Dippel's Inn, where Shelley and Mary probably spent a night in 1814.

Above, Frankenstein's Castle as Mary Shelley would have seen it (*Ernst Selinger*). Below, the castle as it is today – the outer walls and the main towers.

The Barons Frankenstein. Above, their seal and an effigy of Georg, the dragon slayer (*both Dieter Keller*). Below, Frankenstein effigies in the church at Sibiu (*Calvin Floyd*).

Mary Shelley (*National Portrait Gallery*) and Percy Bysshe Shelley (*Bodleian Library, Oxford*). Below, a boating trip on Lake Léman with, presumably, Byron, Shelley, Mary Shelley, Claire Clairmont and Polidori (*Claire Elaine Engel*).

Claire Clairmont (*Newstead Abbey*) and John William Polidori (*National Portrait Gallery*). Below, the Hôtel de l'Ancre at Ouchy, where Byron and Shelley stayed on their *Tour du lac* (*University of Geneva*).

Lord Byron on the terrace of Villa Diodati (*University of Geneva*). Below, the Castle of Chillon (*Claire Elaine Engel*).

Louis-Edward Fournier's *Funeral of Shelley* (*John Mills Photography*).
Below, the tomb of Mary Wollstonecraft Godwin, William Godwin, Mary
Shelley and Shelley's heart at St Peter's Church, Bournemouth.

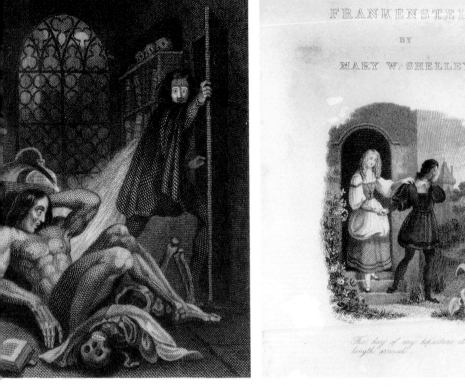

Above, an engraving of the monster by Chevalier and the title page from the 1831 edition of *Frankenstein* (*both Bodleian Library, Oxford*). Below left, a wood engraving of the monster by Lynd Ward in the 1934 edition of the book (*Lynd Ward*) and a poster for the play, *The Monster and the Magician*, showing Thomas Potter Cooke as the monster, performed in Paris in the 1820s (*Bibliothèque Nationale, Paris*).

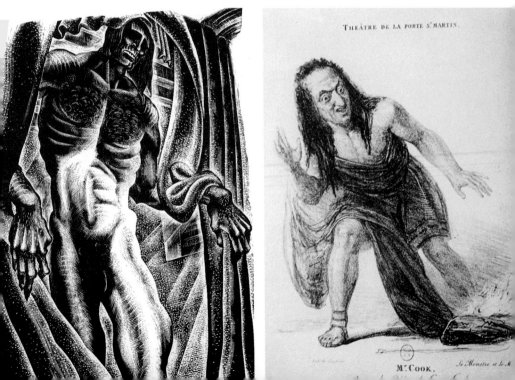

Above, Boris Karloff as the monster and Elsa Lanchester as Mary Shelley in the film *The Bride of Frankenstein*, 1935. Below, Robert Urquhart, Peter Cushing and Christopher Lee in *The Curse of Frankenstein*, 1957.

Above left, physician and alchemist Paracelsus and, right, Albertus
Magnus, creator of an early mechanical man (*both University of Geneva*).
Below left, *Prometheus and the Vulture* (*Bibliothèque Nationale, Paris*)
and, right, an old engraving of the alchemists at court (*British Museum*).

have no wish to form new. ... Life is the desert and the solitude – how populous the grave.'[37]

Shortly after Byron's death, Hobhouse wrote in his diary:
'Of the five that often dined at Byron's table at Diodati:
Polidori, Shelley, Lord Byron, Scrope Davies and myself; the
first (Polidori) put an end to himself, the second was drowned
(Shelley), the third (Byron) was killed by his physician (not
entirely true) and the fourth (Scrope Davies) is in exile.'[38]

Hobhouse seemingly had forgotten to make note of yet
another tragic death among Diodati's guests: that of Gregory
'Monk' Lewis. In May, 1818, barely two years after Diodati,
'Monk' was seized by convulsions in the mid-Atlantic, on
board a ship that was carrying him back from his West Indian
plantation. His groans and sighs, mixed with the voodoo
incantations of his Jamaican servants, could be heard the
length and breadth of the ship. On 14 May, Lewis lay on his
deathbed, felled by yellow fever. Upon his death, a roughly
hewn wooden casket was fashioned, and he was thrown into
his grave, the sea.

Barely eight years after the haunted summer of 1816, the
only members of the original Diodati group who remained
were Mary and Claire. (Godwin had finally died of catarrhal
fever and was buried on 14 April 1836, expressing the desire
in his will that, 'my mortal remains be deposited as near as
may be to those of the author of *A Vindication of the Rights
of Woman'*.)

With the death of Sir Timothy Shelley in 1844, Mary had
finally in the name of her son inherited the estate from which
she and Shelley had been exiled in their youth – Field Place,
Sussex. There she lived out her later years in seclusion with
only a small circle of friends, preserving the memories of her
loved ones, and collecting and publishing Shelley's poems and
letters. Although Mary may have been proposed to by several
men, among the most serious being the French poet Prosper
Mérimée, she never seriously considered remarriage; in her
mind Shelley remained alive. Her devotion was rather
directed towards her only surviving child, Percy Florence,

whom she brought up in a conventional way, educating him at Harrow and Trinity College, Cambridge. In Percy's company she returned to the Continent in 1840, revisiting many of Mary's earlier haunts, and inspiring the writing of one of Mary's best works, her *Rambles*.

Mary died at her London residence at 24 Chester Square, on the first day of February 1851, at the age of fifty-four. A letter from Percy, her son, to Isabel Booth, dated 3 January, stated that paralysis had set in during the last week of her illness. She was buried at St Peter's Church, Bournemouth, in the very tomb where William Godwin and Mary Wollstonecraft had already been laid to rest.

The last member of the Diodati group, Claire Clairmont survived with her memories to a venerable old age – dying at the age of eighty-one. Romantic and tiresome to the end, her later years were difficult times for her, and she was forced to fend for herself. For many years she worked as a governess for various wealthy families, sojourning in European capitals, and even travelling to Moscow. Towards the end of her life she settled in Florence, Italy, and was provided for by her nephews and nieces, the children of her brother Charles. There she died and was buried at Campo Santo della Misericordia de St Maria d'Antella. The inscription on her tomb reads:

In Memory of
Clara Mary Constantia Jane Clairmont
born April 27th 1798, died March 19th, 1879.
She passed her life in sufferings, expiating not only
her faults but also her virtues.

7

Frankenstein: In Print and on Stage

Although Mary and Shelley had difficulty finding a publisher for the novel *Frankenstein*, once published it became an instant success. During Mary's lifetime (she died in 1851) the book was brought out in several editions and revisions, was translated into several languages, and was adapted success-fully to the stage.

Frankenstein editions

The last page of the *Frankenstein* manuscript was corrected by Mary and Shelley at Marlow on 14 May 1817, and Mary wrote in her journal for that day: 'Shelley ... corrects "Frankenstein". Write Preface. Finis.' But the most pressing problem was finding a publisher: Mary was turned down at least three times in spite of Shelley's notoriety, and his solici-tations on behalf of his 'friend'. The manuscript was initially submitted to Byron's publisher, John Murray, who liked the story well enough to send it to one of his literary advisers, William Gifford, the editor of the *Quarterly Review*, for advice. Gifford, considering the book too radical, advised Murray to turn it down. Shelley wrote next to his own pub-lisher, Ollier, on 3 August 1814; but Ollier's refusal of the manuscript was even more prompt; it came back within three days. Perhaps in desperation, Shelley sent the manuscript on 22 August to the publisher Lackington, Allen, and Co.; Lackington's father James had made a fortune by specializing in potential best-sellers and cheap sensational novels, especially those on necromancy and the occult. Lackington and Allen expressed some interest although negotiations continued through September. It is clear from Shelley's letter that the editors were concerned about flaws and errors in the manuscript.[1]

Shelley to Messrs Lackington, Allen, and Co.

GENTLEMEN,

I ought to have mentioned that the novel which I sent you is not my own production, but that of a friend, who, not being at present in England, cannot make the correction you suggest. As to any mere inaccuracies of language, I should feel myself authorized to amend them when revising the proofs. With respect to the terms of publication, my first wish certainly was to receive on my friend's behalf an adequate price for the copyright of the MSS. As it is, however, I beg to submit the following proposal, which I hope you will think fair, particularly as I understand it is an arrangement frequently made by the booksellers with authors who are new to the world. It is that you should take the risk of printing and advertising, etc., entirely on yourselves, and, after full deduction being made from the profits of the book to cover these expenses, that the clear produce, both of the first edition and of every succeeding edition, should be divided between you and the author. I cannot in the author's part disclaim all interest in the first edition, because it is possible that there may be no demand for another, and then the profits, however small, will be all that will accrue.

I hope on consideration that you will not think such an arrangement as this unreasonable, or one to which you will refuse your assent.

Gentlemen, I am
Your very obedient servant,
PERCY B SHELLEY.

Great Marlow, Bucks, August 22, 1817.

The terms were accepted by Lackington, and Mary sent the final proofs from Marlow on 24 September; she was still busy correcting *Frankenstein* with Shelley (according to her journal) as late as December 1818. The book was finally published by Lackington in March 1818.

The book was dedicated to William Godwin, author of *Political Justice, Caleb Williams,* etc. No further clue as to the author's identity was given. A two-page Preface by Shelley was also anonymous. The book appeared in three thin volumes: the first volume comprised six chapters; volume two, nine; volume three, seven. The publication was drab, even by the standards of the time, with a dull-grey cover and poor binding. It looked cheap and formed part of Lackington's novel series. In spite of its defects, the novel sold rapidly, and might be aptly described, with Stoker's *Dracula,* as one of the best-sellers of all time.

One of the first reviews came surprisingly from the pen of William Gifford of the *Quarterly Review,* who called it a fabric of absurdities as horrible as they were disgusting that were intended to pervert public taste and judgement. It was called the dream of a madman (no one guessed that it was written by a woman), written in the language of a madman. It was not surprising, stated the reviewer, that the book chose to link itself with the discredited Godwinian school. Gifford nonetheless took note of the 'rationality' of the Preface which Shelley had written. The *Edinburgh Review* noted that 'Our taste and our judgement alike revolt at this kind of writing, and the greater the ability with which it may be executed the worse it is – it inculcates no lesson of conduct, manners, or morality; it cannot mend, and will not even amuse its readers, unless their tastes have been deplorably vitiated.'[2] Another review from the *Edinburgh Review and Literary Miscellany*[3] coincided most precisely with the publication of the novel and the reaction of the reviewer, though somewhat more impartial, was generally negative. For him the novel reflected, 'all the faults, but many likewise of the beauties', of the Godwinian school. The critic made note of the author's inexperience and pondered on the reasons why books of this nature should be written in the first place.

To

WILLIAM GODWIN,

AUTHOR OF POLITICAL JUSTICE,
CALEB WILLIAMS, &c.

THESE VOLUMES

Are respectfully inscribed

BY

THE AUTHOR.

Dedication page from the 1818 Lackington edition. (By permission of the Harvard College Library.)

The first favourable review, interestingly enough, came from the conservative *Court* magazine in March and also in a magazine entitled *La Belle Assemblée*.[4] Following a lengthy analysis, the novel was judged perhaps 'impious', but also original, audacious, and written in an excellent style; reasons which the reviewer felt assured its success. The ultimate praise for *Frankenstein* originated from an entirely unexpected and prestigious quarter – no less a literary personality than Sir Walter Scott, who paid Mary the supreme compliment of declaring that he preferred *Frankenstein* to any of his own romances. Scott firmly believed that Shelley had written the novel, since he had sent him a copy of the manuscript on 14 January. Writing in the prestigious and well-read *Blackwood's Edinburgh Magazine*,[5] Sir Walter Scott noted that the author seemed to disclose uncommon powers of poetic imagination. He added that the feeling with which the reader perused the unexpected and fearful, yet allowing the possibility of the event, a very natural conclusion of Frankenstein's experiment, could shake one's nerves. The review went on: 'It is no slight merit in our eyes that the tale, though wild in incident is written in plain and forcible English ... the ideas of the author are always clearly as well as forcibly expressed: and his descriptions of landscapes have in them the choice requisites of truth, freshness, precision, and beauty ... [Improbability might be found in] the self education of the monster considering the slender opportunities of acquiring knowledge that he possessed. We should also be disposed ... to question whether the monster, how tall, agile and strong, however, could have perpetrated so much mischief undiscovered ... but ... upon the whole, the work impresses us with the high idea of the author's original genius and happy power of expression. We ... congratulate our readers upon a novel which excites new reflections and untried sources of emotion.'

With such critical acclaim, albeit mixed, the publication of *Frankenstein* in 1818 was somewhat of a major literary event. Peacock wrote to Shelley in late August: 'I went to the Egham Races. I met on the course a great number of my old acquaintances, by the reading portion of whom, I was asked a multitude of questions concerning "Frankenstein" and its author. *It seems to be universally known and read*' (author's italics).[6] The authorship was, of course, a subject of speculation, and many questioned who could have written such an 'audacious' and 'impious' novel? Certainly no one guessed that the novel came from the pen of a nineteen-year-old woman. Most critics attributed the book to Shelley, the amoral atheist and expatriate. Mary could hardly help being flattered by so much critical attention, and from Italy she watched for the reviews of *Frankenstein* and may even have been disturbed by their hostility.

The catalyst for the publication of a second edition of *Frankenstein* came some five years later from the success of the first play based on Mary's story, entitled *Presumption, or the Fate of Frankenstein* by Richard Brinsley Peake. Godwin had seen the play with Mary at the English Opera House, and always anxious to make money, was determined to capitalize on its success. Since Lackington had chosen not to reprint a second edition at that time, Godwin negotiated with G and W B Whittaker, and a two-volume version of the 1818 edition appeared in 1823.

The second edition brought forth fewer critical reviews than the first, but, on the whole, those who chose to review the book gave a more favourable verdict. For instance, the reviewers for *Knight's Quarterly Magazine*[7] described *Frankenstein* as 'the best instance of natural passion applied to supernatural events'. They also liked Mary's emphasis on the monster's isolation in the world; 'What it must be, then – what it is to feel oneself alone in the world'. The idea of solitude so precious to the romantic tradition of the Gothic novel of the time was beginning to make an impression on the public, and particularly on the exceptional romantic who yearned for an isolated place outside the social community. The reviewers did continue to criticize, however, certain literary flaws: deficiencies in grammar and style, and haste of composition.

Perhaps because they were sensitive to this criticism, Mary and Shelley began to correct the 1818 edition as soon as it was published, and up to the time of his death in 1822, Shelley undoubtedly had had a great deal to do with the revision of the manuscript; he, after all, had written the Preface to the first edition, had made some substantial corrections demanded by Lackington, and had continued to help Mary revise the book, a task which she completed alone after Shelley's death. A copy of the manuscript that Mary gave to an admirer, Mrs Thomas, in 1823 in Italy, and which is now in the J Pierpont Morgan Library in New York, contains numerous marginal notes and corrections in Mary's handwriting that were obviously intended for a revised edition. Unfortunately, Mary and Mrs Thomas did not continue their acquaintance after Mary returned to England, and her annotated copy was lost to her. These corrections, however, are the source of the revisions for the 1831 edition, which is by far the best-known and most popular version of *Frankenstein*.

In recent years, there are still a few admirers of the earlier edition, such as Marilyn Butler, who feel that Shelley's corrections did not improve the style and that, in fact, several detract from the imagination and integrity of the original narrative.

However, Mary herself was not pleased with the earlier edition. In Chapter Two, she noted, 'If there were ever to be another edition of the book, I should rewrite these first two chapters. The incidents are tame and ill-arranged – the language sometimes childish. They are unworthy of the rest of the narration.' Apart from polishing up grammar and style, a host of small details were changed: one chapter was added (twenty-four instead of twenty-three); a few content changes were made to de-emphasize some small improprieties. For example, Frankenstein's fiancée, instead of being his 'cousin', became his 'friend' to avoid any suggestion of an incestual relationship. Other changes may have been due to Mary's new-found Italian inclinations. For instance, instead of spending their honeymoon in Cologny on Lake Geneva, Frankenstein and his bride were to go to Lake Como; yet other changes are more difficult to account for: Frankenstein's father Alphonse no longer dabbled in physics; on the contrary, he was ignorant of science. Mary also decided to insert as much of Shelley as was possible: she abstracted a good deal of the Mont Blanc episode from his writing.

FRANKENSTEIN;

or,

THE MODERN PROMETHEUS.

◆

IN THREE VOLUMES.

◆

Did I request thee, Maker, from my clay
To mould me man? Did I solicit thee
From darkness to promote me?—
PARADISE LOST.

———

VOL. 1.

══════════

London:
PRINTED FOR
LACKINGTON, HUGHES, HARDING,
MAVOR, & JONES,
FINSBURY SQUARE.

———

1818.

Title page of the 1818 Lackington edition. (Henry W. and Albert A. Berg Collection. The New York Public Library. Astor, Lenox and Tilden Foundations.)

Mary's introduction to the third edition was re-written entirely: largely autobiographical in nature, as we have noted, it contained, nevertheless, a series of inaccuracies which may have included the improvisation of her so-called dream. By far the least accountable correction was her statement that Shelley had had little to do with the work. Ready to accept the fame she had already enjoyed, Mary dared reveal her true identity, which simply confirmed what most of the reading public already knew to be a fact: that she was the daughter of two distinguished literary celebrities, Mary Wollstonecraft and William Godwin.

This time Mary had less difficulty in selling the rights to *Frankenstein*, although in spite of her fame she experienced at least one refusal. As early as 1827 she had written to Shelley's publisher Ollier for a reconsideration of the revised manuscript, and had received a negative reply. She next tried Henry Colburn and his partner Richard Bentley, a publisher specializing in current fiction at popular prices, using Ollier as a middleman. It is extraordinary to reflect that even then Mary was not sanguine of success. She wrote to Charles Ollier in January 1827, 'I suppose there is no chance of his purchasing the copyright of Frankenstein.'[8] Her pessimism on this occasion was unwarranted, however, and Henry Colburn published *Frankenstein* in one volume under Mary's name with the new caption: 'Revised, corrected, and *illustrated* with a new introduction by the author'. The book was introduced as Number 9 of the *Standard Novel Series*. Simultaneously, Bell and Bradfute published the novel in Edinburgh, and Cumming in Dublin. Opening the first page of the far more attractive one-volume 1831 edition the reader could still notice that Mary's *Frankenstein* continued to be associated with another Gothic story, namely Schiller's *Der Geisterseher*.

The desire to link *Frankenstein* to the older Gothic traditions is also evidenced by the illustrations in the 1831 edition which, perhaps for promotional reasons, were commissioned to the engraver, Chevalier. Mary had given virtually no descriptive details of the so-called 'laboratory' where the monster was manufactured. Her only details were that the 'filthy work' was performed 'in a solitary chamber, or rather cell, at the top of the house, and separated from all other apartments by a gallery and staircase'. Chevalier created on the frontispiece of the 1831 edition the laboratory which the Frankenstein movies have used ever since: the narrow room with high ceilings and huge window created a Gothic effect, while on the left were strewn the chemical and alchemical apparatus, test tubes, flasks, retorts, which Mary had simply labelled the 'instruments of life'. To the right the book shelves were lined with old tomes and topped by three skulls. At the foot of the monster, an open book, in part covered by a towel and diverse bones representing the remains of the skeletons that Victor Frankenstein had used. The artist's conception of the monster presumably followed closely enough Mary's description in the novel. 'His yellow skin scarcely covered the web of muscles and arteries beneath; his hair was of a lustrous black, and flowing; his teeth of a pearly whiteness; but these luxuriances only formed a more horrid contrast with his watery eyes, that seemed almost of the same colour as the dun white sockets in which they were set, his shrivelled complexion and straight black lips' – a far cry from Pierce's famous make-up for Boris Karloff that has created the current popular conception of the monster.

Since the book was already, known by two previous editions, the third edition of *Frankenstein* did not draw the number of reviews that followed the initial publication of that work. To all intents and purposes, *Frankenstein* had already made literary history and the revelation of Mary Shelley's name at that late date was hardly newsworthy. Rather, whenever mentioned in the press or in literary reviews, *Frankenstein* was now regarded almost as a classic, and evaluated in terms of its place in the history of the Gothic novel. For instance, the *Evening Chronicle*[9] in an article devoted to the Gothic novel, used *Frankenstein* as a kind of watershed to characterize the opposing schools of classicism and romanticism. The symbol of the monster, a being created in the image of man but still cold and lifeless, in the author's mind represented classicism; once animated by its creator with the spark of life, it indeed became monstrous even though alive.

There followed many editions of the 1831 text, both in England and America. Colburn reprinted *Frankenstein* again in 1832 and Richard Bentley who took over the firm after his partner's death brought out another edition in 1849.

Mary presumably had not given Colburn and Bentley exclusive rights, for the book was printed in 1833 in Philadelphia by Carey, Lea, & Blanchard and by Blaseland in England. In 1856, it was published by Hodgson in the Parlour Library (vol. 144). After Mary's death in 1851, it appeared in Cambridge in 1869 (Sever, Francis, & Co.). G Routledge and Sons as well as J W Lovell (Lovell's Library, No. 5) printed it in 1882; Routledge again in 1886 (Routledge's World Library, No. 25), in 1888 (Routledge's Pocket Library, No. 31) and in 1891. The Home Book Company in New York had *Frankenstein* as one of its titles in 1893 and L Gibbings of London, 1897, the year of the publication of Stoker's *Dracula*. It was published again by Routledge in 1899. In the late 1800s, two publishers, H M Caldwell Company of New York and Donohue Henneberry & Co. of Chicago decided, for reasons of their own, not to reveal the exact date of publication. London and Toronto's J M Dent and Sons took up the rights from Routledge in 1912 and were identified with the printing of Frankenstein for many years. (Their New York counterpart was E P Dutton.) The Dent publication marked the introduction of *Frankenstein* in the famous Everyman's Library. Altogether, there were no less than fourteen editions in that series from 1912 to 1967. In 1959, *Frankenstein* was number 616 in Everyman's Library and printed in a new format. Other editions continued to appear independently of Dent, one, by Brentano's of New York in the 1900s (no precise date is mentioned), and another by the Mershon Co. is equally undated. In 1932 there appeared an interesting edition of the novel by Illustrated Editions Co., fascinating because of the illustrations by Nino Carbe, probably the first illustrated *Frankenstein* since the 1831 edition. There were two other limited illustrated editions; one by Harrison Smith and Robert Hass (the artist responsible for the woodcuts was Lynd Ward) published in 1934. The other illustrated limited edition with an introduction by Edmund Lester Pearson and illustrated by Everett Henry was also published in 1934 by the Limited Editions Club. A special digest edition of *Frankenstein* which is now a collector's item was printed in 1942 for the benefit of the US Armed Forces in Germany (No. 909 in that series). Presumably the Armed Service, Inc., a non-profit organization established by the Council of Books in Wartime (New York), believed that the reading of *Frankenstein* could galvanize the furore of the GIs against their German foes, to be identified with Frankenstein's monster.

The first paperback edition marks art important step in the large-scale distribution of the novel, and was printed by J M Dent in 1960 in the Everyman's Library Series. Between 1960 and 1967, there were no less than three editions of *Frankenstein*. In hardcover the 1963 edition, with a new introduction by Robert E Dowe and D J Palmer and an updated bibliography is to be recommended. It was last printed by Dent in 1970.

Undoubtedly, one of the best of the recent hardcover editions of the 1831 version of *Frankenstein* is that published by the Oxford University Press, in 1969 and reissued in paperback in 1971, edited, and with a very useful introduction by N K Joseph. The most recent and most accurate version of the 1818 version has been published by the Oxford University Press in 1994, edited and with an Introduction by Marilyn Butler. It provides a useful comparison between the 1818 and 1831 texts and gives interesting new insights previously unknown in the gestation of *Frankenstein*. One should also make note of a number of audio versions of the original classic, the latest read by actor Kenneth Branagh.

Frankenstein is now in the public domain, and it would be useless to list here its many other paperback editions, many of which have exploited the popular effigy of Boris Karloff on the title page to augment the number of sales. Equally pointless would be a list of reprints and foreign editions, starting with the first French edition in 1821. The book has now been translated into every conceivable language, including Japanese, Urdu, Arabic, and Malay, and a good Russian edition appeared in 1965. Of the foreign editions, the best translation, by far, is that in French by Michael Boujut, published by the Cercle Bibliophile in 1959, with a most scholarly introduction.

Given all these editions and translations, it is entertaining to speculate on how many copies were sold in all. What were Mary Shelley's royalties during her lifetime? What royalties accrued to her sole surviving son, Percy Florence? How long were *Frankenstein* royalties collected by the Shelley estate after Percy Florence's death? How do the *Frankenstein* royalties compare with those of Bram Stoker's *Dracula*? Since the statement 'best-seller of all time' has been attributed to both these horror twins, which of these books, in fact, sold more, and which made the greater profit?

Since Mary had a genuine aversion to discussing money matters – she once told Murray that she had made a vow never to exploit her acquaintance with Byron for financial gain – she was careful enough to leave no evidence of any financial transaction, so it would be hopeless to try to gauge the total royalties that *Frankenstein* yielded its author. It would be even more difficult to estimate the total sales accruing to the various publishers since *Frankenstein* reverted to the public domain. Insofar as Mary was concerned, it is possible, however, to make an educated guess concerning the profitability of the sale of *Frankenstein*, based on the expected revenues of other novels at the beginning of the nineteenth century. Although totally unknown as an authoress, Mary could not have sold the copyright of *Frankenstein* to Lackington for less than £500, a modest sum by the standards of the time. (Dr Robertson received £600 for his *History of Scotland*, though well-known authors such as Wordsworth got £1000 for their poems.) If the terms of Shelley's letter to Lackington were accepted – 50 per cent of royalties after deduction of publicity and other expenses – Mary could not have made less than £200 or £300 from the proceeds of the royalty. The 1831 edition by Colburn sold for five shillings, the equivalent of our modern paperback, a price which Colburn had introduced in 1830 to combat the high prices of novels that made their purchase by the masses almost impossible. Even a successful play like *Presumption* could bring its author from £350 to £700, the usual distribution being as follows: £300 for the first nine nights, £100 on the twentieth night and £150 for the copyright, and for a special success, the play could command even higher fees.[10]

In time Mary probably became concerned with the exploitation of her novel by various playwrights and plagiarists. She finally succeeded in changing the closing scene of *Presumption* in 1826 so that the play was in conformity with the end of her original story. One can well sympathize with Mary's frustrations at having her plot exploited and spoofed, even if it did help to sell books or plays. As plagiarism continued unabated, a friend of Mary's, George Lamb, brought before Parliament the first copyright bill which aimed at giving a writer undisputed control over his or her own property. The bill was given the royal assent on 10 June 1833, after the publication of the third edition of *Frankenstein*. In order to enforce the act, a dramatic authors' society was formed to protect their rights.[11] Despite the passage of the Copyright Act, Mary still considered it unworthy to involve herself in lawsuits. When Crabbe Robinson was busy organizing his own copyright petition to Congress, he wrote to the poet Wordsworth: 'Only three writers of note refused to subscribe, Mrs Shelley, because she had never asked a favour of anyone and never would, Lord Brougham and W.' Author Grylls finds the clue to such an attitude in Mary's 'supersensitive pride'.[12]

The literary history of Mary's later years represents somewhat of a disappointment, attributable in part to the loss of Shelley's guidance and encouragement after his death, and to her increasing need for money to support herself, Percy Florence, and Godwin (whose publishing firm went bankrupt in 1822). Mary later used her influence to obtain a sinecure for her father, which granted him a small income for life, and she worked to obtain a publisher for his last book *Lives of the Necromancers*. (Till his death at the age of eighty, Godwin continued to be a financial parasite on his generous daughter.) These motives may have contributed to the increasing conventionality of Mary's later works, as she guided her writing to the literary tastes of the nineteenth-century English reading public, although her last travelogue, *Rambles in Germany and Italy, in 1841, 1842, and 1843*, published in 1844, was perhaps her greatest literary achievement. After *Frankenstein* her novels included *Valperga* (1823),[13] the *Last Man* (1826),[14] *Perkin Warbeck* (1830),[15] *Lodore* (1836),[16] and *Falkner* (1837).[17] She also compiled numerous short stories and reviews which she sold to various magazines, and busied herself with biographies for *Lardner's Cyclopaedia*, translations of French verse, and, of course, her own Journal and correspondence. Her fame, however, continued to rest on her first novel, and her publishers always added to her name 'by the author of *Frankenstein*'.

Apart from her own literary activity, Mary dedicated herself in her later years to collecting and publishing Shelley's poems and letters, guiding others in their writing on Shelley, and selecting her recollections and memories for a biography of Shelley, although she only finished eleven pages before her death. (These are now in the Bodleian Library.) Her *Life of Godwin* remained equally unfinished, although it was abstracted by Kegan Paul for his *William Godwin: His Friends and Contemporaries*. With the lifting of Sir Timothy Shelley's strictures upon his death that the Shelley name not appear lest Mary's small pittance be discontinued, Mary was more free to shepherd the Shelley legend, a role which she cherished till her death in 1851.

The Plays

Mary had a long-standing interest in the theatre, stemming from her earlier theatre-going days at Skinner Street. She had in fact published two plays, *Proserpine* and *Midas*, written under Shelley's guidance, although she was dissuaded from further playwriting by Godwin's criticism. In retrospect, it is unfortunate that Mary relinquished her role as a playwright, for adaptations of her famous story proliferated after 1818.

The first play, *Presumption, or the Fate of Frankenstein*

opened at the English Opera House (Lyceum) on Monday, 28 July 1823; it had been adapted to the theatre by Richard Brinsley Peake, and was produced by S J Arnold. James Wallack starred as Dr Frankenstein and Thomas Potter Cooke, a well-known villain of the stage, stole the show as the monster.

Mary was travelling in Turin when the play premiered in London, and shortly thereafter she was informed of its reception in Paris on her way back to England by a friend Horace Smith, who told her that they had brought out *Frankenstein* at the Lyceum and Cooke (the actor) 'had vivified the monster in such a manner as caused the ladies to faint away and a hubbub [to ensue] – however they diminished the horrors in the sequel, and it is having a run.'[18] Four days later in Paris Mary had apparently received new information on the play and found that it was not true that the ladies were frightened at the first appearance of Frankenstein. When she reached London on 25 August, she decided to stay with her father who had moved from Skinner Street to 195 The Strand. *Presumption* was still playing and Mary was sufficiently curious to attend an actual performance at the Opera House. Her reaction to the performance is worth reproducing in full.[19]

But lo and behold! I found myself famous. 'Frankenstein' had prodigious success as a drama, and was about to be repeated, for the twenty-third night, at the English Opera House. The playbill amused me extremely, for, in the list of *dramatis personae*, came '—, by Mr. T. Cooke;' this nameless mode of naming the unnameable is rather good. On Friday, August 29th, Jane, my Father, William, and I went to the theatre to see it. Wallack looked very well as Frankenstein. He is at the beginning full of hope and expectation. At the end of the first act the stage represents a room with a staircase leading to Frankenstein's workshop; he goes to it, and you see his light at a small window, through which a frightened servant peeps, who runs off in terror when Frankenstein exclaims, 'It lives.' Presently Frankenstein himself rushes in horror and trepidation from the room, and, while still expressing his agony and terror,('—') throws down the door of the laboratory, leaps the staircase, and presents his unearthly and monstrous person on the stage. The story is not well managed, but Cooke played —'s part extremely well; his seeking, as it were, for support; his trying to grasp at the sounds he heard; all, indeed, he does was well imagined and executed. I was much amused, and it appeared to excite a breathless eagerness in the audience. It was a third piece, a scanty pit filled at half price, and all stayed till it was over. They continue to play it even now. . . . On the strength of the drama, my Father had published, for *my benefit*, a new edition of 'Frankenstein'.

Although the play had been picketed and protested by some of the more conservative members of the London public, the playbill for 14 August announced that 'Presumption: or the Fate of Frankenstein notwithstanding the abortive attempts which have been made to prejudice the Publick, being fully established, will be acted until further notice,' the play ran until October and was removed by its popular successor, *Der Freischütz*.

That year there were two other versions of Mary's story playing in London, one at the Coburg, the other at the Royalty, as well as a trio of burlesque versions of *Frankenstein* at the Surrey, the Adelphi, and at Davis's Royal Amphitheatre. These were variously titled *Frankenstitch* (who created his monster from the corpses of nine men using needle and thread), *Frank-n-Steam* (a story of an ambitious student who steals a still-living though seemingly dead body), and a third burlesque about a Parisian sculptor who animates a statue of Aesop. Cooke again played the role of the monster in *Presumption* in 1824 at the English Opera House and the New Covent Garden, and again in Paris in 1826 at the Grand Guignol. In 1824 a burlesque which opened at the Olympic on 13 December may have been the logical precursor to Mel Brooks's *Young Frankenstein*; it was entitled *Frank-n-stein, or the Modern Promise to Pay*. While in Paris Cooke also played at the La Porte de St Martin in an adulterated version of Mary's story by Merle and Anthony entitled *The Monster and the Magician*. *Presumption* also played in New York in 1825. When Cooke returned from Paris in 1826, he played in a revival at the Coburg entitled *Frankenstein; or, the Man and the Monster*. Another 1826 dramatization of Mary's story was *The Devil Among the Players*, and featured a trio of monsters: Frankenstein, Faust, and the Vampire. After 1826 there was hardly a season in London, Edinburgh, Paris, Vienna, New York, in English provincial theatres or at the universities, where some melodramatic or burlesque adaptation of *Frankenstein* was not performed by either professional or amateur groups. These plays were widely reviewed in theatre magazines and on the whole remarkably well attended. In modern parlance they were for the most part box-office successes.

In most of these early performances, Cooke as the monster occupied centre stage, miming and grunting, but inviting the sympathy of the audience. His brilliant and sympathetic portrayal probably in part accounts for the extraordinary durability of the play. He was indeed the Boris Karloff of the day, having played the role of the monster no less than 365 times during a total period of seven years. As the nameless monster occupied centre stage and the person of Frankenstein his creator, played by Wallack and others, was relegated to a secondary role (in *Presumption*, Frankenstein already had an assistant called Fritz, the Ygor of our time), the public began to confuse the two. Gradually the monster so completely superimposed himself upon his maker that, to all intents and purposes, he *was* Frankenstein, a substitution which still confuses the public. The Frankenstein movies have simply completed this mystification. By 1930, Cooke had relinquished his monster role to O Smith, who was to become associated in the English mind with the monster, and was once referred to by the English humour magazine *Punch* as 'Lord Frankenstein'.

Other actors had made their fortune with the play, either in the role of the monster or that of his creator: Wallack, Rowbotham, Bennett, Baker, Perkins, Diddear, even Henry Irving, the actor whose stage career began in earnest under the management of Bram Stoker, the future author of *Dracula*. We know little of the early Frankenstein plays beyond the summaries of their scenarios, a few billboards, the reviews and the names of the actors and writers. One thing is certain: they caught the public eye and enjoyed widespread success. Another interesting dimension in the monster legacy is that the Frankenstein and vampire monsters, born together during the summer of 1816, continued to terrorize the stage during the 1820s. (Between the publication of Polidori's *The Vampyre* in 1819 and 1830, there were no less than five or six different theatre adaptations of his story that played in many of the theatres where *Frankenstein* was performed.) With reference to this vampire–Frankenstein popularity, the 1820 period bears some remarkable analogies to the more recent *Dracula* and *Frankenstein* movie revival with such films as *Bram Stoker's Dracula* (Francis Ford Coppola, 1992, Tristar) and *Mary Shelley's Frankenstein* (Francis Ford Coppola and Kenneth Branagh, 1995, Tristar).

The last version of *Frankenstein* to be produced during Mary's lifetime was a burlesque written by the Brothers Brough entitled *Frankenstein; or, the Vampire's Victim*. The play opened at the Adelphi on Boxing Day in 1819. At the time it was universally recognized that Mary Shelley was the author of the original story; this may have been one reason why the actor, Otto von Rosenberg, apologized to the audience at the beginning of the play, calling attention in rhyme to the many obvious digressions from the book:[20]

> You must excuse a trifling deviation
> From Mrs Shelley's marvellous narration.
> You know a piece could never hope to go on
> Without Love – Rivals – tyrant pa's and so on.
> Therefore to let you know our altered plan
> I'm here to represent the 'nice young man'
> And in the hero's person you'll discover
> On this occasion the obnoxious lover.

One can only speculate on Mary's reaction to the stage version of her story, for the stage, as the movie, had to concentrate on the horrific aspects of the story; it had to emphasize the monster while de-emphasizing the other dimensions, including the creator, Dr Frankenstein. Elizabeth Nitchie notes:[21]

> The exigencies of the theatre left no room for the character of Walton, whose scientific curiosity and loneliness reinforce the two major themes of the novel, and no time for the gradual development of the Monster's acquaintance with the world, the sequence of his abortive attempts to serve the men and women whom he was so ready to love, and the repeated experiences which turned that love into hatred and a desire to injure and even to destroy his creator. There was no time either for the moral struggle of Frankenstein over the creation of a mate for the being whom he had doomed to loneliness, or for his long, relentless pursuit of the Monster after the death of Elizabeth. The dramatist must concentrate on the horror of Frankenstein's presumptuous experiment. He must condense and knit together the scattered episodes of the novel and devise an ending to replace the dramatically impossible death of Frankenstein from exhaustion and exposure on Walton's ship and the departure of the Monster over the ice fields to the North Pole, there to make of his sledge his own funeral pyre. He must, in conformity to the conventions of the melodrama, introduce songs and incidental music and produce some comic relief.

In fact, Mary's monster proved more durable than she perhaps had ever expected. At the 1823 English Opera House version of *Presumption* he perished in an avalanche, at the Coburg that same year by fire, in a church. In 1826 in Paris he was killed by a thunderbolt, and at the Coburg, again, he leapt into a crater. Certainly the twentieth-century versions of the monster's death are more terrific – the favourite film version in the 1950s was to kill the monster by dropping an atomic bomb!

After Mary's death, the adaptations continued, one of the most curious being the burlesque titled *The Model Man* by Richard Butler and H Chane Newton, presented in 1887 at the Gaiety. This time Frankenstein was played by a woman (Miss Nellie Farren), the Gaiety's top star. Fred Leslie played the monster, although he was not very terrifying, and part of the time cavorted on stage as a ballerina. The opening on Christmas Eve was a flop, and was punctuated by riots and uproar from the audience, who were complaining about their seats in the pit.

Perhaps the most famous and sympathetic rendition of Mary Shelley's story, and the one that was adapted to the film in 1931 by Universal Pictures' James Whale, was Peggy Webling's *Frankenstein*. The play opened in London at the Preston in 1927 and featured Henry Hallat as Dr Frankenstein and Hamilton Deane as the monster. (Deane had adapted Stoker's *Dracula* to the stage in 1924.)

In 1936, a faithful version of Mary's story was written by Gladys Hastings-Walton, and premiered in Glasgow, Scotland. In 1940, a comic version, titled *Goon with the Wind* starred the actor James (Byron) Dean as the monster, made up with a high forehead – soon to be seen on Karloff. A 1944 Broadway digression, *Arsenic and Old Lace* starred Karloff himself, and was written by Joseph Kesselring. The play was immensely popular, and ran on Broadway for some 1444 performances.

The most creative modern version of *Frankenstein* is surely that performed by The Living Theatre of Julian Beck and his wife, Judith Malina, although the play only vaguely resembles Mary Shelley's story. It premiered at the Venice Biennale in 1965. In this version the cast is seated around a woman who, when she fails to levitate, is tossed into a coffin, a scene followed by mimicked murders and executions on the part of the cast into which Dr Frankenstein enters to dismember the corpses and give the dead new life. Blood is transfused into Frankenstein's monstrous creation, and a third eye is implanted into the monster's navel. When the monster comes to life the cast translates his thoughts although they are rewarded in the third act by death – at the hand of the monster. The play ends with the monster and Dr Frankenstein performing acts of love.

On stage, as well as on film, there were revivals of the original Frankenstein story. The 1970 musical *I'm Sorry, the Bridge is Out, You'll Have to Spend the Night* by Sheldon

Allman and Bob Pickett is far more sympathetic to Mary's theme than was The Living Theatre, although it combines the contemporary cast of horror's creatures: Dracula, the Mummy, Wolf Man, Ygor, and, of course, the Monster. That these monsters will live to terrify and haunt us may be taken from the sequence of the musical, where the cast of monsters was destroyed by various nefarious means. As each one came back to life, however, the villagers in the musical chorused that 'the monsters always came back because that was the way the fans wanted it.'[22]

8

Mary Shelley and the Gothic Novel

In what literary tradition can the novel *Frankenstein* be placed? Is it a Gothic novel? A moral tale? A tale based on the theme of the Noble Savage or the Wandering Jew? Or is it the first book of science fiction?

'It is Gothic,' says one commentator. 'It is science fiction,' responds another. 'It is philosophical allegory.' 'It is twaddle.' As might be expected, there is some merit to all of these attempts to categorize Mary Shelley's novel, including the last, but there is still no simple way that we can make them all fit together and quite define her extraordinary creation. One thing is clear, however. Although the novel may play on some of the most archetypal obsessions of Western man, it still belongs very much to its place and period. There is a slant, an angle of vision to the work, that ties it firmly to the early nineteenth century, as does the tint of its own particular melodrama.

Because of the notoriety of its modern-day versions, it would be easy to overestimate *Frankenstein*'s importance in the early nineteenth century. It is not the central document of the Romantic Movement, yet in many ways it is one of the most typical. However, the novel did help to shape the imaginations of two of the greatest novelists of that time – Emily Brontë and Herman Melville.

To read Mary Shelley's *Frankenstein* is to experience its great power. The first sense is one of being in contact with an archetypal story, for the novel is a collection of themes and ideas at once the most attractive and the most forbidden in the post-Renaissance West. Its power derives, however, not only from its use of the myths of Prometheus, Pygmalion, and the legend of Faust, but also from the very crudity of its fictional devices. Its structure of concentric tales within tales; its frequently overwrought rhetoric; its archaic science – all secure the powerful effect of the primitive, the elemental, and the prototypical. The novel has a legacy not only because it portrays the deep and ambiguous human longing to be Rebel and God-Defier, but also because it recounts with labour and seriousness, events and characters of such outrageous improbability that skilful rationalizations would only weaken the telling.

In this respect, the example of some of Mary Shelley's successors is instructive. For instance, Robert Louis Stevenson is a more skilful novelist than Mary Shelley. Yet his well-known story, *The Strange Case of Dr Jekyll and Mr Hyde*, which derives its inspiration from *Frankenstein*, is the incomparably weaker exercise. Rationalized, moralized, allegorized, the great Promethean symbols of *Frankenstein* are reduced to the level of ingenious triviality. Indeed, Mary Shelley's power in *Frankenstein* is to act as a medium for some of the great themes and preoccupations of her age, to make of her hideous monster, in the words of Byron's Prometheus, a 'symbol and a sign/To Mortals of their fate and force'.

Literary Sources

In the final analysis, the novel is almost certainly a compendium of themes, bearing on Mary's germinal idea, that filtered through her reading list in 1814, 1815, and 1816. As her journal documents, Mary and Shelley read voraciously – about sixteen hours a day – and often aloud to each other. But as Mary began to work exclusively on *Frankenstein* in the winter of 1816–1817, her reading became defined by several salient literary themes and works that resurface in the novel, and that we will discuss at length in this chapter. (Her scientific sources and reading will be examined in the chapter on the artificial man.) Some of the books that Mary read so impressed her that she gave them to the monster as reading: Goethe's *The Sorrows of Young Werther*, Volney's *Ruins of Empire*, Plutarch's *Lives*, and Milton's *Paradise Lost*. With the exception of Volney's *Ruins of Empire*, for which we have no listing (we presume that Mary read it before 1814; her reading list begins with her journal, starting in 1814 with the elopement), these classics were all read in 1815 and 1816, while *Frankenstein* was being written. Pertinent questions to this chapter are the extent of Mary's indebtedness to a variety of classical and eighteenth- or nineteenth-century authors, as well as the influence of Shelley, William Godwin, Mary Wollstonecraft, and others in her immediate entourage. We shall also question what, if any, material survives this dissection to determine how much of the work is Mary's own.

As previously suggested, the writings of both Mary's parents left indelible marks on her in terms of content, philosophy, and style. The indebtedness to her father was freely acknowledged by Mary in the Preface to the first edition and also in the Introduction to the third edition, and most of the early critics lost no time in highlighting the 'Godwinian style' and 'philosophy' contained in Mary's lines. A few thought that Godwin himself had written the book. Indeed, the libertarian and utilitarian philosophy of the author of *Political Justice* (Mary had read the book carefully during one month from 20 September to 19 October in 1814) emerges no matter how artfully woven into Mary's science–monster disguise. The political message, however, is understated and *Frankenstein* could not have survived if it had been a mere pretext for decrying the inequities of mankind, or of demonstrating Godwin's attitude that education determines character.

Beyond the subtle influence of Godwin's philosophy lies the more direct impact of her father's novels. Godwin's *Caleb Williams* (1794), which Mary read twice in 1814 and again in 1816, and his *St Leon* (1799), which she read in 1814, clearly form part of the imaginative background of *Frankenstein*. *Caleb Williams* is a more powerful and suggestive work of art than it is a finished one. It is the story of one man bound to and haunted by another by a knowledge of his secret crime. The 'innocent' Caleb Williams, obsessed by curiosity about his employer, Falkland, discovers that the latter is guilty of a particularly dishonourable murder for which he has allowed another man to be condemned. Elements of this incident are echoed of course in Mary's novel. But more significantly, Williams's obsessive curiosity is as archetypal a Faustian desire as Frankenstein's, although the comparison may at first seem strained. No sooner does Williams succeed in prompting a confession of murder and cowardice from Falkland than he is repelled by the very knowledge he so eagerly sought and is disgusted by his own curiosity. Falkland transfers some of the onus of his guilt to Williams and proceeds to hound and persecute him with the same almost supernatural power that Frankenstein's creation also possesses. Like Frankenstein, Williams becomes totally isolated from other human beings by the burden of his secret and his transferred 'guilt'. The relationship between Falkland and Williams also has much of the ambiguity, love, and hatred, that marks the relationship between Frankenstein and the monster.

Godwin's *St Leon* (1799) is now little known and less read. Although it is a weak novel, its preoccupations parallel somewhat those of *Frankenstein*, and shed some light on the meaning of the latter. Like Caleb Williams, St Leon combines attributes of Faust and Prometheus. He is a restless seeker, inquisitor, and would-be benefactor of mankind (and himself). In the course of his life, he meets with a mysterious and ominous stranger who turns out to be Godwin's version of the Wandering Jew. St Leon assumes the burden of the Wanderer's immortality in exchange for the secret of the philosopher's stone and the access this talisman opens to wealth, knowledge, and power. He discovers soon that his 'gift' is a curse that dooms him to a life of solitary roaming. Thus the novel evolves into a cautionary tale against that same Promethean spirit which would soon emerge in the poetry of Shelley and the fiction of Godwin's daughter. In *Frankenstein*, Captain Walton abandons his Promethean quest through the polar regions because Frankenstein's story serves as a cautionary tale to him.

Though most scholars have acknowledged Godwin's impact upon *Frankenstein*, few, if any, have noted the equally pervasive influence of the writings of Mary Wollstonecraft, which Godwin himself had noticed when he wrote to Mary, 'I am afraid you are a Wollstonecraft.'[1] The Shelleys read and re-read Mary Wollstonecraft's *Letters Written during a Short Residence in Norway, Sweden, and Denmark* during their journey down the Rhine in 1814. The scenic descriptions in *Frankenstein* (of the Geneva area, of Mont Blanc and the Rhine) can be said to owe a debt to the excellence of this now-forgotten travelogue.

Few people in Mary's entourage, however, had more of a literary impact on *Frankenstein* than Shelley himself – a fact we have already noted. Mary may never have written *Frankenstein*, at least not in book form, were it not for Shelley's encouragement to expand her essay into more than an article for a review. Since Shelley corrected the final proofs from Lackington in 1817, oversaw his wife's manuscript at every stage of development, corrected grammar, spelling, and even suggested some of the themes and ideas contained within the novel, one may well wonder with James Rieger whether Shelley was merely an editor or a minor collabora-tor.[2] We know that when the whole manuscript was revised at the request of Lackington, Shelley in essence had assumed responsibility for the revision (his very letter to Lackington, cited in the last chapter, implies as much). Finally, it was Shelley who wrote the three-page Preface to the first edition of *Frankenstein*.

We have noted in Chapter Seven how, before his death in 1822, he helped Mary to polish up her work in preparation for the third edition. Indeed, some passages contained in that edi-tion, such as the crucial Mont Blanc episode, were taken straight from Shelley's own travel descriptions. It would be misleading to belabour the degree of Shelley's influence by stating, as Wade and a few other critics do, that Shelley wrote most of the novel, but it may be true that Mary's real genius died with her husband. We prefer to conclude that the idea of Frankenstein and the conception of the novel were entirely Mary's own, and the relationship with Shelley was that of mutual stimulation rather than total dependence.

Though Mary worshipped Byron and felt a genuine pang of grief when she learned of his death, Byron's impact upon *Frankenstein* is more difficult to detect. The substance of Byron's influence on Mary lay perhaps in the stark, desolate, and melancholic effects that the mountains had upon his own poetry (unlike Shelley, who was exhilarated by the majesty of the Alps), and which had some bearing on Mary's own use of the mountains in the plot. Also the anti-Turkish attitude displayed by Safie, against her own Turkish kinsmen (the Greeks at the time were in revolt against the Turkish Sultan), as well as the emphasis on the destructive side of sexuality in the novel, were similarly Byronic in influence.

Of the Diodati group, if one had to single out the influence of any one additional person in the composition of *Franken-stein* it would be Matthew Gregory Lewis, whose famous horror romance *The Monk* (1796) had been read by Shelley prior to his arrival at Diodati. (Mary first reported reading *The Monk* on 2 September 1819.) When Matthew Gregory Lewis related his German horror stories at Diodati in August and began translating the first part of Goethe's *Faust*, Mary recorded most of these stories almost verbatim in her journal.

Mention of Shelley's acquaintance with 'Monk' Lewis provides a convenient point for considering *Frankenstein*'s relation to the Gothic vogue which raged at the end of the eighteenth and at the beginning of the nineteenth centuries. The classic Gothic novel deals in gloomy castles, exotic scenery, persecuted maidens and real or imagined supernatural occurrences, all furniture which is conspicuously absent from *Frankenstein*. The novelist who set the standard for this earlier type of gothicism, though she did not originate it, was Ann Radcliffe whose most influential novels were published between 1789 and 1797. (We know that Mary read her *Mysteries of Udolpho* in 1815 and *The Italian* in 1814. Mary had also read Walpole's *Castle of Otranto* about the same time.) By around 1800 Radcliffe's romances had been superseded by more luridly melodramatic and radical fiction, the impious, unrestrained 'horror Gothic' which took its popularity, its tone, and its interest in great crimes and heightened states of perception from Mrs Radcliffe, but left much of the paraphernalia of 'classic Gothic' behind. It is to this later phase of Gothic that the novel *Frankenstein* belongs, along with those other flawed masterpieces, Lewis's *The Monk*, Charles Maturin's *Melmoth the Wanderer* (1820), and James Hogg's *Private Memoirs and Confessions of a Justified Sinner* (1824).[3]

Aside from a common interest in promoting physiological symptoms of fear in the reader, what underlies both phases of gothicism is the prominence of a new type of protagonist in whom several overlapping traits can be detected. He is rebel and outcast, sometimes Satan, Cain, Ishmael, Prometheus, or Ahasuerus. Mrs Radcliffe's carefully tempered fascination with the villain type helped prepare for a revolution in values – a revolution in which Mary Shelley participates. In addition, the gothicists shared an assumption that terrible or catastrophic experiences were the only aesthetically significant ones. Thus it is most accurate to say that Mary's imagination was liberated by earlier gothicists to wildly melodramatic subject matter and her debt remains general rather than particular.

In remarking the relations between *Frankenstein* and other Gothic novels, it is useful to remember that we are dealing with literature written before Freud had provided either a model of, or terminology for, subrational reality. The lack of a model and a terminology does not mean that pre-Freudian writers were unaware of the subconscious or of the *Id*, but rather that the only way they could depict their intuition of such reality was through the Gothic devices of melodrama, the supernatural, and *Doppelgänger*.

The work which had perhaps the single greatest literary

impact on the evolution of *Frankenstein* was no Gothic novel at all, but Milton's *Paradise Lost,* which the Shelleys read and re-read during their stay at the Villa Diodati (where some scholars believe that Milton may have stayed during his Italian journey in 1639). The following lines from Book X of *Paradise Lost* form the epigraph to *Frankenstein*: 'Did I request thee, Maker, from my clay/To mould me Man, did I solicit thee/From darkness to promote me?' Mary has the monster educate himself and form his dual identity as fallen Adam and fallen Satan. Milton's poem enriches at least one level of meaning in Shelley's novel by turning it into a sort of allegory. The monster represents a startlingly 'modern' and absurdist version of mankind, created and endowed with intelligence only to suffer the more hideously from self-consciousness. But if Miltonic allusions enrich the meaning of Frankenstein, they also complicate it. For not only does the monster see himself as fallen Adam and fallen Satan, so too does his creator Frankenstein. If the monster rebels against his maker, Frankenstein has committed a similar sin by rebelling against the limits of his nature and by trying to create life, that is, by usurping the divine prerogative. Part of the power of *Frankenstein* comes through this highly ambiguous use of Milton and the traditional theology he represents.

The last of the major literary influences on *Frankenstein* was that of Samuel Taylor Coleridge's *The Rime of the Ancient Mariner.* Coleridge was affiliated with Godwin's literary circle and was a frequent visitor to Skinner Street. The episode of Byron reading Coleridge's 'Christabel' and the drama that ensued has already been alluded to in Chapter Five. To mention only her most obvious debt, Mary uses Coleridge's symbolism of the 'land of mist and snow'. It is in such regions that Frankenstein's tale of isolation unfolds to Captain Walton and where Walton himself is diverted from his own Promethean and possibly self-destructive quest. The literary device of a tale within a tale (the monster tells his tale to Frankenstein who tells it to Walton) is indebted to the *Ancient Mariner,* as is the role of the sympathetic listener: Walton plays Coleridge's Wedding Guest in the *Ancient*

Mariner, but has penetrated deeper into significant experience than his predecessor ever did. Walton's intense attraction to the nearly burnt-out Frankenstein may have been the attraction toward an alter ego. For Walton, Frankenstein is a projection of the dangerous side of his own longing. As he initially flees the monster, Frankenstein echoes Coleridge's Ancient Mariner who:

> Like one who, on a lonely road,
>   Doth walk in fear and dread,
> And, having once turned round, walks on,
>   And turns no more his head;
> Because he knows a frightful fiend
>   Doth close behind him tread.

At the end of Mary's story, however, the level of unreality is removed, as Walton comes face to face with the monster.

The foregoing account of writers who directly stimulated Mary's imagination, mentions mainly those of the first magnitude. But there are others, like the relatively obscure American novelist Charles Brockden Brown (1771–1810), himself an imitator of Godwin and whose *Wieland, or the Transformation* (1798) Mary read in 1815, and whose *Edgar Huntley* (1799) she read in 1814. Shelley had apparently introduced Mary to Brown and held so high an opinion of him that he could compare him with Schiller and even with Goethe. Christopher Small suggests that not only is the influence of Brown apparent in the general form of *Frankenstein* but Mary may have derived some particular incidents and phrases from him, for example the 'brawny and terrific' figures of the Indians may have come from *Edgar Huntley*. And in *Wieland*, the protagonist Carwin exclaims 'had I not rashly set in motion a machine, over whose progress I had no control, and which experience has shown me was infinite in power?'[4]

Living in Rousseau's Geneva, admiring his statue at Plainpalais, Mary and Shelley could have hardly avoided his influence. Mary had read Rousseau's *Dreams*, and both Mary and Shelley had read *La nouvelle héloïse* in 1816 several times. It was the reading of that book that had impelled both Byron and Shelley to seek the 'Bosquet of Julie' at Clarens, an event Shelley sentimentalized on the occasion of the historic lakeside tour. But Mary's main debt to Rousseau is for his concept of the Natural Man in the depiction of the monster. His creator having fled at the sight of him, the monster goes out into the woods to live on berries and spring water, being delighted by the songs of the birds and feeling pleasure at the rising moon and stars, even though he does not know what they are. Although he enters the world as a ready-made grown-up, his reactions to his surroundings and to people have a childlike quality, and he is formed kind and good; it is his interactions with society that corrupt him. Like Rousseau's heroes in *Emile*, the monster initially trusts his heart, not his reason.

From other writers of the Enlightenment, Mary obtained much of her information as to how ideas were formed in the monster's mind. Early in the composition of *Frankenstein*, Mary had studied Locke's *Essay Concerning Human Understanding*. Following the lead of Shelley, she read it daily from 15 November 1815 to 13 December 1816. The basic Lockeian theories of learning and understanding reappear in the monster's depiction; his mind at his creation was free of innate ideas, and became enlightened by ideas induced by his perceptions of light, cold, and heat. Mary may also have been indebted for her theories on the growing of consciousness to Diderot and Condillac. She had read Diderot's *Family Picture*, and his *Letter on the Deaf and Dumb*, and Condillac's *Treatise on Sensation*, and with Shelley's help, Buffon's *Natural History*, while she was writing *Frankenstein*. But surely the primary influence on Mary's theories of the innate goodness of man, and her ideas about education come, as we have noted, from William Godwin.

Unlike Milton's Adam, in *Paradise Lost*, there is no God to serve as a teacher; the monster's creator has fled. Mary has the monster learn the fundamentals of language, and become acculturated by observing the de Lacey family through a hole in the wall from his secret hiding place in the adjoining cottage. The monster learns French by listening to young de Lacey tutor his newly arrived girlfriend Safie in French, and the monster learns about culture and literature from the daily interactions of these French expatriates. Since the theme of Orientalism was a popular one during the Gothic period, it is not surprising that Safie is of Turkish origin.

Having explored some of the literary and philosophical influences on the novel, let us review the members of Mary Shelley's entourage for models of some of the more salient characters. For example, we have already suggested that the scientist, Victor Frankenstein, was a composite of many persons – Dippel and Shelley being the most obvious. Yet very rarely indeed does Mary betray Shelley as a model for Frankenstein. William Walton in his letters to his sister comments on Frankenstein, 'I never saw a more interesting creature: his eyes have generally an expression of wildness, and even madness; but there are moments when if anyone performs an act of kindness towards him, or does him even the most trifling service, his whole countenance is lighted up, as it were, with a beam of benevolence and sweetness that I never saw equalled. But he is generally melancholy and despairing; and some times he gnashes his teeth, as if impatient of the weight of woes that oppresses him.' Again, in Chapter Two, Frankenstein describes himself in Shelleian terms:

> My temper was sometimes violent, and my passions vehement; but by some laws in my temperament that were turned, not towards childish pursuits but to an eager desire to learn, and not to learn all things indiscriminately. I confess that neither the structure of languages [Shelley was not a linguist], nor the code of governments, nor the politics of various states, possessed attractions for me. It was the secrets of heaven and earth that I desired to learn; and whether it was the outward substance of things, or the inner spirit of nature and the mysterious soul of man that occupied me, still my enquiries were directed to the metaphysical, or, in its highest sense, the physical secrets of the world.

There are allusions in the novel to Shelley's contempt of mathematics; the very name 'Victor' was a well-known pseudonym that Shelley had adopted in his youthful writing.

Is it possible to detect in Frankenstein's father Alphonse, some reflection of William Godwin? 'My father', states Frankenstein, 'was respected by all who knew him, for his integrity and the indefatigable attention to public business. ... a variety of circumstances had prevented his marrying early, nor was it until the decline of life that he became a husband and father of a family.'

The two professors from the University of Ingolstadt, Krempe and the amiable Waldman, can be recognized from Shelley's descriptions of his teachers at Eton. Keats, whom Shelley disliked, may have corresponded with Krempe; and Adam Walker, the professor of chemistry and physics, whose experiments so fired the poet with enthusiasm, perhaps as much as Dr Lind, could have been the prototype for Waldman. Descriptions of the University of Ingolstadt, an ancient citadel of learning, established by Pope Pius II in Bavaria during the fifteenth century, could have been supplied by Shelley himself who was an admirer of a secret society called the *Illuminati*, which had been organized by students of the university during the eighteenth century. The university became reputed as a centre for the study of science ever since Jesuits became associated with it.

Henri Clerval, Victor Frankenstein's best friend, has been identified as another aspect of Shelley himself; though he also shows some characteristics of Shelley's best friend, Thomas Jefferson Hogg, who was essentially literary and not scientific in his interests. Clerval at times even reminds one of Lord Byron, 'He was a boy of singular talent and fancy. He loved enterprise, hardship, and even danger, for its own sake. He was deeply read in books of chivalry and romance. He composed heroic songs, and began to write many a tale of enchantment and knightly adventure. He tried to make us act plays, and to enter into masquerades in which the characters were drawn from the heroes of Roncesvalles, or the Round Table of King Arthur, and the chivalrous train who shed their blood to redeem the holy sepulchre from the hands of the infidels.'

If Mary's intimate friends and relatives can be listed as 'sources' for *Frankenstein*, so too perhaps can some of the conflicts of her own subconscious. But before we try to draw a portrait of the author that is based on psychological patterns in the novel, a major caution should be borne in mind. A novel is an exercise in conscious artistry. The novelist subjects the raw material and energy with which the subconscious may supply him to much shaping and arranging. As they form part of the artistic pattern of the novel, the personal psychological data of the author are no longer pure enough to be trusted completely. Remembering this, we can proceed to look at some of the inferences that have been drawn about the psychological meaning of the novel. In his *Life* article,[5] Samuel Rosenberg suggests that one psychological 'source' of the monster can be found in Mary's own loneliness and in the grievance she harboured against the man William Godwin who created her and then denied her love when she failed to be a substitute for his prestigious lost wife. And though we may not go as far as Rosenberg, it is clear that the characterization of the monster, and the astonishing sensitivity to his rage, his loneliness, and his incapacity to love that Mary brought to this creation could only have come out of her direct experience. Although the theme of loneliness haunts much of Mary's writing, her depiction of the monster's solitude and isolation are final; his world is filled with barriers and rejection. The wall that separates him from the de Lacey family confirms his isolation and, when longing for companionship he begs Frankenstein to create a mate for him, the destruction of the female monster dooms him to a life of solitude and wandering through the uninhabited regions of the earth. Other authors, perhaps only half-seriously, have seen in the monster a reflection of the personality of Mary's stepsister, Claire, the bane of her life since she was three years old, who constantly cohabited with Mary and Shelley, pursued her, never gave her peace and, like the monster, was present on her wedding night.

Another commentator, Ellen Moers[6] gives a rather circum-scribed, but nonetheless provocative reading of the novel by suggesting that it is a Gothic meditation on human birth. Moers reminds us that Mary Shelley is not only a woman but one of the few major women novelists of the eighteenth or nineteenth century who were also mothers (one major excep-tion was Elizabeth Gaskell). Moers argues that the depth of Frankenstein's revulsion for his newly created monster could only have been imagined by a woman who had experienced a similar moment at the birth of her child and its attendant guilt and shame. We should add that Mary was a singularly unfortunate mother whose complicated pregnancies and the death of whose successive newborn children made her suffer deeply. Indeed the pain experienced after the death of her first baby, the one-month-old girl whom Mary later dreamt came back to life, may have helped prompt an interest in the idea of an artificial man.

Yet no matter how startling the biographical details, it should be remembered that the archetype for Frankenstein's revulsion, though it can certainly include the dismay of a new mother, perhaps even take its tone from it, is still more significant as representing all the other falls from innocence in the life of the individual, and in a larger sense, in the life history of mankind.

Overshadowing all other birth traumas, however, was the death of Mary's own mother a few days after she was born. This rejection is recalled in a singularly striking passage in the novel when Frankenstein finally succeeds in giving life to his creature, and, racing out of his laboratory, collapses in his bedroom, falls asleep, and has a nightmare in which he sees his fiancée walking in the streets of Ingolstadt. Delighted and surprised, he embraces her, but as he imprints the first kiss on her lips, they become livid with the hue of death, and he beholds the corpse of his dead mother in his arms, a shroud enveloping her form, and graveworms crawling in the folds of the flannel.

Others have observed that Frankenstein reflects Mary's divided feelings about Shelley and her father. Robert Kiely in

his book states, 'In places the narrative seems chiefly to provide the occasion for Mary to write a tribute to her father's
idealism and a love poem to her husband.'[7] Elsewhere the
novel seems to repudiate the Promethean idealism of her husband and appears to be reserved about the pessimism of
Caleb Williams: in this sense it can be read as a portrait of
the quiet war between her affections and her rational intelligence.

The Literary Impact of the Frankenstein Theme

From the foregoing account, it is clear that Mary Shelley's
novel, however deeply rooted in her life and in the intellectual climate of her day, still gave 'classic' utterance to a
theme of great popularity and contributed a science fiction
idea to posterity which has yet to exhaust itself. We can
detect two kinds of influence on writers that came after her.
The more direct is on those who worked variations on the
themes of creating new life and resurrecting the dead. Robert
Louis Stevenson's *The Strange Case of Dr Jekyll and Mr
Hyde* or George Eliot's all but forgotten story, *The Lifted Veil*
(1859) were both influenced by *Frankenstein*. Often we find
we are dealing with minor writers or with minor works by
major writers. However, a subtle but more important
influence can be detected in the works of two major novelists of the nineteenth century, Emily Brontë and Herman
Melville.

Readers familiar with *Wuthering Heights* (1847) and
Frankenstein only through modern movie versions may be
surprised to hear these two titles linked to one another, but
literary critics have long since noted compelling resemblances. The resemblances are, however, all we have in the
case of Emily Brontë. Though no documentary evidence
exists that Emily Brontë knew Mary Shelley's novel, the
internal evidence is still strong that she knew not only
Frankenstein, but also Mary's *Valperga* (1823), as well as the
fiction of Radcliffe, Hogg, and Charles Maturin.[8] *Wuthering
Heights* grows directly out of the romantic strain (where

Frankenstein bulks large) of the early Victorian novel rather than from the realistic tradition.

In the character of Heathcliffe, Brontë refashioned Frankenstein's monster. Heathcliffe has origins metaphorically identical with the Shelleyan charnel house or some hellish corner of the human spirit. The similarity between the moral predicaments of Heathcliffe and of Frankenstein's monster has also been noted by Lowry Nelson, Jr.[9] Like the monster, who responds viciously when the world is hostile to him, Heathcliffe becomes evil and vindictive when his love for Cathy is thwarted and, embarking on a massive and calculated retaliation, he degenerates into a 'haunted wanderer'. Although of lesser significance, another point of resemblance can be detected between Shelley and Brontë: both writers use frame narrators as a sort of buffer zone between the world of the reader and the incredible world of the tale. But since this device is common in eighteenth-century narrative, perhaps it can be de-emphasized in the case of *Frankenstein*.

As for Herman Melville, we at least know that he owned a copy of *Frankenstein* and presumably read it: his editors had made a present of it to him in 1849. Like Brontë, Melville mined the ore of fictional romance for expressive symbol, and what he found in Frankenstein and his monster were suggestive prototypes for the deep ambivalence that he would make recur in his depiction of Captain Ahab and the Whale. The obsessive pursuit through the waste regions of the world are similar in both novels, as are the strong suggestions that pursuer and pursued are actually one being at war with itself.

The most familiar heirs of *Frankenstein* are nearer our own day. In them the science-fiction rather than the symbolical potential of Mary Shelley's novel is realized and exploited. H G Wells compares his own fiction with *Frankenstein*; 'These stories of mine ... do not pretend to deal with possible things; they are exercises of the imagination in a quite different field. They belong to the class of writing which includes ... the story of *Frankenstein*.'[10] Two of his novels show obvious debts to Mary Shelley, *The Island of Dr Moreau* (1896) and *The Invisible Man* (1897). The personality of Griffin in

The Invisible Man is one of Wells's last versions of the romantic scientist or scientist-magician of the Victor Frankenstein variety.

It is impossible within the context of this chapter to assess completely the extent to which the imaginations of nineteenth- and twentieth-century authors were stimulated by Mary Shelley's life-creating theme. In this respect, Mary's monster is the legitimate precursor of the robot, the synthetic (or semi-artificial) man and of the innumerable romances which purport to describe the creation of life. It would be difficult and probably pointless to evaluate the role of *Frankenstein* in this formidable array of robot literature, which is still quite popular in our time; since the coming of the twentieth century the borrowings have become indirect. We shall never know whether Ambrose Bierce, Samuel Butler, Karel Čapek and Clyde C Campbell read *Frankenstein* when they wrote *Moxon's Master* (1893), *Erewhon* (1872) and *RUR (Rossum's Universal Robots;* 1921), and *The Avatar* (1935), but the basic theme pervades all these works. (Ambrose Bierce describes an automaton chess player that becomes angry at a checkmate and destroys his creator.)

Another mechanical man story, Eando Binder's *Adam Link's Vengeance* (1941) is so similar to Mary's tale (though garbed in twentieth-century robot language) that one may assume that the author was familiar with either the Boris Karloff movie (1931) or the novel. A sinister scientist, Hillory, who at first glance does not seem to share many traits with Victor Frankenstein, constructs a mechanical robot called Adam, who is as disenchanted as Mary's monster with his mechanical existence, and seeks to commit suicide by disconnecting the wires of his consciousness. Hillory frustrates this plan and re-connects Adam's neural system, but is finally convinced, as is Victor Frankenstein, that Adam needs a mate. (In the end Adam destroys his creator and his mate.) Another twentieth-century Frankenstein is Cummings's *The Man Who Masters Time* (1900), the story of a scientist who works in a laboratory containing the artificially made organs of man and joins them together by a network of vessels.

It is pertinent to say a word about the influence of *Franken-stein* on French literature by mentioning the *Frankenstein* plays which were performed in Paris in the 1820s. Once again, it is a topic which deserves greater exploration, and Mary Shelley scholars have rarely alluded to such influences. Mary, like her mother, was very much at home in Paris and had important literary friends such as Prosper Mérimée, who had proposed marriage to her. At Geneva we made note of the fact that Balzac visited Villa Diodati on two separate occasions: one wonders whether it was not in part curiosity about the summer residents of 1816 that motivated his first visit with Madame de Castries in 1832 (barely sixteen years after Byron's and Shelley's stay). With the portrait of Byron hanging above the lacquered Louis XV furniture, memories of the summer's legend still vivid, and the successes of the *Frankenstein* plays in Paris comparatively fresh in his mind, it seems likely that Balzac read Mary's novel in addition to Byron's and Shelley's works. He returned during the winter of 1833–4 in the company of the aristocratic countess Eveline Hanska and waltzed with her down the long living room at Diodati which faces the lake, attempting to recapture a few sparks of the sentimental atmosphere of 1816 with the Countess who became his one and only true love. In the following year (1834), Balzac composed his work *The Quest of the Absolute* which, in essence, contained a plot of the alchemist Balthazar Claës searching for the philosopher's stone.[11] Four years before (1830), Balzac had written *The Elixir of Life* which bears some similarity to the Frankenstein plot.

Even Victor Hugo, one of the most prolific of the nineteenth-century writers, has a work entitled *Han d'Islande*, which is indebted to *Frankenstein* and *Melmoth*. Victor Hugo's 'monster', Han d'Islande, seems as repulsive as Mary's, and likewise learned to detest men. There were many lesser authors in Paris who exploited Mary's theme: one was Miss Bodin, a prolific but mediocre novelist, who published a book appropriately called *The Monster* (1824) collaborating with a certain Lamerlière, though the ugliness of her particular monster was more moral than physical.

As these titles already serve to imply, the process of exploiting Mary's material by third-rate writers had begun in fiction as well as on the stage and the name Frankenstein came to acquire a commercial significance which is still present in our day. We have mentioned an obscure novel by Thomas Alexander Boswell, entitled *Recollections of a Pedestrian*, written in 1826. One of the principal characters is a German traveller named Frankenstein whose peregrinations throughout Europe are totally unconnected with Mary's hero. It was no accident that the book was published in 1826 by Saunders and Otley, at the peak of *Frankenstein's* stage success. Though it does not figure on her reading list, we know that Mary had read the book, since in 1957, a copy of it in three volumes, bearing her autograph, was discovered in the possession of a London book dealer.

It would be idle to mention the numerous books, articles, spoofs, even contemporary comics that have since used and abused the Frankenstein name and theme for commercial success. One anecdote will suffice to explain the rest: in the 1950s, a French novelist, Benoit Becker, was certain of increasing the sale of his book by appending the name of Frankenstein to his various titles. He wrote no less than six books, all of them featuring the Boris Karloff effigy on the cover: *The Tower of Frankenstein*, *The Step of Frankenstein*, *The Night of Frankenstein*, *The Seal of Frankenstein*, *Frankenstein Roams*, and *The Cave of Frankenstein*, none of which had any genuine connection with Mary Shelley's plot.

One of the most scurrilous of recent works is by a German, H C Artmann, called *Frankenstein in Sussex*, published in Munich, which created a tempest in a teapot. The interest of this book is largely due to the pornographic illustrations of a Swedish artist and created a scandal in Germany. Frankenstein's monster is endowed with an enormous phallus in continuous erection, which outraged even the liberal West German censorship. As a result of the public outcry, the editors published a new edition in which the monster was emasculated.

There is, finally, another kind of literature that has

emerged in recent years connected less with Mary's monster story than with the story about the story, and the summer of 1816. One of the best among that group is Derek Marlowe's *A Single Summer with Lord B*. It is an extraordinarily entertaining and well-written book, though largely fictional. A very recent edition on that theme largely inspired by science fiction is Bryan Aldiss's *Frankenstein Unbound*.[12] The author places the whole context of the story in an imaginary Geneva in the year 2002 and, using the time-slip device, the hero, a Texan called Joe Bodeland, driving his atomic-powered 'Felden' is suddenly thrust back to the year 1816, where he encounters and even makes love to Mary Shelley on Lake Geneva. 'The Frankenstein mentality', states Bodeland, 'had finally triumphed in my day as the monster finally rises. Two centuries was all it needed.'

9

The Frankenstein Films

While one could hardly ascribe any Machiavellian intent on the part of motion picture producers and writers, it is a rather well-established fact that the film medium generally has been less than accurate in adapting screenplays from literary source material. An excellent case in point is the way Mary Shelley's *Frankenstein* has made the thorny transition from printed page to celluloid. To date countless theatrical and television films have claimed to be the inspired progeny of the 1818 novel, yet not a single version has correctly followed the format or grasped the spirit of the original. Unfortunately such literary devices as the concentric tales or multiple flashbacks in Mary Shelley's novel are extremely difficult to adapt to the film medium. Screenwriters, therefore, have been forced to produce their own written creations using only key fragmentary ideas from the original conceptions. The basic framework of man playing God and, to his later regret, creating a man (or creature) in his own image has formed the principle plotline of most film productions, but the humanistic motivations engendered in the original novel have given way to increasingly monstrous aberrations. The kindly doctor-scientist has degenerated into a progressively decadent madman, and his literate, articulate, hand-crafted creation has become an increasingly grotesque and despicable monster. Young Victor Frankenstein's creation, through continued misplaced usage, has now assumed the very name of his creator and the mere mention of 'Frankenstein' conjurs up visions of horror and maliciousness that were surely never envisaged by Mary Shelley.

This inappropriate tone of abject horror was established in the very first version of the tale brought to the screen. In 1963, while researching an article on *Frankenstein* for *Screen Facts* magazine, film historian Edward Connor was the first person to unearth a rare 15 March 1910 issue of the *Edison Kinetogram* containing a review of the earliest known motion picture version of the story. Featured on the cover was a picture of Edison Stock Company actor Charles Ogle as a hideously conceived version of Frankenstein's creation. The film ran a scant ten minutes and therefore had little time to devote to exposition. Frankenstein was portrayed as a young student who became absorbed in the secrets of life and death. In his quest to create a perfect human being, he produces only an abhorrent monster. He flees from the creature only to be pursued from place to place. Finally, on his wedding night, he confronts the monster and in a strangely mystical scene (very reminiscent of a Dr Jekyll and Mr Hyde) we see the monster's image, reflected in a mirror, disappear as Frankenstein's unholy mind is filled with the purer thoughts of love for his intended bride. This plot gimmick of utilizing a 'dream' to resolve a complicated story was over-worked in silent films, but somehow seemed uniquely suited to this particular version. Press releases on the film described the creation of the monster in a 'cauldron of blazing chemicals' (as opposed to the later dependency on electrical energy), as 'probably the most remarkable ever committed to a film'. Since no known prints of this film have survived, we can only take these publicity-inspired comments with a degree of caution. What we do know, however, is that this prototype established at once the image of grotesqueness and horror that all subsequent film versions were to exploit in one way or another.

Five years later a second silent version of the story was filmed. *Life Without Soul* ran for almost a full hour and featured the distinguished English actor Percy Darrell Standing as a very human-appearing monster. Produced by the Ocean

Film Corporation of New York, this version portrayed the creature as a more sympathetic figure, 'awe-inspiring but never grotesque'. Like its predecessor, this version also ended with the creation being a product of the hero's imagination and dreams. Even less material seems to have survived concerning this production and, again, no known prints seem to exist.

In 1931 Universal had scored a spectacular film triumph with Bela Lugosi in *Dracula*. Anxious to capitalize on their new-found star, the studio sought an equally impressive story to use as a follow-up. Director Robert Florey suggested *Frankenstein* and the studio assigned him to fashion a screenplay loosely based on Shelley's novel (but with a creature more horrible than she had described). In the finished script that Florey and Garrett Fort wrote, Lugosi was visualized as portraying 'Henry' (rather than 'Victor') Frankenstein. The only link to the novel was the premise of a man creating life from parts of dead bodies. Universal, however, felt that the public associated their new star with pure horror and wanted him to play the creation rather than the creator.

Jack C Pierce, Universal's make-up artist extraordinaire, was given the awesome task of creating the look of the monster. He researched in morgues and mortuaries and studied medical texts. Pierce used undertaker's wax and created new make-up application techniques to fulfil his vision of what a man stitched together from dead bodies and resurrected might look like. His vision was genius. However, Lugosi, after doing a screen test, felt that Pierce's make-up would hamper his performance and walked away from the production. Universal, disgusted by the wasted efforts, dropped Florey from the production and brought in their new hot property, James Whale, to direct.

Whale took control by immediately hiring Francis Edwards Faragoh to rewrite Florey's script and hired an unknown English actor by the name of Boris Karloff to play the monster. The rest is history.

Universal's 1931 release of *Frankenstein* was a blockbuster. The film scared people so well that stretchers had to be brought into the theatres and kept on stand-by for audience members who fainted from fright. In fact, the actor Edward Van Sloan, who plays Dr Waldman, warns the audience in a prologue that precedes the opening credits of the film that what they are about to see may shock you . . . it may even horrify you!'

As to the plot itself, the story began immediately with Dr Frankenstein, played by Colin Clive in a masterfully manic, over-the-top performance, gathering up the mutilated body parts he would ultimately incorporate into his masterpiece. Anticipating that a creature with a normal brain (like Shelley's) would not be hideous enough to create screen mayhem, this script had Dwight Frye, as Clive's assistant 'Fritz' (in a marvellous supporting role that often had unique touches of humour), steal an abnormal brain. This damaged brain accounted for the monster's lack of speech and predilection for violence. The creation sequence was visually exciting, with electrical pyrotechnics setting a fine example for future film versions, and Karloff's first appearance as the monster was truly a shocker for the unsophisticated viewers of the day. We see a door slowly opening and the creature backs in. As he slowly turns, the camera cuts in to a full close-up of the now well-established famous make-up. The only missing ingredient was the sudden burst of music for emphasis. (One of the film's main flaws is a lack of background music.) Also established in this first Universal feature was the scene most filmgoers always associate with horror films: the mob of villagers pursuing their monstrous quarry with flaming torches. It has been suggested that the idea for the monster's fiery death in the blazing windmill came about because Robert Florey lived in an apartment over a Van de Kamp Bakery in Los Angeles whose trademark was a small turning windmill. Of such trivialities are great endings made!

The success of *Frankenstein* set the stage and the Hollywood sequel machine began chugging. Over the next dozen or more years Universal pumped out at least seven Frankenstein films. The first of these sequels, and by far the best, was *The Bride of Frankenstein* (originally the working title was *The Return of Frankenstein*). Here was a case where all the elements of film-making meshed together to form a nearly perfect feature. The original screenplay was fashioned by William Hurlbut based upon his and John L Balderston's adaptation from 'events in the 1818 novel by Mary Wollstonecraft Shelley'. Actually, the only idea to come from the novel was the idea of creating a bride for the monster. Shelley's creature wanted the mate for companionship, and when he was denied, fearful consequences ensued. In *Bride*, Henry Frankenstein is forced to create the grisly mate when the sardonic Doctor Praetorius uses the monster to abduct his bride, Elizabeth. *Bride* was impressively photographed, utilizing huge macabre Gothic-like interior settings that tended to dwarf the human participants. Franz Waxman, one of Hollywood's most illustrious film composers, created a background score so dynamically different that Universal re-used his compositions countless times in the late thirties and forties to supply the accompaniment for a wide assortment of features and serials. Whereas in *Frankenstein* the camera tended to be stationary a great deal of the time, now Whale utilized its vast potential in huge panning and travelling shots. The viewer is literally caught up in the chase as Karloff moves swiftly through the stylized cemetery with the incensed villagers hotly in pursuit. The creation sequence becomes infinitely more expansive as we witness long overhead crane shots and pan along with the bride's cadaver as it is elevated skyward to receive its jolt of life-giving electricity.

The original *Frankenstein* ended on a happy note with Henry's father toasting the recovery of his son after having been thrown from the fiery windmill. So as to tie the new version together with the old and not confuse audiences, this ending was excised from all prints of the first film that were still in circulation at the time. The scriptwriters on *Bride* then came up with a fascinating gimmick to tie the two together. In a long establishing shot we find Elsa Lanchester, who also portrayed the 'Bride', essaying the role of Mary Shelley, and telling her husband and Lord Byron that the story of the monster had not ended with the creature's fiery death at the windmill. Instead, the monster had fallen to an underground cistern and was still alive. The pivotal role in *Bride*, however, was not that of Karloff's monster, but rather that of Dr Praetorius, played by Ernest Thesiger. Whale, in his cunning, has given us the maddest of all mad scientists. Praetorius's sardonic soliloquies lend a style and flavour to the film that tends to elevate it from horror films in general and place it more in the macabre-fantasy vein.

If there is a slight flaw in this gem, it is in trying to humanize Karloff's characterization. In a scene in which the monster goes to a blind man's cottage and learns to grunt words and smoke a cigar, the creature is reduced to engaging in a kind of buffoonery that Karloff and most audiences found totally out of place within the framework of the entire piece. Whale's final touch of irony – that of having the reconstructed bride recoil in horror upon gazing at her mate – was a superbly cunning slice of macabre comedy. It can seldom be said of sequels that they are superior to the original, but in the case of *The Bride of Frankenstein* that is exactly what has occurred.

When the monster pulled the switch blowing up the laboratory, his bride, and Dr Praetorius at the end of *Bride*, it was felt that he had earned a permanent peace. Such was not to be the case, for a scant four years later Universal once again revived him for the final qualitative entry in the studio's series, *Son of Frankenstein*. With the completion of *Bride*, director James Whale's career took a decided plunge. The magic he had shown in so many ways seems to have deserted him, and he was to finish his life as a pathetic 'has-been'. With Whale gone, the studio assigned Rowland V Lee to direct *Son*. The screenplay was fashioned by Willis Cooper, who had the decency to claim that his story was merely based on 'characters created by Mary Shelley', rather than attributing any misguided analogy to her original work. The plot of *Son* is relatively unimportant: another case of the monster being revived only to be destroyed again. What is different is the elaborate production accorded the story and the exquisite performances by an outstanding cast. The huge

interior sets of the castle seemed to be inspired by the dis-
torted expressionistic German films of the twenties (i.e., *The
Cabinet of Dr Caligari* etc.), and the laboratory with its open
sulphur pit bubbling ominously was a mad doctor's delight.
And what a gallery of performers: Bela Lugosi, who had
missed his chance to play the monster, now created a gem of
a role as the deformed Ygor, who had been hanged, but
survived with a twisted neck. It was Ygor who rescued the
monster and guarded him in a semi-comatose state until he
could be re-vitalized. Basil Rathbone as 'Wolf' Frankenstein
was appropriately benign until his quest for success where his
predecessors had failed almost resulted in mass destruction.
Another brilliant caricature was added in the person of Lionel
Atwill, who portrayed the Police Inspector with a wooden
arm, brought about as a consequence of having the monster
tear his real one right from its socket. The macabre humour
of Atwill sticking darts into his wooden appendage during a
crucial meeting with Rathbone was gallows humour at its
best. With *Son* Karloff had decided that he was finished with
the role. He was extremely grateful to what he called 'his dear
old Monster'. After all, it had made him a star. But he did not
like what the scriptwriters were doing to his creation. The
simplicity of the original was constantly being tampered
with; first by giving him speech and then by changing his cos-
tume (in *Son*). The monster deserved better.

The monster's apparent demise in *Son* by being kicked into
the sulphur pit by Rathbone was again to be short-lived. By
1942 in *The Ghost of Frankenstein*, Lugosi, once again playing Ygor in what was to be that actor's last real role of any
merit, encouraged two new scientists (Sir Cedric Hardwicke
and Lionel Atwill) to free the monster from his temporary
tomb of solidified sulphur and restore him to full potency.
Hardwicke plans to clear his ancestral name by putting a normal brain in the creature, but Atwill switches Ygor's brain at
the last moment and it looks as though we are in for real
trouble until we find that Ygor's blood was a different type
and the monster becomes a blinded maniac. In his rage, the
creature destroys almost all in a blazing finale. Lon Chaney,

Jr as the monster was far from satisfactory, perhaps because we had come to accept Karloff's appearance and attitude as definitive, and could accept no substitutes. One particularly annoying scene was that in which the monster carries a little girl to the roof of a building to retrieve a balloon, with the frightened townspeople fearing he will throw her to her death. A point should be made here that most Universal *Frankenstein* films had scenes in which children played an important role. From the famous deleted scene in *Frankenstein*, where he drowns the little girl, to the monster's attempt to get back at Rathbone in *Son*, by throwing the latter's son into the sulphur pit, a continuing relationship, for good or ill, had been established. In the fifties, when horror films had made their way to television, the Frankenstein monster became a favourite with children who viewed him not as a monster, but rather as a sympathetic deformity. This was an affinity which pleased Karloff no end, for he always maintained his monster was very child-like in nature. *The Ghost of Frankenstein* bore no tie-in with Shelley's work at all, nor did any of the remaining entries in the series produced by Universal. As a film, *Ghost* was a good programmer, with little money or creativity being expended. For all intents and purposes, the monster really should have been laid to permanent rest.

The Wolf Man, a 1941 release by Universal, had been one of the studio's better excursions into horror and fantasy. It was only natural that an enterprising studio member would come up with the suggestion to pair up its two favourite monster creations in a single film and the 1943 *Frankenstein Meets the Wolf Man* was the end result. As an individual film, it wasn't all that bad. The monster really played a very small part in the production, the bulk of the plot concerning Larry Talbot's (Lon Chaney, Jr's) quest to find Frankenstein's notebooks on the 'Secrets of Life and Death', so that he could find a way to die, forever ending the curse that had been placed upon him. He travels to the ruins where Frankenstein perished, finds the monster frozen and, after thawing him out, tries to locate the valuable books. He is unsuccessful and is forced to get Ilona Massey, playing a Frankenstein relative, to get them for him. It is decided by Patric Knowles, again portraying a doctor whose quest for knowledge of the unknown gets the better of him, to drain off the energy from both Talbot and the monster. Instead, he gives them more power and the result is a tremendous battle between the titans of terror, which ends when an embittered citizen of the town blows up a dam and floods the castle (in a very good miniature sequence). Bela Lugosi, who missed his chance in 1931, finally portrayed the monster this time around. It would be kind to say only that he was awful in the role; he looked completely alien to the role, which itself had some ambiguity to it. The monster, blinded in *Ghost,* appeared to be without sight in some sequences, and to possess 20/20 vision in others. Lugosi ideally had little to do except a few brief sequences and close-ups. Most of the real doubling for the creature was done by stuntman Eddie Parker. One of the best elements of the film was its fine musical score by Hans Salter, alternating gypsy motifs with thematic passages. One can never underestimate the value of a good musical score, especially where horror films are concerned.

That same breed of Universal Studio thinker who thought two monsters would be very commercial finally decided that five would be even better, so in 1944 the Frankenstein monster was joined by the Wolf Man, Dracula, a hunchback, and a mad doctor in another routine, though well-produced fable called *House of Frankenstein.* This time around Karloff, as the doctor, and his assistant with the hunchback, J Carrol Naish, try to help Larry Talbot (Lon Chaney, Jr) rid himself once again of his lycanthropic curse by going to find Frankenstein's record books. Once again they find the monster refrigerated in the underground catacombs and release him. After the elimination of Dracula (early on in the picture in his own little sequence), the Wolf Man, and the hunchback, the monster carries off Karloff into a quicksand bog where, as they sink slowly into oblivion, we feel we have finally seen the last of the monster and his succession of administrants. Having used up their first string of players

(Karloff, Chaney, Lugosi), they settled on Western heavy Glenn Strange to portray the Frankenstein monster. His natural height and rough-hewn features gave a new dimension to the creature's character.

The following year the last 'serious' treatment of the Frankenstein theme was brought to the screen as *House of Dracula*. Another charming quintet of monstrosities were on view again. Dracula, played here as in the preceding film by John Carradine rather than Bela Lugosi; the Wolf Man, again by Lon Chaney, Jr; the monster, by Glenn Strange in a second go-round; the hunchback, this time played by Jane Adams in order to give equal ugliness to the ladies, and the mad doctor, essayed to perfection by Onslow Stevens, were enough to make audiences and studio heads alike feel that they had virtually milked Mary Shelley's creation to the bone. This time they rescued the monster from an underground cave where they had been searching for some rare fungus with which they hoped to cure Larry Talbot of his hirsute malady, a task which bore eventual fruition when he *was* cured. How the monster got from the quicksand bog to the cave is still a mystery! Once again the monster had little to do except cause havoc in the final reel and perish once again in flames. The screenplays for these last two films were written by Edward T Lowe, who apparently excelled in banality.

In the forties the comedy team of Bud Abbott and Lou Costello had practically rescued Universal single-handedly from bankruptcy. Their comedies, turned out at a rapid pace to capitalize on their success, were extremely entertaining and filled with delightful routines and song numbers (featuring the Andrews Sisters in the first two in the series, *Buck Privates* and *In the Navy*). However, like most fast successes, their following greatly diminished by the mid-forties. Now, with two faltering comics and a retinue of used-up monsters, a suggestion was advanced to combine the two in a single new feature. The result was *Abbott and Costello Meet Frankenstein*, made in 1948. The blending was fortuitous, for not only was the film rated as an extremely funny satire on the horror genre, but a fairly good fright film in itself. Bela

Lugosi made a reappearance in his most famous role as Dracula; Lon Chaney, Jr, who had finally been cured of his curse in the preceding film, had suddenly re-acquired all the dreaded attributes of the Wolf Man; Glenn Strange was standing tall as the monster for his final appearance, and Lenore Aubert was the scientist who hoped to implant the brain of chubby Lou Costello into Frankenstein's creature – all in the original screenplay by Robert Lees, Frederic Rinaldo, and John Grant. Frank Skinner, one of Universal's first-string composers, concocted a very effective background score. Considering that the film was aimed primarily at younger audiences, it is rather unique that there was as much violence as the restrictive Hays Office would permit (i.e., Frank Ferguson's throat is slashed by the Wolf Man, and all of the monsters are destroyed). All the basic ingredients for a horror film existed: a remote castle with a laboratory ready and waiting for the brain transplant, underground caves, swamps, etc. The most successful ingredient, however, was the script which gave Bud and Lou a chance for pun after pun. An example is when Bud berates Lou for being afraid to open Dracula's coffin and tells him that all that stuff about Dracula rising from the dead is a lot of 'bunk'. Lou replies by pointing to the coffin and saying, 'That's what I'm trying to tell you. That's *his* bunk!' Later in the film, Lou poses a question to Lenore Aubert who says, 'I'll bite'. Lou shakes his head and replies, 'Oh, no. You gotta stand in line.' Gag after gag is thrown out, and each seems funnier than the last. The film, of course, made no pretence of being a continuation of the earlier series. We first find Dracula and the monster's remains being shipped to a museum where Bud and Lou are the delivery men who become entangled in the intrigue. As pure comedy, *Abbott and Costello Meet Frankenstein* is probably the funniest film of its type, bettered only, and this of course is open to dispute, by Mel Brooks's brilliant satire of 1974, *Young Frankenstein*.

For almost a decade the Frankenstein monster was allowed to remain dormant, until it once again rose from the dead with a vengeance in 1957 in Hammer Films' *The Curse of*

Frankenstein. It was like *déjà vu* setting in. During the early fifties, with television keeping a great many movie viewers home watching the likes of Milton Berle, movie makers seem to have given up on human monsters and turned their attention to creating havoc with the insect population. We had giant ants (*Them*), giant spiders (*Tarantula*), giant praying mantis (*The Deadly Mantis*), etc., all aimed at the teenage viewing audience. They were very successful commercially, but one longed for a more down-to-earth and sympathetic human type of monster. It was in this spirit that Hammer Films, a distinguished English producing company since 1936, decided to take the Universal classics and remake them in colour. Dracula, The Wolf Man, and the Mummy were all to be revived in superb productions, but it was left up to Mary Shelley's classic man-made monster, Frankenstein, to serve as the initial product. Although it was claimed that the screenplay was to be more faithful to the Shelley original, it really followed the 1931 film more closely. This time around they restored the scientist's name to 'Victor', rather than the 'Henry' of Colin Clive. Peter Cushing, a distinguished actor, was chosen for the dominant role and Christopher Lee, a likewise fine actor, was cast as the monster. The film, *The Curse of Frankenstein*, turned out to be so successful that the two new stars found a completely new career carved out for them as the English equivalents of the likes of Karloff and Lugosi. As in the earlier film, Frankenstein sets about to create a human being from assorted bits and pieces. In a fight with his earnest assistant, the brain slated for implantation is damaged. The result: another creature with irrational tendencies, dooming him to eventual destruction. Of course we had seen it all before, but it now seemed much more enjoyable done in beautiful colour and with lavish sets and fine period costuming. The dialogue was literate and the playing straightforward, completely lacking the staginess of the earlier version. If there was a flaw it was in the occasional excessiveness of the blood and gore. Hammer was to film all its horror epics with fangs dripping blood and decapitations, etc. Although this carnage was in keeping with the subject matter, it did at times become repugnant to good taste. By now we had become fairly used to the standardized make-up of the Universal Frankensteins, so it was something of a minor shock to see what they did to Lee's face in this version. It was a bit overly grotesque, and changed drastically from film to film as a series of different actors played the role. Cushing never changed, though, consistently trying to create a creature all the world would admire.

Since the character of Frankenstein had long since passed into public domain, the subject was available to any studio to do service with it, so it was unfortunate that the very same year that *Curse* was released in the United States, American-International Pictures turned out an incredibly cheaply made feature called *I Was A Teenage Frankenstein*. Made to capitalize on the demands of the youthful theatre audiences, it had Whit Bissell making a twisted and scar-faced monstrosity out of young Gary Conway. It further denigrated the character, which many felt had reached a low point when it had become a foil for Abbott and Costello. However, Frankenstein had survived greater perils than this film.

The enormous success of *Curse* (it was the largest money-maker in England during the year that it was released), encouraged Hammer to turn out *Horror of Dracula* the following year as well as a first sequel to *Curse*. Called *The Revenge of Frankenstein*, this new film began just where the previous one had ended, with Peter Cushing about to be beheaded by the guillotine. A clever substitute is found and Cushing, changing his name to 'Dr Stein', takes up right where he left off by trying to create another monster. Christopher Lee was replaced as the monster in this version by Michael Gwynn. Both films for Hammer were directed by the talented Terence Fisher with style and a flamboyance that transcended its subject matter.

The year 1958 also marked the return of Boris Karloff to the Frankenstein legend. Allied Artists, another relatively low-budget film-producing company, was trying to turn out a better quality product (for years they had produced Bowery Boys, Charlie Chan, and B-Western features). Their entry in the

Frankenstein saga was called *Frankenstein – 1970*. Now, nineteen years after he had played the monster in *Son of Frankenstein*, Karloff found himself playing a disfigured 'Victor' Frankenstein, set in contemporary times, who brings back his ancestor's much earlier creation by means of an intricate atomic device. When the creature is finally revealed, its likeness turns out to be that of a much younger Boris Karloff. The whole thing seems like an incredible 'inside' joke that the scriptwriters, Richard Landau and George Worthing Yates, had concocted. This was to be Karloff's final official appearance in a theatrical Frankenstein film. He did, however, do the voice for his famous monster in a full-length cartoon produced in 1967 called *Mad Monster Party* and, as a nostalgia piece, he appeared in an episode of the American television series *Route 66* in 1964 wearing the Frankenstein monster make-up (rather a bad imitation thereof) in a story which found him being joined by good friends Peter Lorre and Lon Chaney, Jr. The trio agrees to meet at a large motor inn and test whether their old monster creations are still capable of scaring modern-day viewers. With Karloff donning the Frankenstein outfit, and Chaney once again sporting his Wolf Man trappings, they roam about the inn and succeed in their scary mission. The whole thing was done humorously, and a simple love story was interwoven into the plot. It was an interesting farewell appearance to the characterizations that had survived in our memories for such a long time.

In 1959 Astor Pictures released a low-budget quickie called *Frankenstein's Daughter* that had very little merit. John Ashley was supposedly the son of Frankenstein and called himself 'John Bruder'. The female was portrayed by Sandra Knight.

As we entered the sixties interest in man-made monsters looked as though it was beginning to wane. We were beginning to see another return to gigantic, this time prehistoric, creatures like *Godzilla* (a fire-breathing dragon), *Mothra* (a giant moth), *Ghidrah* (a three-headed monster), *Gamera* (a turtle with teeth), *Ebirah* (a colossal crab), *Gappa* (a beaky lizard), *Viras* (a giant squid) and *Gyaos* (a fanged, flying fox).

Almost all of these incredible movie inventions came out of the Toho Studios in Japan with men in rubber suits substituting for long and costly creative animation. The films, done in colour, were very successful in the United States. The great horror films of the past seemed to lose much of their effectiveness when the prints were rescreened unceasingly on television. Somehow you are not easily frightened when you are watching a small picture in a television set while you are comfortably seated at home with the lights on. So horror gave way to fantasy, big screens, and lots of miniature destruction and the Japanese reaped a fortune.

Other countries got into the action as well. Mexico turned out a large number of good quality films, mostly done in black and white, with Aztec mummies, zombies and a seemingly endless supply of Dracula imitations leading the list. In among these were thrown at least two Frankenstein sagas, *El Infierno del Frankenstein*, done in 1963, and *El Testamento del Frankenstein*, done the following year.

After a six-year respite from Frankenstein story-telling, during which they concentrated on remaking tales featuring other Universal stalwarts like the Mummy, the Wolf Man and the Phantom of the Opera, as well as many original concepts, Hammer Films decided to revive the monster once again in 1964's *The Evil of Frankenstein*. Freddie Francis directed this time around and Peter Cushing was back to do laboratory duty once again as Baron Frankenstein. The plot was a novel one, and many feel that *Evil* was the best of the Hammer Films Frankenstein productions. On the run, as usual, from a mob of angry townspeople, the Baron finds the body of the Frankenstein monster frozen in a glacier. After careful defrosting, a hypnotist is brought in to help restore the creature's mental facilities. Once the hypnotist gains control of the creature's will, however, he utilizes him to perform a series of robberies and murders. The Baron puts an end to this unholy alliance, but the creature, consuming a devastating dose of chloroform, wreaks havoc and the whole plot is resolved in a fiery finale. Kiwi Kingston played the monster.

The year 1965 turned out to be busy, but thoroughly undistinguished, for Frankenstein monsters with three low-budget efforts being produced. *Frankenstein Conquers the World* (*Furankenshutain Tai Baragon*) was a Toho production from Japan thrown in with their series of rubber monsters. American actor Nick Adams played a leading role, but was hardly a huge drawing card. The monster was a strange concoction looking more like a prehistoric caveman than a piecemeal conception. With fangs and a hair-covered torso, the creature did combat with an incredible array of rubberized studio creations. *Frankenstein Meets the Space Monster* was hardly more palatable to our pre-conditioned tastes. Released by Vernon Films, this very lowgrade adventure had an interplanetary robot as its monster. When its mechanism goes awry, the resultant carnage produces the usual destructive ending. The last of the three had some production values and was filmed in colour, but suffered from agonizingly bad acting. *Jesse James Meets Frankenstein's Daughter* was the unlikely title of this Embassy Pictures release directed by the veteran B-Film helmer, William Beaudine. The daughter of the film's title was played by Narda Onyx, who emoted like an amateurish grade-school novice. Her creation was Cal Bolder, a well-built young man whose only deformity in the film was a circular scar placed around his shaved head. These three films left scars in the minds of viewers everywhere!

Director Terence Fisher, who had directed Hammer Films' first two Frankenstein films, came back in 1967 to put Peter Cushing and an excellent supporting cast through its paces in the fourth of that studio's continuing series on man-made creations, *Frankenstein Created Woman*. Although the title might suggest a possible remake of Universal's *Bride of Frankenstein*, this was far from being the case. The film began with Peter Cushing, as Baron Frankenstein, being re-animated by close friends with the aid of electrical energy. Once back to full strength, the Baron revives the body of a drowned young girl and transfers into her body the soul of her boyfriend who has recently been guillotined. Thus acting as the boyfriend's method of revenge, she carries out a series of murders as a kind of retribution for branding the unlucky lover with false crimes. Eventually the girl takes her own life a second time. Susan Denberg played an exceedingly voluptuous monstress, with no scars visible to mar her skin. Now might be a good time to point out that almost all of the horror films turned out by Hammer Films tended to exploit the physical attributes of their leading ladies. Somehow it seemed a more heinous crime if the victims of the monster turned out to have amply proportioned and generously exposed bosoms. It was gratuitous, to be sure, but it added enormously to the popularity of the films. Another extremely beneficial ingredient in these productions was the careful detail applied by the set designers. All the laboratory sequences were carefully set in period, with appropriate equipment tailored to meet the needs of the current undertaking. The Universal films depended almost solely upon Kenneth Strickfaden's elaborate electrical contrivances, but the Hammer tales, especially since they were all filmed in colour, had all kinds of beakers and flasks bubbling with their multi-hued imitations of life-producing fluids. It was play-acting at its stagy best.

The year 1967 also gave the tiny tots their own little monster production in the guise of a full-length animated cartoon released by Embassy Pictures labelled *Mad Monster Party*. All the horror favourites were in attendance: the Frankenstein Monster, the Wolf Man, the Mummy, Dracula, etc. Boris Karloff and Phyllis Diller were among those who supplied the soundtrack voices.

Hammer Films' final horror production of the sixties was 1969's *Frankenstein Must Be Destroyed*. Terence Fisher, now an old hand at handling various Frankenstein creations, once again put Peter Cushing through his paces as Baron Frankenstein. The plot was an interesting departure from the run-of-the-mill, man-made monster themes. Cushing kidnaps a surgeon whose insanity masks knowledge he feels will be helpful to him in his then current project involving brain transplants. Unfortunately, the man dies before he can be of much assistance. Cushing then implants his brain into the body of a dead professor. When the professor revives, he returns home to the surgeon's wife who becomes terrified of him. Bitter and resentful of what Cushing has done to him, the professor (played skilfully by Freddie Jones) lures the Baron to his home in which he has prepared a deadly fire trap. In a blazing finale, they both perish, putting an end to the current peril. Hammer Films' penchant for making audiences uncomfortable with their excess of blood-letting reached a new high in this picture when we were subjected to Cushing drilling into the shaved scalp of his subject with a period brace and bit. We witness close-ups of Cushing grimacing as he applies pressure and the soundtrack echoes with the grinding sound of breaking bone and resultant spurting blood. Without attempting to moralize, a strong case can be made that these Hammer Film productions, with all their excesses in blood and gore, have helped to de-sensitize viewers to the values of human life. Hammer set a trend that was soon followed by the *Bonnie and Clyde* and *The Wild Bunch* syndrome of extremely graphic picturization of brutal death. Producers claimed that they were only providing realism. Death *was* gory. The same kind of rationale is always used, however. 'We are just giving the people what they want to see. This is life. This is what it is all about.' This, of course, is sheer nonsense. It has resulted in films being forced to reduce themselves to pleasing the lowest common denominator, rather than maintaining a quality and dignity to remain above base demands. For all their screen success, Hammer Films may have left us with a terrible legacy.

As the new decade began, even Hammer Films seemed to be somewhat bankrupt in the field of originality. For their 1970 entry in the series, *Horror of Frankenstein*, the scriptwriters went back to the basic plot of the 1931 Universal film. Ralph Bates gave Peter Cushing a breather as he portrayed 'Victor' Frankenstein, a descendant of the original Baron. After some elementary attempts at reviving life in dead animals, Victor turns to the more rewarding task of creating a human being. Once again the brain which is to be implanted, this time in the head of a professor Victor has poisoned, is dropped and damaged. After giving the creature life by charging it electrically during a violent storm, the monster, because of its malfunctioning brain, takes off on a murder spree. Victor ultimately finds a way to control his creation and utilizes him to commit several convenient murders when demanded. The monster, portrayed in a rather clod-like manner by David Prowse, is finally destroyed in gruesome fashion by plunging into an acid vat. Hammer, after having treated its earlier Frankenstein films with a rather substantial degree of dignity, almost seemed to be parodying itself as *Horror* was filled with touches of macabre humour. Victor Frankenstein's light-hearted approach to evil even results in the unlikely circumvention of justice when he goes scot free because evidence of his creation has been destroyed in the acid.

In 1971 two low-budget film producers, Al Adamson and Samuel M. Sherman, created somewhat of a monster themselves. After having shot a motorcycle-terror film, variously released as *The Blood Seekers*, *Blood Freaks* or *Satan's Blood Freaks*, this enterprising duo shot new footage featuring Count Dracula (Zandor Vorkov) and the monster (John Bloom) in a sub-plot and integrated it into the original production. The result, *Dracula vs. Frankenstein*, came out as a serviceable programmer, but little else. Kenneth Strickfaden, who had provided the trend-establishing special effects for the 1931 *Frankenstein* film, was brought in to create the laboratory sequences here, but with a decidedly lower budget. The film's one rather dubious distinction is the final screen appearances of two fine actors, Lon Chaney, Jr and J. Carrol Naish, both of whom had played such an important part in earlier Hollywood features.

The following year Independent-International Films, which had made and released *Dracula vs. Frankenstein*, released the Spanish-made *La Marcha del Hombre Lobo* with the Americanized title of *Frankenstein's Bloody Terror* substituted. Although the film had the creative enhancements of being filmed in 70 mm, and 3-Dimension, the story itself had nothing whatsoever to do with the Frankenstein monster. It was basically the story of a werewolf on the prowl once more, but the film's distributors tried to somehow justify their title and advertising by calling the lycanthropic creation 'Baron Imre Frankenstein'. These last two films were frequently paired up as a double-feature release.

The tales of Frankenstein and Dracula were done many times on radio and television through the years, but in 1972 a really first-class production was constructed for presentation in two parts (16–17 January) on the American Broadcasting Company's 'ABC Wide World of Entertainment' series. For the very first time an attempt was made to try and stay reasonably close to Mary Shelley's original conception of the monster. With Robert Foxworth as 'Victor Frankenstein' and Susan Strasberg as 'Elizabeth', Bo Svenson emerged as a literate, well-spoken and sensitive 'monster'. Although the plot once again had the creature created electrically rather than biologically, director Glenn Jordan adhered to Shelley's desire to have her monster seek a mate in order to pacify his destructive impulses. Admittedly, the intricate flashback mechanism of the novel was again shunted aside, but at least a sincerely admirable linkage between printed page and movie (or rather TV in this case) screen was attempted.

A year later Universal Pictures, which had not made an original Frankenstein saga since their *Abbott and Costello Meet Frankenstein* in 1948, implied that Mary Shelley's tale would at last be faithfully transferred to celluloid in their *Frankenstein: The True Story*. Such was not to be the case. Director Jack Smight had a very literate script fashioned by Christopher Isherwood and Don Bachardy. It began with a ship navigating through the Arctic ice like Shelley's novel, but soon strayed off course. However, the direction in which the script strayed was brilliant, creating a new and unexpected dimension to the story that gives this version bite and the audience surprise. Leonard Whiting as 'Dr Frankenstein' creates a handsome literate creature, played by Michael Sarazin, whom he at first loves like a son! Dr Frankenstein teaches his sweet, good-natured creation to read, write and speak. Sarazin's creature is even shown off by his creator, introduced at parties as a visting Count where he becomes not only the toast of the town but the object of the sexual advances of many a young lady. The brilliant twist comes as the Creature slowly begins to degenerate. The resurrected cells begin to mutate, like a virus. Dr Frankenstein is unable to stop the process and must watch helpless as his beautiful creation is reduced to a hideously deformed thing. With the loss of his beauty so goes the admiration of the public and the women, even his creator turns his back on the wretched Creature. Shunned by all, the Creature is forced to flee alone into the night only to return for revenge and to beg Dr Frankenstein for a mate with which to share his life. Aided by a tremendous supporting cast which included Sir John Gielgud, Sir Ralph Richardson, James Mason, David McCallum and Jane Seymour, this version, filmed at Pinewood Studios in England and unbelievably lavish for a made-for-television movie, was originally aired in two parts and is still the best version of the tale ever told. Mary Shelley would have surely been proud of the extra elements of social commentary added to this version, a sweeping indictment of our society's over emphasis on beauty which rings even truer today than when the film was first made.

In 1974 a French-Italian production called *Flesh for Frankenstein* eventually made its way to the United States where it became *Andy Warhol's Frankenstein*. Written and directed by Paul Morrissey, and filmed in 3-D, this version is perhaps the most grisly of all the versions. Cheaply and quickly made, the film is an obvious satire on the blood-letting Hammer Films features. But it is satire with a vengeance, as the audience is deluged with severed limbs, bloody human entrails, and assorted other gobs of glob as it is literally thrown in their faces thanks to the 3-D process. Morrissey had a background of churning out cheaply made features which few people found worthy of serious attention, although his *Trash* and *Heat*, both made for Warhol, did attract some notoriety. In with all the blood and gore are woven as many tasteless sexual excesses as can be tolerated in the film's running time. An incredible scene in which 'Frankenstein' mounts his female construction and announces that 'to know Death,

Otto, you have to fuck Life ... in the gall bladder', serves as an adequate example of the tastelessness of the whole affair.

Peter Cushing made a reappearance the same year, 1974, in his sixth portrayal of a Frankenstein bent on creating a perfect man-made creature in *Frankenstein and the Monster from Hell*. Calling himself 'Dr Victor', Cushing creates his monster, this time from parts of inmates in an asylum where he is the attending physician. As usual the monster creates havoc and is destroyed, this time, when he is forced into a battle with a band of raving lunatics who succeed in tearing him to pieces. Again Hammer infused some slightly macabre humour into the performances, particularly in Cushing's case.

By 1974 the endless barrage of Frankenstein films had begun to wear their material thin. Audience's eyelids were hanging heavier than Karloff's. It seemed somehow appropriate that the era of the classic Frankenstein horror films should end with the ultimate parody, Mel Brooks's *Young Frankenstein*. Based on an original concept by Gene Wilder, who co-authored the script with Brooks and who plays 'Dr Frederick Frankenstein' in the film, *Young Frankenstein* seems to have spared no element of the multi-covered subject matter from its needled barbs. First, it was filmed in black and white, something that is rarely done today, because producers look forward to television sales which demand colour, and it featured a musical score (composed by John Morris) which incorporated the mandatory gypsy motifs and appropriate 'scare' and 'chase' themes. Kenneth Strickfaden was once more brought in to perfect a new series of electrical contrivances for the laboratory sequences. However, these are aesthetic benefits. The real success of the film is based on the inspired zaniness of the script. Only Brooks could give us a monster with zippers where scars should be, or a scientist whose lecture to his students includes stabbing himself in the leg with a scalpel. Peter Boyle was a delightfully clumsy monster, and a superb supporting cast headed by Cloris Leachman, Madeline Kahn, and Marty Feldman (as a delightful 'Igor', pronounced 'eye-gore', whose hunchback hump keeps changing position), added to the overall fun. With so many laughs in evidence, it is hard to single out only a few, but certainly highlights included: the monster's first public appearance, where he does a tap dance to 'Puttin' On the Ritz'; the monster's meeting with the blind hermit (a splendid cameo by surprise guest Gene Hackman), in which his finger rather than a cigar is set on fire; and the scene where the monster and a little girl are throwing things down a well and when the girl wants to know what else they can throw down the monster does a perfect eye-raising 'take' right into the camera. All of this nonsense if done by less-skilled hands could have turned into a type of disaster which has marked so many other attempts to satirize horror films. *Young Frankenstein* leaves one with the feeling that Mary Shelley might have been somewhat pleased to see how her novel could have inspired so much attention and humorous respect after so many years.

The mother of all cult B-movies, *The Rocky Horror Picture Show*, was brought to us in 1975. Written by Jim Sharman and Richard O'Brien and directed by Jim Sharman. This ultra-cool rock and roll 'transvestite' musical was adapted from a London stage play and pokes fun at all the bad Frankenstein films over the years. It stars Tim Curry, in an amazing performance, as Dr Frank-n-Furter, a garter-belt and fish-net-stockinged alien from the planet 'Transexualvania', who creates Rocky Horror, the perfect blonde-haired, blue-eyed, muscle-bound playmate for himself. Of course, Frank-n-Furter must first deal with his original creation, played by Meatloaf. He must also keep an eye on his castle full of freaks while attempting to seduce two stranded honeymooners with car trouble, Brad and Janet, played by Barry Bostwick and Susan Sarandon. The film took the youth crowd by storm and still plays in many cinemas to this day, encouraging 'audience participation'. It is a wonderously ingenious parody that gets better each time you see it. The songs are fantastic, you will walk away singing catchy lines like '. . . I'm just a sweet Transvestite from Trans–sexual–Vania'!

In 1985 the first post-modern telling of the tale came to the screen, with what was essentially a remake of *The Bride of*

Frankenstein entitled simply, *The Bride*. Aimed at the MTV generation, the film was a visual delight, creating a wonderfully gothic mood with lavish sets and extravagant costumes. However, the film was all sound and no fury. Keeping with its MTV motif, director Franc Roddam starred music's chart-topping Sting in the role of Dr Frankenstein and Jennifer Beals fresh from the success of her musically charged mega-hit *Flashdance*. Both proved to be somewhat less than adequate in their roles. The story dealt with the Creature, wonderfully played by character actor Clancy Brown, finding work by joining a travelling circus freak show. At the circus he makes friends with a midget played by David Rappaport. Later, the Creature, wanting a mate, returns to his creator and demands that he make him one. Dr Frankenstein after making his mistakes creating his original creature gets it right the second time and creates the beautiful Jennifer Beals. However, the good doctor takes one look at his new creation and falls in love. He decides to keep her for himself. This sets up the inevitable showdown between Creator and creation. The film was a bomb at the theatres and with reviewers. Beals' and Sting's one note, down-beat performances essentially ended their acting careers and let Brown and Rappaport steal the film and make it almost worth watching.

After the débâcle caused by *The Bride* one would think Hollywood would give up. Instead, that same year came John Hughes' comedy *Weird Science* and a year later horror-meister Wes Craven's *Deadly Friend*. Although neither film was directly a Frankenstein film they were both thinly veiled euphemisms for Shelley's novel. In *Weird Science* two computer nerds use their micro chips to conjure up Kelly LeBrock as an answer to their sexual frustrations. All in all it wasn't a terrible film, it did have its share of laughs but it was virtually indistinguishable from the numerous other teen sex comedies of its day. *Deadly Friend* covered some of the same territory only with unintentional humour and a great many gory scares. A teenager in love with the beautiful girl next door is devastated when she is killed. Unable to accept her death, he steals her body and, through the use of implanted computer chips, manages to resurrect her. This leads to the usual consequences, death and destruction for all. In anyone else's hands this could have been trash at best, but the talented Wes Craven manages to pull it off and, believe it or not, create some real emotional moments. Both films were moderate successes and *Weird Science* went on to become a syndicated television series.

Later in 1986 British film-maker and master of weirdness, Ken Russell, took a different approach to the Frankenstein story and told the tale of the creation of the novel in the now cult classic *Gothic*. The film tells how Mary Godwin, played by Natasha Richardson in her film debut, and her lover Percy Bysshe Shelley, played by Julian Sands, come to the home of the great poet Lord Byron, played in a wonderfully mad performance by Gabriel Byrne. There the three are joined by Byron's friend Dr Polidori, performed by Timothy Spall. While a storm rages outside all come to realize that they are plagued by demons in their personal lives. As the group rediscover their sexual orientations and experiment with different sexual partners – all in a very implied way – they begin to exorcise each other's demons. This exorcism turns the demons loose inside the house where they begin to haunt Mary and the others to the breaking point of madness. In a final attempt to vanquish their demons forever to the written page the group write a series of gothic horror stories. Mary's of course, is the now famous *Frankenstein* and Polidori's is *The Vampyre*, which many believe was one of the inspirations for Bram Stoker's *Dracula*. This vanquishing of demons turns out to be only temporary as the future fate of the group is revealed at the film's conclusion.

Overall, *Gothic* is masterpiece of style and is, without a doubt, a thinking person's horror film. Too highbrow for the average movie-going audience, the film was a financial failure. It is only on video and cable that the film found its audience. *Gothic* is perfect for an evening of frights since it does not follow a conventional horror film set-up. Yet, as a historical record of the meeting of two of England's greatest poets it is far from accurate.

For a more historical account of the events of that meeting one can turn to 1988's *Haunted Summer*. A slow, laborious picture that, keeping pace with the eighties, deals more with the group's sexual antics and drug experimentation than with its characters' remarkable lives. In this adaptation of that famous, or should I say infamous, summer, Mary is played by Alice Krige, Percy by Eric Stoltz, Philip Anglim appears as Byron and Alex Winter, of *Bill and Ted's Excellent Adventure* fame, as Dr Polidori. After watching the performances in *Gothic*, these young players all leave something to be desired – as does the film. At best, the film gives you a glimpse into the poetry of these great 'revolutionary' writers and an itch to travel to your nearest library and find the true story out for yourself. At its worst, the *Haunted Summer* of the title seems to be nothing more than a meeting of the minds of spoiled little rich kids looking to be devilish. All of the characters, as they are presented by director Ivan Passer, appear more pathetic than sympathetic and the writing of Mary's *Frankenstein* is mentioned only in a one-sentence epilogue at the film's conclusion. However, there is one implied reference to the novel that only its most avid fans may pick up. While sitting at dinner one night, Lord Byron announces how sad he feels it is that man needs women to reproduce. Mary, like the feminist she was, takes offence at this statement. The scene suggests that Mary's Victor Frankenstein held some of these same beliefs as he attempted to make life himself without the benefit of woman. The results, of course, are tragic.

Later in 1988, came the inevitable B-movie-makers Shapiro–Glikenhaus' *Frankenhooker*, written and directed by Frank Henenlotter of *Basket Case* fame. This movie is not for everyone (especially the squeamish), but fans of *The Rocky Horror Picture Show* will love it. This is typical cult, 'midnight movie' stuff. James Lorinz is excellent as an electrician/inventor who accidentally kills his overweight girlfriend while testing his new invention, a remote control lawnmower. Needless to say Lorinz decides to bring her back from the dead *á la* Mary Shelley. However, knowing his girlfriend's wish to have a sexy body, he puts her head on the body parts of prostitutes that he murders. Of course the experiment goes awry when his resurrected girlfriend wants to charge him money for sex and keeps having the urge to hit the strip in fish nets and high heels. This is gory, demented fun and Patty Mullen has a ball as the confused monster.

Still trying to cash in on gothic horror, like in his great B-movie versions of Edgar Allen Poe's horror stories, cheapie director Roger Corman assembled a talented cast for what was to be his first directorial effort in nearly twenty years, 1990's *Frankenstein Unbound*. In an attempt to bring new life to a tired tale Corman starred John Hurt as a time traveller from the twenty-first century who gets sent back to the time of Mary Shelley, played by Bridget Fonda, and actually gets to meet Mary during that haunted summer she spent with Lord Byron, played by Michael Hutchence of the rock group INXS, and her lover Percy Bysshe Shelley, played by the extremely talented Jason Patric. To the time traveller's surprise he finds that Shelley's story is not fictional but that Dr Frankenstein, played excellently by Raul Julia, is real and so is the monster. In traditional, campy B-movie style everything goes amok and Hurt's character must prevent the murderous monster from escaping to the future. The fault of this film is not the script, it could have worked with Corman's old crew, Vincent Price, Peter Lorre, Jack Nicholson and Boris Karloff who were used to playing for camp. However, the fine group of actors Corman assembled played it straight, thus the movie seemed too unbelievable and Julia's vivid portrayal of a haunted, driven and slightly mad Dr Frankenstein, the best ever filmed, is totally wasted.

History has a way of repeating itself. Hot on the heels of the blockbuster success of Francis Ford Coppola's *Bram Stoker's Dracula* in 1992, Ted Turner's cable television station, TNT, rushed into production the cleverly titled *Frankenstein* starring Patrick Bergin as Dr Frankenstein and Randy Quaid as the monster. Nothing new here, just the same old thing done again. Another snoozer.

Then came the announcement that Frankenstein fans

around the world had been waiting for. At last Hollywood was going to make a big budget Frankenstein movie with all the trappings and, best of all, it was going to be faithful to Shelley's original novel. The film was to be produced by Francis Ford Coppola and James V Hart, the team that brought *Bram Stoker's Dracula* to the screen. It was to be directed by and star as Victor Frankenstein, Kenneth Branagh, the talented young English actor and director who won acclaim on the English stage doing Shakespeare and in film with his wonderful thriller *Dead Again*. Then, in what was deemed by the press as the 'casting coup of the decade', Robert de Niro accepted an offer to play the monster. This new version, to capture the legacy of *Bram Stoker's Dracula* was to be titled, *Mary Shelley's Frankenstein*. It seemed like the perfect union, a promising young director experienced in thrillers and trained in Shakespearean tragedy, a mastermind of a producer, one of the greatest American screen actors of all time and of course one of the most enduring writers in literary history.

The hype surrounding this new film was incredible. In fact it was so huge that the film would have to have been a masterpiece just to live up to it. Therefore to be fair the film opened with a major strike against it. Too much hype is never a good thing. Unfortunately, the hype was not the film's only flaw. As predicted, it did capture the legacy of *Bram Stoker's Dracula* and, just like *Bram Stoker's Dracula*, it was closer to the original novel than any other version, but it was still miles away from the author's original vision. The film, although lavish and beautiful to look at, was marred by the narcissistic approach of Branagh who seemed to love to look at himself and thought the audience did as well. His constant close-ups, bare-chested scenes with stomach muscles drawn on to his body with make-up, and his hogging of the storyline upset the balance of the film, leaving the monster with very little to do. Branagh's uneven interpretation of the character left someting to be desired as well. He went from sane and loving to mad and obsessed to angry and bitter with almost reckless abandon. Victor was a new person in almost every scene. Branagh never caught on to the sad, haunted and driven character that was at the root of Shelley's work. In an excellent cameo *Monty Python's* John Cleese infused his portrayal of Dr Waldman with all the elements that Branagh should have brought to Victor. The film shines for the brief few moments that Cleese is on screen and when he goes so does the movie. Robert de Niro's brief appearance out of make-up as a one-eyed and peg-legged murderer with an Irish brogue reminds us how great an actor he is. Unfortunately, the resurrected de Niro, covered from head to toe in latex, can barely speak understandably – forget about expressing any emotion – and his terribly underwritten character does not gain any sympathy from the storyline. Branagh took great care in overseeing the development of the monster's make-up and making it look like real operation scars that slowly heal throughout the film. If he had taken that much care in developing the script there might have been a good movie here. The deepest cut of all is that there is nothing scary about this film. Branagh decided to go for action scenes and gore rather than gothic horror. We are given a blistering soundtrack by Patrick Doyle and grand filler scenes of the monster jumping across ice caves and chases on horseback but these scenes are hollow. They leave no emotional impact, there is nothing in this film that even comes close to rivalling that first appearance of Boris Karloff, in Jack C Pierce's make-up, backing out of that doorway sixty years earlier. Mary Shelley deserved better.

It is interesting to note that although the film was not received well around the world, Branagh's version of Frankenstein was successful in Romania, the home of Dracula. It is also interesting that *Bram Stoker's Dracula* was a commercial flop in Romania.

Incredibly, done originally as a promotional vehicle for the Branagh film, Nicholas Stein's made-for-television production of *The Real Frankenstein* was infinitely more interesting than any of the films done in the eighties or nineties. Due to the box office failure of *Mary Shelley's Frankenstein*, this documentary was not aired until after the film's release in

1995 in an attempt to separate the interesting theories presented in the piece from the critically devastated film. Hosted by Sir David Frost and shot at the actual Frankenstein Castle located on the shore of the Rhine River in Germany, the documentary presented the theory that Mary Shelley's Dr Frankenstein character was actually based on a mad scientist and alchemist known as Konrad Dippel who at one time lived in the Frankenstein Castle. It further suggested that Mary and her lover Percy may have stayed in or near the castle and heard the tale of Dippel from the local villagers. The theories were presented by this book's author and the camera took us to the actual historical locations where these events may have taken place.

Will Mary Shelley's story ever be told on screen as it was written? Probably not. Mary Shelley, who wrote Frankenstein in 1817, did not have Hollywood in mind when she put pen to paper. Nor was her great intellect held hostage by the promise of the obscene studio royalties she would be paid for the rights to her book if she reached the widest possible audience. In other words, she had no ulterior motive when writing her story. Therefore, the book as it was written does not transfer well to film. It is a book that allows the reader's imagination to take control. That is why so many people in Hollywood are drawn to it. Every person who reads the novel, and each time they re-read it, comes away with new ideas and new images. Mary Shelley left much unsaid and Hollywood has been trying to fill in the blanks ever since. Perhaps one day someone will realize that the blanks are not what is important. Surely Shelley did not think so or she would have filled them in herself. What is important is the root of the story, the core itself. The moral that Frankenstein gives us is what counts. That is why the two original Universal films, *Frankenstein* and *The Bride of Frankenstein*, have endured. In these films the message is clear and simple. In these films we see both the worst and the best in ourselves as a race. That is why to this day people still read Mary Shelley's novel, written in answer to a wager, and that is also why when we

10

The Artificial Man

The theme of the creation of an artificial man was not new to Mary Shelley; it has ancient origins. The creation of man by divine intervention can be traced to the myth of Prometheus, or to that of Pygmalion, or even to the older Hebrew legends of the Golem. Many early alchemists like Paracelsus, Agrippa, Albertus Magnus, and even Konrad Dippel, had attempted in their nefarious pursuits to play God by creating humans in test tubes, by the distillation of blood, or by other complicated occult practices. The early scientists of the eighteenth and early nineteenth centuries, like Luigi Galvani, Count Volta, and Benjamin Franklin, all of whom experimented with the powers of electricity, were in their own way, working with the power to infuse the spark of life into inanimate matter. Their experiments, coupled with the manufacture and perfection during Mary's time of mechanical men, or androids, by such men as Vaucanson and Jaquet-Droz reinforced the scientific and occult environment in which Mary was writing her novel.

Our interest in this chapter is to explore some of the important eighteenth- and early nineteenth-century discoveries in science and alchemy that were probably known to Mary Shelley, and that coalesced in her creation of the monster. We shall also examine the extent to which *Frankenstein* can genuinely claim to have a scientific foundation in line with the scientific discoveries of the early nineteenth century. We will ask ourselves questions like: how deeply was Mary Shelley really versed in such subjects as physics, chemistry, biology, medicine, anatomy, physiology, and psychology? Did she really understand Harvey's theory of the circulation of the blood, the manner in which the retina could be attached to the eye, or the latest medical use of the recently discovered power of electricity? The answers to these questions will enable us to determine whether, in fact, *Frankenstein* can legitimately be described as a genuine work of science fiction – in the genre of a Jules Verne – or whether it belongs to a more occult tradition.

Genuine scientific elements are scarce in the novel. In the Preface to the first edition and in the Introduction to the 1831 edition, Mary and Shelley imply at least some actual scientific research in the statement: 'The event on which this fiction is founded has been supposed by Dr Darwin and some of the physiological writers of Germany, as not of impossible occurrence.' (Preface to the 1818 edition, written by Shelley.) In the Introduction to the 1831 edition Mary states: 'They talked of the experiments of Dr Darwin (I speak not of what the Doctor really did, or said that he did, but as more to my purpose, of what *was then spoken of as having been done by him* [author's italics]), who preserved a piece of vermicelli in a glass case, till, by some means it began to move with voluntary motion.' (This seems to be an oblique and unscientific statement, since scientists do not conduct their experiments on the basis of hearsay.) Mary continues, 'Not thus, after all, would life be given. Perhaps a corpse could be re-animated: galvanism had given token of such things: perhaps the component parts of a creature might be manufactured, brought together, and endued with vital warmth.' This statement might lead the reader to suspect some detailed analysis of the use of the powers of electricity in stimulating life, in line with the latest experiments of Volta, Galvani, or Darwin, and reflecting the latest nineteenth-century scientific and medical discoveries – but again the reader will be disappointed. In the crucial chapter on the creation of the monster, instead of an elaborate scientific description of the monster's manufacture, Mary simply notes:

It was on a dreary night of November, that I beheld the accomplishment of my toils. With an anxiety which almost amounted to agony, I collected the instruments of life around me, that I might infuse a spark of being into the lifeless thing that lay at my feet. It was already in the morning: the rain pattered dismally against the panes, and my candle was nearly burnt out, when, by the glimmer of the half-extinguished light, I saw the dull yellow eye of the creature open; it breathed hard, and a convulsive motion agitated its limbs.

No laboratory capturing the elemental powers of the sun or of lightning? No specific reference to the latest discoveries of Erasmus Darwin or Sir Humphry Davy concerning the use of electricity in animating muscles? Even describing the actual construction of the lifeless monster, Mary displays little knowledge of the human anatomy, of the connection of muscles, tissues, arteries, or veins; nor does the chapter reveal any scientific data concerning the details of the human skeleton, the tibia, or the skull. We are left with the explanation that Frankenstein pursued his filthy work in charnel houses. When finally Victor Frankenstein discovers 'the principle of life' which he has studied for months, that discovery is revealed in one simple and disappointing sentence: 'After days and nights of incredible labour and fatigue, I succeeded in discovering the cause of generation and life; nay, more, I became capable of bestowing animation upon lifeless matter.' What explains Mary's extraordinary reticence in revealing any detail that might lead the reader to infer a genuine knowledge of science and medicine? Was it due to a sense of delicacy, a desire not to shock the moral and religious scruples of her sensitive early nineteenth-century readers? Or to the ill-digested nature of the knowledge which she had gathered from others and which she was too timid to reveal?

The Scientific Sources

If Mary's novel has any claim to genuine science fiction, it must rest on the scientific environment of the eighteenth and nineteenth centuries and the discoveries in physics, biology, chemistry, medicine, and surgery. N K Joseph states in his Introduction to *Frankenstein* that Mary linked the myth of Prometheus with 'certain current scientific theories which suggested that the "divine spark" of life might be electrical or quasi-electrical in nature.'[1] Who were the major scientists of the time that influenced Mary's creation?

SIR HUMPHRY DAVY

Within William Godwin's circle of friends there was a remarkable scientist, Sir Humphry Davy (1778–1829), whose career in many respects parallels that of Konrad Dippel. Davy's career began in natural philosophy and metaphysics, and gradually shifted to the study of mathematics. At the age of nineteen, he began to study chemistry, being particularly interested in the use of chemical compounds and gases for curing disease, and at the age of twenty-two, when Mary was barely nine years old, Davy was appointed to the prestigious Chemistry Lectureship at the Royal Institute of London and won universal acclaim for a lecture he delivered in 1806, and subsequently published an article entitled 'On the chemical effects of electricity' which won him a prize from the French Institute. (Quite a remarkable distinction in view of the fact that England and France were at war at the time.) His health weakened as a result of his endeavours, Davy returned to Geneva in 1826 and was one of the few Englishmen in whose honour the Swiss government gave a public funeral on 29 May 1829. At the time Davy was barely aged fifty-one. Appropriately enough he was buried at the cemetery of Plainpalais, where the monster committed his first crime. From her journal it is apparent that Mary started reading Davy's *Elements of Chemical Philosophy* (1812) on 28 October 1816, although she refers to it as 'Introduction to Davy's Chemistry'. At the time Mary was at Great Marlow and was busy writing *Frankenstein*.[2] Davy's book was extolled earlier in the *Quarterly Review*, which Mary read: 'It had most assuredly fallen to the lot of no one individual to contribute to the progress of chemical knowledge by discoveries so numerous and important as those that have been made by Sir H. Davy ... we do not hesitate to rank his researches as more splendidly successful than any which have before illustrated the physical sciences.' The reviewer added that the author's 'discovery relating to electricity' is paramount to that of Franklin and Volta.[3]

As a prelude to Davy, Mary's attention had been riveted to the power of electricity during the lightning storms over Lake Léman. Byron claimed that he had witnessed a dead tree spring to life when hit by lightning, and the conversations at Diodati may have revolved around the electrical discoveries of the time – those of Benjamin Franklin (1706–1790), who, with the aid of his metal and silk kites, flown during thunderstorms, had conclusively proved that lightning *is* electricity. One of Mary and Shelley's favourite sports was flying balloons over the lake. Were they performing experiments of this kind? Shelley's fascination with the electrical powers of the galvanic battery when he was at Eton has been well documented thus far. Although we do not know for sure that Mary read Volney's *Ruins of Empire*, the monster mentions having read it. Indeed, Volney ponders whether electricity might not be the fundamental principle in the universe: 'the more I consider what the ancients understood by ether or spirit, and what the Indians call *akache*, the stronger do I find the analogy between it and the electrical fluid.'[4]

The manner in which Luigi Galvani (1737–1798) produced a continuous flow of electricity has been related many times, as has the episode of the frog's legs, where Galvani's wife happened to notice the convulsive movements produced in a skinned frog when the nerves in the leg were accidentally touched by a scalpel lying on the table that had become charged by contact with an adjoining electrical machine. She communicated her fascination to her husband whose experiments concluded that the source of electricity lay in the nerve and that the metals simply acted as conductors. This theory was later contradicted by Count Alessandro Volta (1745–1827) of the University of Pavia, creator of the Voltaic cell and inventor of the first electric battery, who contended that the electrical power lay in the metals themselves.

ERASMUS DARWIN

Erasmus Darwin (1731–1802), grandfather of Charles Darwin (the most famous theoretician of the evolutionary theory of man and the author of *The Origin of Species*), was an English physician, physiologist, psychologist, chemist, geographer, meteorologist, engineer, botanist, and poet. Reference to the work of this famous scientist in both the Preface to the 1818 edition, and the Introduction to the 1831 edition is highly significant. Both Mary and Shelley had every reason to read the works of this extraordinary physician. His *Zoonomia, or the Laws of Organic Life* (1794–1796) was called the 'most original book ever written by man'. But in addition the Shelleys had a far more personal connection with Darwin. Being an atheist, he shared Mary's and Shelley's scepticism about the Genesis interpretation of the origins of man (he gave the first somewhat timid impulse to his grandson's evolutionary theory); like Mary and Shelley, Darwin was a romantic, a free thinker, and a rebel against eighteenth-century morality; he was sympathetic to Mary Wollstone-craft's practice of free love; like Mary and Shelley, Darwin was an artful mechanic and engineer; he was interested in automatons and had perfected all kinds of robots, speaking machines, copying machines, and somewhat irreverently he had even manufactured a 'speaking priest'. Like the Shelleys, he was also a lover of plants who believed with Peter Tompkins and Christopher Bird[5] that plants have an exis-tence of their own, akin to man. He also had had the unique opportunity of meeting Jean-Jacques Rousseau in 1776; he was a friend of Mary Wollstonecraft's publisher Johnson, of Priestly, and of other members of Godwin's intimate Skinner Street circle. In fact, Godwin had called on Erasmus Darwin in 1797, some two months before Mary Wollstonecraft died. At the time Darwin was away at Shrewsbury, and so the two great radical thinkers of the time did not meet. Godwin later regretted that he did not wait for the return of 'so extraordinary a man, so truly a phenomenon'.[6]

Darwin was undoubtedly one of the most artful medical practitioners of the eighteenth century. Like Polidori, he had obtained his medical diploma from the prestigious University of Edinburgh. He believed in the psychic origin and treatment of most diseases, and had risked his family's life by experimenting with a measles inoculation. Like Galvani, Volta, Franklin, and Davy, Darwin had also seen the future importance of electricity in curing disease, in stimulating paralysed muscles by electric shock at a time when the medical practice considered this new power a mere toy. In *Botanical Garden* he records that: 'The temporary motion of a paralytic limb is likewise caused by passing the electric shock through it; which would seem to indicate some analogy between the electric fluid and the nervous fluid, which is separated from the blood by the brain, and thence diffused along the nerves for the purpose of motion and sensation.'[7]

There can be no question of Darwin's influence, particularly on Shelley, who was enthused by his theory of the possible reanimation of life by the use of electricity. The poet had read Darwin's books: *Botanic Garden* (1791), the *Temple of Nature* (1804), and *Zoonomia, or the Laws of Organic Life* (1794–96) as early as 1811, and inevitably communicated his enthusiasm to Mary, who learned most of Darwin's theories from Shelley (there is no evidence in her *Journal* that she actually read his books, a difficult task for a non-scientist). King-Hele, one of Darwin's biographers, may be exaggerating when he says that 'Darwin stands, then, as a father-figure over this first and most famous work of science fiction.'[8]

Theories of the spontaneous regeneration of matter were also popular during Mary's time, and it is possible that her reference in the 1818 Preface to the animation of man as 'not of impossible occurrence' referred to the work of a German doctor, George Frank von Frankenau (the name is uncannily close to Frankenstein), who was also ennobled by Emperor Leopold for his work, and who might be called the father of the science of *Palingenetics* – or the science of successive rebirths. Von Frankenau, who studied the regeneration of plants and animals, used their respective ashes in attempting to reproduce micro-organisms. His writings may have incited other scientists, such as the Englishman John Turberville Needham (1713–1781), who, by infusing animal and vegetable substances, believed that putrefactions were capable of producing worm-like micro-organisms. Needham also experimented with the regeneration of eels.

The eighteenth century witnessed a number of far bolder experiments of this nature, among them those of René Antoine Réaumur (1683–1757), who studied the regeneration of lost parts of crustaceans. Assuredly the most publicized experiment of this nature was conducted by Abraham Trembley (1700–1784), who was able to demonstrate that water hydra, when cut into pieces, could regenerate 'into as many complete new polyps as there were severed portions of the original one'.[9] Charles Bonnet (1720–1793), a Swiss naturalist and philosopher who was also conducting studies on water hydras and other sea animals who had lost some membrane, proved convincingly that their lost parts could be reproduced by fusion and regeneration. Elected a member of the Royal Society in 1743, he obtained fame with his eight-volume work on natural history and philosophy (1779–83), and in particular for his work *Palingenetic Philosophy*, in which he enunciated a theory on the immortality of all forms of life. Other studies of animal or vegetable regeneration were carried out in France by people such as M. Bichat (1771–1802), whose *Physiological Studies on Life and Death* was published in 1802.

How much science did Mary really understand? Her balloon-flying experiments notwithstanding, the chances are that her mind was of a more literary than scientific bent. She had probably a very slim grasp of the theories expounded by Erasmus Darwin, Sir Humphry Davy, or the 'physiological writers' of Germany. For Shelley it was different, however; in spite of his penchant for the occult, or perhaps because of it, he was fascinated by chemistry and biology, as his early experiments at Eton and later have clearly demonstrated. Besides, Shelley had briefly studied medicine in London. Dr John Polidori was also a scientist, having trained at one of the best medical schools in Britain, the University of Edinburgh. We know that Polidori had had ample opportunity, during the week that Byron and Shelley were on the *Tour du Lac* to elaborate on the conversation of 'first principles' for Mary. N K Joseph, in his Introduction to *Frankenstein*, suggests that Victor Frankenstein's change of emphasis from alchemy to chemistry and electricity surely suggests the lesser influence of Godwin's occultism and the greater influence of Shelley and Polidori, whose interests in electricity made it, rather than alchemy, the animating force for the monster.

The Creation of Man by Divine Intervention

THE PROMETHEUS MYTH

The subtitle of *Frankenstein – the Modern Prometheus –* implies that Mary was familiar with the legend of *Prometheus plasticator*, that ancient Greek god who revolted against Zeus, stealing the fire from heaven. Zeus, in retribution, chained Prometheus to a mountain top in the Caucasus, prey to an eagle who daily devoured his liver piece by piece, while it daily grew back to prolong his punishment. According to the Roman version of the Promethean myth, this god created, or re-created mankind by animating a figure made of clay. By about the third century AD, these two elements of the legend had fused together, and the fire stolen by Prometheus had become the fire of life. Ovid described Prometheus in his *Metamorphoses* as the creator of man and animals. From the Renaissance through the eighteenth century, a popular literary theme was Prometheus as a symbol of insubordination to the Christian God.

The myth of Prometheus can be said to have reached its literary apogee among the members of the Diodati group. Byron, who had translated part of Aeschylus's *Prometheus Bound* while at Harrow, wrote his poem 'Prometheus' in July of 1816, while Mary was composing her first lines of *Frankenstein*. The Promethean aspect of Byron's hero in *Manfred*, which he began that September, may have been a topic of conversation at Diodati. Shelley, for his part, read Aeschylus in 1816 (perhaps even aloud to Mary) and entitled his greatest poem *Prometheus Unbound* after that of the Greek author. Shelley as an atheist may have been titillated by the theme of Prometheus's revolt against God. If a minor Greek god could steal the 'fire from heaven' and animate man out of clay, it was but a short step to contemplate man himself usurping that same power of creation, without divine intervention.

PYGMALION

A hasty entry in Mary's *Journal*, dated 24 July 1816, and written during her Mont Blanc excursion, comments: 'We arrived back [at the Hôtel de La Ville de Londres], wet to the skin. I read Madame Genlis's *Nouvelles Nouvelles*, and write my story' (meaning *Frankenstein*). (Mary had also read Madame de Genlis's *Adèle et Théodore* in 1816.) Who was Madame de Genlis? What does that obscure reference to *Nouvelles Nouvelles* mean? Historians are familiar with a Madame Stéphanie de Genlis, a member of the French aristocracy, a lady in waiting and mistress of the regicide, Philippe 'Egalité' who voted the death of his cousin Louis XVI. The lady later became the tutor of his children, which included Louis-Philippe, the future bourgeois monarch of France who succeeded to the throne in 1830. What is less well-known is the fact that Madame de Genlis was part of Mary Wollstonecraft's small circle of radical friends in Paris and shared with Mary many of her political and moral ideas. We do not know how well Mary Wollstonecraft knew Madame de Genlis, but the latter was one of the intimate friends of Helen Maria Williams, whom Mary and Percy unsuccessfully sought out during their 1814 visit to Paris. Mary Wollstonecraft had made mention of Madame de Genlis (somewhat unkindly) in her *A Vindication of the Rights of Woman*, and again in her

Letters Written during a Short Residence in Sweden, Norway, and Denmark. For a variety of reasons, then, Madame de Genlis's name was riveted in Mary's mind.

One of the stories in the book *Nouveaux Contes Moraux et Nouvelles Historiques* (Paris, 1802) was entitled *Pygmalion and Galathea*, or *The Statue that Lived for Twenty-four Hours*, and refers to the myth of Pygmalion. This myth is the story of a Greek sculptor from Cyprus who one day carved a woman so beautiful that he fell in love with his sculpture and then prayed to the goddess Aphrodite so earnestly that the statue actually came to life. Of course there may have been other sources in Mary's readings for the notions of clay statues coming to life by divine intervention – or otherwise.

THE GOLEM LEGENDS

A version of a clay-like brutish monster that predated Mary Shelley's monster by some 300 years relates back to the sixteenth-century Golem legends. According to this tradition, a monster is animated from clay by divine intervention – this time by the Jewish God. According to the legend of the Golem, various holy men animated clay through a secret name or word of God. The Jewish *Talmud* describes the creation of man as follows: 'In the first hour, his dust was collected; in the second hour, his form was fashioned; in the third, he became a shapeless mass [a golem] . . . in the sixth [hour] he received a soul; in the seventh hour he rose and stood on his feet.'

The Golem tales embroidered this theme of creation, making the rabbi the life-giving force, who dances around the lifeless statue, pronouncing holy words and uttering the secret name of God. Finally the rabbi writes on the forehead of his creature the word 'Emeth' which means 'truth' in Hebrew, thus giving the statue the seal of creation. Endowed with life, in accordance with the magic rite, the Golem becomes the faithful servant of his master.

Unlike Mary Shelley's monster, but like his characterization in many films, the Golem was a mute creation, blindly following the instructions of its creator. According to the *Talmud*, the destruction of the monster is comparatively easy ... all the rabbi had to do was to erase the letter 'E' from its forehead. Without the letter 'E' the Hebraic inscription read 'Meth', which means 'death'; the erasure results in the immediate disintegration of the monster.

Most of the known Golem legends which have survived are East or Central European in origin, although the most famous is probably the *Golem of Chelm*, where Rabbi Elijah created his Golem in the sixteenth century by writing down the secret *Shem-Hamforesh* on a parchment which he placed on the monster's forehead. The Chelm monster turned into a horrific creation, wreaking destruction on the city of Chelm, and the unfortunate rabbi. In one version of the Golem tale, the rabbi was killed by the savage blow of a Golem that he could no longer control. In yet another version of the tale the rabbi ordered his giant clay servant to take off his boots, hoping in the process to wipe off the letter 'E' surreptitiously; the strategy failed when the Golem fell upon the rabbi, whose head was crushed by the sheer weight of the mass of clay falling on him. By far the best-known Golem story, and the inspiration for numerous literary themes and the film concept of the monster is that of Rabbi Loew of Prague who died in 1609, and whose tomb in the famous Jewish cemetery of that city can still be seen. In this version of the Golem legend, Rabbi Loew, agonizing over the oppression of the Jews by the gentiles during the sixteenth century and the miserable conditions in the ghettoes of what is now the Czech Republic, created a powerful and mute Golem from clay to protect his people, and to prowl the ghetto streets:[10]

> Then, Rabbi Loew bade the *Kohen* walk seven times around the clay body, from right to left, confiding to him the *Zirufim* (charms) which he was to recite while doing this. When this was done, the clay body became red, like fire.
>
> Then Rabbi Loew bade the Levite walk the same number of times, from left to right, and taught him also the formulas suitable to his element. As he completed his task, the fire-redness was extinguished, and water flowed through the clay

body; hair sprouted on its head, and nails appeared on the fingers and toes.

Then Rabbi Loew himself walked once around the figure, placed in its mouth a piece of parchment inscribed with the *Schem* (the name of God); and, bowing to the East and the West, the South and the North, all three recited together: 'And he breathed into his nostrils the breath of life; and man became a living soul.'

According to the legend, the Golem could not be used by the rabbi for non-sacred tasks. One day the Golem went wild and threatened the destruction of the Jewish quarter of the city. There followed a poignant scene in which Rabbi Loew, praying at the synagogue in Prague, was informed of the Golem's rebellion during the service; he rushed out in search of the monster to destroy the writing on this creature's forehead and reduce it to dust and then, all out of breath, rushed back to complete the service in the synagogue. This particular scene has been exploited both in literature and in films for its powerful visual impact.

A story from what was then Czechoslovakia, reported by the international press, suggests that the tradition of the Golem monster is not yet dead.[11] Some years ago a respectable engineer who lived on the famed Zlata Ulicka in Prague was found dead under the debris of a red statue of clay. The police inspector who reported the incident during the Czech May uprising of 1968, told Western journalists that he saw the statue melt under his very eyes, in the end disintegrating into a reddish shapeless mass. Neighbours residing on Zlata Ulicka became terribly excited and spoke of the 'return of the Golem' which according to them still haunted the street and walked in the direction of Hradčany, whenever a major untoward event was about to disrupt the city. (This occurs on an average cycle of once every thirty-three years.)

In some respects the Jewish Golem resembled Mary's conception of Frankenstein's monster. It was an alter ego or a projection of its creator, and was of gigantic size. And in many of the Golem versions, like Frankenstein's monster, the Golem was forced to avenge itself on its master; the difference being that, unlike the monster, the Golem could be easily destroyed.

The Alchemists

There is a great deal of evidence to suggest that Mary was well acquainted with the occultism of Godwin. Let us recall that Mary had her father's book *Lives of the Necromancers* printed in 1834, two years before Godwin's death, and probably at her own expense, being a book she greatly admired, even though it was judged in its day offensive to public taste and religion. Godwin probably cultivated and shared his interest in the occult with Mary from her childhood, and the topics covered in the various chapters of Godwin's book: Albertus Magnus, Paracelsus, Cornelius Agrippa, the Rosicrucians, Faustus, and Raymond Lully were frequently discussed at Skinner Street, and later at Godwin's home on The Strand. In fact, Godwin's heroes are those fallen angels that Victor Frankenstein eventually abandons.

PARACELSUS

A name often cited by Victor Frankenstein, as one of the 'lords of imagination', and a teacher initially respected by him was Paracelsus, one of the first who claimed that it was possible to create 'a little man or homunculus'. Philipus Aureolus Theophrastus Bombastus Paracelsus von Hohenheim (1493–1541), better known to us simply as Paracelsus, was, like Frankenstein, a son of Switzerland – he was born around 1493 in Einsiedeln in a house that was destroyed (like Mary Shelley's Chapuis) only in the last century, appropriately located near the Teufelsbrücke, meaning Devil's Bridge. Castrated at the age of three (either medically or accidentally by a pig), Paracelsus acquired a reputation as a physician in addition to practising palmistry, spiritualism, alchemy, and black magic. He also drank to excess and was a misogynist (perhaps because of his castration). His tramp-like existence led him to Transylvania, Dracula's homeland. Paracelsus felt that an homunculus could be created without a natural mother, and that it would grow to full age, like a monstrous dwarf and other creatures, would be victorious over its enemies, and know secret things that men otherwise could not know. Paracelsus's precise recipe for the creation of an homunculus is as follows:[12]

> If the sperm, enclosed in a hermetically sealed glass, is buried in horse manure for about forty days and properly 'magnetized', it begins to live and to move. After such a time it bears the form and resemblance of a human being, but it will be transparent and without a corpus. If it is now artificially fed with the *arcanum sanguinis hominis* until it is about forty weeks old, and if allowed to remain during that time in the horse manure, in a continually even temperature, it will grow into a human child, with all its members developed like any other child, such as may have been born of a woman, only it will be much smaller. We call such a being a homunculus, and he may be raised and educated like any other child, until he grows older and obtains reason and intellect, and is able to take care of himself. This is one of the greatest secrets, and it ought to remain a secret until the days approach when all secrets will be known.

Godwin attributes to Raymond Lully, also known as Doctor Illuminatus (1235?–1315) and a native of Majorca, the discovery of the 'elixir of life', by which means, according to Godwin, he could keep off the assaults of old age, at least for centuries.

CORNELIUS AGRIPPA

Another alchemist, Cornelius Agrippa (1486?–1535), and favourite of Godwin, became physician to Louisa of Savoy, the mother of Francis I, and wrote an occultist treatise on 'The Precept for the Art of Magic'. Agrippa was an astrologer, and delved into black magic; a devil attendant upon him in the shape of a black dog accompanied him in all his travels and he pursued his magic, presumably the creation of life, with formidable and various apparatus and the aid of the supernatural powers of the dog. Godwin relates a tale of Agrippa involving a youthful boarder in his house, who was punished for his insatiable curiosity. Agrippa being out of town, the youth fell upon one of the alchemist's books of spells and incantations, which when read aloud by the youth caused a demon to appear. Upon being told by the startled youth that he had been called forth for no purpose, the demon became so enraged that he fell upon the youth and strangled him. The episode forced Agrippa to take up his residence in a distant province, according to Godwin.[13]

The use of the mandrake root was another method of creating the artificial man that fascinated Godwin and the early necromancers. The root when extracted bore a remarkable resemblance to the head, body, and limbs of 'a little man', and was fabled for its narcotic powers. (Legend has it that man originally appeared on this earth in the shape of a monstrous mandragora.)[14] Alchemists believed that the plant was initially derived from the sperm of an innocent hanged man. At the moment of being hung, the muscles of the culprit relaxed and a sperm ejaculation was noticed. The seed, falling to the ground, produced a mandrake root which could only be picked on a Friday morning before dawn by a black dog. Once the root had been picked, the owner had to wash it and feed it with milk and honey – some writers said with blood. In this manner the mandragora accentuated its human features, growing hair, opening its eyes, and reaching the size of a newly born child. If then kept in a secret place, it looked after the well-being of its owner.

The Rhineland region through which Mary travelled in 1814 was reputed for its commercial exploitation of the mandragora plant, known in the area as *Galgen Mänchlein*, which literally means 'little man of the gallows'. A few commercially minded aristocrats in the State of Hesse, such as Baron Riedesel, made a fortune by the sale of such plants (he dressed his little root-men in fine clothes). (Emperor Rudolph

II of Germany bought two such homuncular mandragora plants in 1600, which can still be seen fully dressed in the Art Museum of Vienna.)

One of Konrad Dippel's professors at the University of Giessen, Dr David Christianus, who also studied at Strasbourg, prescribed the fabrication of an homunculus as the following: to take the egg of a black chicken, remove an even quantity – about the volume of a big broad bean – of the white of the egg, replace the bit taken out by *sperma viri* (sperm of a man) and seal the slot of the egg by applying a little slightly moist virgin parchment. The egg then must be placed in a layer of dung during the first day of the moon in March. After thirty days of incubation, there will be a little something that leaves the egg, resembling somehow the human shape, which has to be kept hidden in a secret place and fed with an aspic seed (lavender) and earthworms. Christianus continues 'as long as it is alive, you will be happy in everything'.[15]

Dippel as we know was concerned also with the principle of life, and may have written an anonymous treatise entitled: *Monthly Conversations with the Empire of Spirits*. (It would have been dangerous for Dippel to publish such theories under his own name.) One of the theories propounded in that work was 'that there are quite extraordinary mysteries in the blood of men and animals, as I have shown myself and in the experiments of others ... after the successful distillation of blood, the whole human being emerges in a monstrous way.' The formula, of course, resembles Dippel's prescription for his famous oil to prolong life and cure disease, based, as you will recall, upon the distillation of blood.

Of all this sorcery, Mary and Shelley were probably most interested in Dippel's concept of the 'philosopher's stone' and the elixir of life, which can be traced to Shelley's and Godwin's interest in a secret society called the Rosicrucians. Godwin notes in his *Lives of the Necromancers* that 'Nothing very distinct has been ascertained regarding the sect, calling itself Rosicrucians. It is said to have originated in the East from one of the crusaders in the fourteenth century; but it attracted no public notice till the beginning of the seven-teenth century. Its adherents appear to have imbibed their notions from the Arabians, and claimed the possession of the philosopher's stone, the art of transmuting metals, and the *elixir vitae*.'[16]

Christian Rosenkreuz, the alleged founder of this secret sect, had written a book, entitled *Chemical Wedding*, that attempted to explain his art by using the Phoenix as his sym-bol for the regeneration of a king and queen who were killed and then resurrected by use of the secret alchemical formula. We know that both Godwin, in his novel *St Leon*, and Shelley in his *St Irvyne, or the Rosicrucian*, made use of that device. It would probably be fairer to say that Shelley was less the author than the translator of two occultist German tales. Shelley had always been attracted to the occult and he pursued this interest with an enthusiasm which almost amounted to a belief, which he attempted to share with Mary.[17]

The alchemists' dream of creating an homunculus by dis-tilling blood, bones, precious metals, urine, various minerals, horse dung, acids, mandrake roots, and male sperm, con-tinued to exercise the imagination of the alchemists up to the eighteenth century. The most notorious of these early crea-tors of homunculi, who printed the results of his weird experiments, was the Austrian Count Johann Ferdinand von Kueffstein, a Templar, Freemason, and necromancer, who worked in concert with the Italian abbot Geloni in a monastery in Calabria, and allegedly manufactured no less than ten homunculi in test tubes: a king, a queen, a knight, a nun, a monk, an architect, a miner, a seraph, a blue spirit and a red spirit. Operating faults caused the death of the monk; the lewdness of the king – who at all costs wished to visit the queen – was fatal to his further growth and he also died. Count Kueffstein's diary was transcribed by one of his ser-vants, a man called Kammerer, and first published by Karl Kieserweller in 1807. It provides fascinating reading (we don't know whether the Shelleys read it) and served as a piquant script for the movie *Bride of Frankenstein*, which contained a brief allusion to the homunculus.

The Artificial Man 237

The Mechanical Man

Another important source of inspiration for Mary in her conception of the monster is the android, automaton, or mechanical man. In contrast to the creation of man by divine intervention or by alchemy, the manufacture of an automaton is a scientific endeavour, even if the science is somewhat limited and certainly does not presume to infringe upon the work of the Deity.

ALBERTUS MAGNUS

We know to what extent Shelley had been fascinated by the engineering of these mechanical toys. Victor Frankenstein also makes reference to Albertus Magnus (1206?–1280), also called Doctor Universalis, as one of his early and discarded mentors. Godwin in his *Lives of the Necromancers* relates of Magnus that he made an entire man of brass, putting together its limbs under various constellations and occupying no less than thirty years in its formation. This man would answer all sorts of questions, and was even employed by Magnus as a domestic. Godwin continues that at length the machine became so garrulous that St Thomas Aquinas, being a pupil of Albertus, became so enraged at the robot's abstruse speculations and uncontrollable loquacity, that he beat it to pieces with a hammer. According to other accounts, the man of Albertus Magnus was composed, not of metal, but of flesh and bones like other men.[18]

The eighteenth century was of course a time in which the manufacture of machines bearing human likeness and performing the functions of humans was raised to such perfection that the inventive talents of their creators could be compared to that of the great inventions of any period in history. Switzerland, a nation internationally famous for the excellence of its watches and musical clocks (in particular the Neuchâtel and Geneva regions), became known in the seventeenth century as one of the chief European centres for that particular art. The city of Neuchâtel, where the history museum still houses some of the most famous automatons created during that period, was, as we have noted, most likely visited by Mary and Shelley during their 1814 elopement to the Continent.

At another museum located in the village of L'Auberson and owned by the brothers Baud, among the many fascinating exhibits, we were shown two remarkable life-sized drummers, bearing the French uniforms of the eighteenth century, which the owners of the museum had purchased some time before from Coppet, the former property of Madame de Staël. According to the museum, these drummers announced the visit of famous personages to Coppet by rolling their drums at the château entrance. As these drummers performed for us it was easy to imagine a scene in which the arrival of Lord Byron and John William Polidori was announced at one of their many visits to Coppet, to the roll of these two drums. Such a conversation piece would surely have been mentioned at Diodati, and Mary must have been aware of these remarkable androids; in fact she may even have seen them perform.

These new-style Swiss automatons of the seventeenth and eighteenth centuries were a far cry from the early 'talking brass men' of Albertus Magnus. They were human-like figures which not only opened their eyes and talked, but walked, danced, composed music, drew, played chess (often outwitting their adversaries), and even created the impression of thinking by answering difficult questions. Such figurines seemed alive, and their performances were so well known that they often went on touring exhibitions, drawing enormous crowds wherever they went. (Judging by the crowds we witnessed at the automaton museum in L'Auberson and Monte Carlo, there seems to be a current resurgence of popularity for these figurines.) Though today they are an object of curiosity, in the early nineteenth century such robots must have invited comparison with the work of Prometheus or Pygmalion.

Jean-Jacques Rousseau, the most distinguished citizen of Geneva, and one whom the Shelleys so greatly admired, was the son of a watchmaker who was greatly impressed by the manner in which his father could assemble the complicated machinery of a clock; he introduced the word *automaton* to the French language. An automaton, in Rousseau's sense, was a term devised to designate men and women appearing to be machines. The term 'android', however, was more often used in the works of the period only to be replaced by the word Robot, introduced by the Czech writer Karel Čapek, in 1921, with his play *RUR, Rossum's Universal Robots*. The notion of the automaton also figured prominently in all the great encyclopaedias of the period, read by the Shelleys, and it is likely that Mary was acquainted with nineteenth-century works popularizing the automaton, such as those by E T A Hoffman, who wrote *Automatons* (1812) and the *Sandman* (1814). According to Donald Glut, 'Hoffman's stories considered the possibility of man and machine becoming interchangeable.'[19]

JACQUES DE VAUCANSON

Although there were many creators of androids, the Frenchman Jacques de Vaucanson (1709–1782), a former student of the Grenoble Jesuits, was the most skilful. This gifted technician created robots like a three-dimensional duck which drank, ate, digested, cackled, and swam – the whole interior apparatus of digestion exposed, so that it could be viewed; the flute player who played twelve different tunes, moving his fingers, lips and tongue, depending on the music; the girl who played the tambourine, the mandolin player that moved his head and pretended to breathe – a somewhat uncanny spectacle for the many onlookers. Vaucanson actually attempted to manufacture a complete human model of an automaton with heart, veins, muscles, and arteries, though he died with his robot incomplete.

PIERRE JAQUET-DROZ

Even more spectacular creations belong to the Swiss engineer, mechanic, artist, and musician, Pierre Jaquet-Droz (1721–1790) and his son, Henri-Louis (1753–1791), both of

Geneva, who won universal acclaim. Many of their automatons were exhibited from 1789 onwards all over Europe and a few have survived to this day at the History Museum at Neuchâtel. Droz's automatons imitated the human figure and movements almost to perfection. In 1774 he created a life-sized and lifelike figure of a boy seated at a desk, capable of writing up to forty letters. (He still functions at the History Museum in Neuchâtel.) Droz created another figure called 'the Artist', personified by a boy that could draw up to four different sketches, improving on the average work of his human counterpart. A third well-known figurine is that of a young girl called 'The Music Lady', who played the clavichord by the pressure of her fingers on the keyboard.[20]

These fascinating mechanical devices became collector's items in Europe, and particularly in England. For instance, in 1792, when King George III wished to make an impressive gift to the Chinese Emperor, he ordered Droz to make a copy of his 'Writing Boy', and ordered him dressed in Chinese clothes. (There is a copy of the 'Writing Boy' in the Philadelphia Research Museum.) Vaucanson's automatons were shown in England in 1742 and elsewhere in Europe. One English performance by these Swiss robots, dating back to 1784 is recalled by some billboards and posters of the period which have survived to this day. 'Having been honoured with the presence and approval of Their Majesties [the musical lady] is now exhibited at Wigley's great promenade room. Spring Garden.' Visiting hours were from 10 a.m. to 4 p.m. and from 6 p.m. to 10 p.m. The fee was one shilling during the day, and one and six pence at night. Another poster, dated 22 March 1811, described the automaton 'as a perfect imitation of nature reminding one of the mythological Greek statue that Prometheus brought to life'. For the twentieth-century person, weaned on television, and educated in the conquest of space, these mechanical attempts at imitating the work of Prometheus seem trivial, but to Percy and Mary, they must have been true marvels of inventiveness. Hitherto, only a very few scholars have laid emphasis on the impact of these man-machines on Mary's conception of Frankenstein's monster. One of the few is Mario Praz, who questioned the impact of conversations at Diodati on 'those French precedents of the artificial man.'[21]

In the last analysis, however, Mary's monster is more the child of the alchemists and occultists than of the scientists. We assume this to be the reason for Mary's silence on the precise circumstances attending Victor Frankenstein's creation of the monster, and prefer to conclude with Rieger (in his Introduction to the 1818 edition of *Frankenstein*) that '[I]t would be a mistake to call *Frankenstein* a pioneer work of science fiction. Its author knew something of Sir Humphry Davy's chemistry, Erasmus Darwin's botany, and, perhaps, Galvani's physics, but little of this got into her book. Frankenstein's chemistry is switched-on magic, souped-up alchemy, the electrification of Agrippa and Paracelsus. Things simply unknown or undone do not engage his attention; he wants the *forbidden*, unknown and undone. He is a criminal magician who employs up-to-date tools. Moreover, the technological plausibility that is essential to science fiction is not even pretended at here. Mary Shelley . . . skips the science.'[22]

11

Mary Shelley's Prophetic Vision

Although Mary Shelley was not a scientist, she may have been a prophet. She possessed a 'sixth sense', a kind of second vision, and had a gift of divination which was particularly noticeable in her dreams about her immediate family; she foresaw the death of her son William three years before the event, when she had the monster kill the image of her son, at Plainpalais. Mary had a similar premonition concerning Shelley's drowning in the novel *Mathilda* (1819), and again one week before he actually drowned. This gift of prophecy caused Mary great anguish, making her worry constantly about her loved ones.

On a less immediate level, one critic, Muriel Spark, described *Frankenstein* as a novel of 'scientific speculation in which the germ of prophecy necessarily resides'. The case for Mary, the prophet, emerges more forcibly in her novel *The Last Man* (1826), her only original work other than *Frankenstein*, in which she forecast that the English Royal Family would adopt the name Windsor – a decision only made in 1917 during World War I, when it was considered desirable to give up German names. In that same work, she prophesied that flying would be a mode of travel in the future (since she loved balloons, she saw these as a vehicle), but she did miscalculate the time – Mary thought it would take 48 hours to fly from London to Scotland.

Going beyond incidental visions, Muriel Spark noted further that 'Mary had a certain intuitive farsightedness by which she anticipated the ultimate conclusions to which the ideas of her epoch were heading.' In this respect, *The Last Man* advances hypotheses that were clearly judged so wild by contemporaries that the critic of one English newspaper, *John Bull*, wondered whether the book would find any readers at all. In an age when atomic or biological destruction of the planet earth is a terrifying reality, Mary's description of an end of civilization seems strangely apocalyptic.

Her scenario for *The Last Man* is set in the year 2073, barely 77 years hence. England has become a republic, not by any means a far-fetched idea in an age of tottering thrones and an increasing criticism of the high moral and financial cost of the English monarchy (there are many in England today who would wager that Prince Charles will never succeed to the throne). Mary sees humanity reduced to just one man, her hero, owing to a swift, incurable and fatal disease coming from Eastern Europe that will sweep across Europe to the Americas. This vision assumes a certain stark reality if we consider the ominous statistics of the spread of AIDS and the outbreaks of other deadly viruses such as Ebola in Africa or the possibility of the use of germ warfare by Iraq during the Gulf War. Reading our daily newspaper headlines, Mary's symptoms of the end of the planet earth appear in the guise of current conversational topics. In the novel, humanity has abandoned itself to the hedonism of the day: mystical religious leaders, sects and false prophets proliferate; politicians exploit the public trust for personal gain; men and women dig up public parks to grow food; would-be tyrants lurk in every corner, ready to establish their dictatorship – how much more relevant could she have been? Let us recall that the words were written in the sound, stable and solid dawn of the Victorian age.

What of Mary's concepts of the possibility of an artificial man manufactured by Victor Frankenstein from the spare parts of cadavers, sewn together in a rough sort of way by this self-appointed plastic surgeon of his day and endowed with a spark of life by some galvanic battery? Given the scientific possibility of the last quarter of the twentieth century, does that vision lie within the realm of possibility? Are we on the threshold of finally achieving the age-old dream of the alchemists in having men play God and create life?

Judging by the startling accomplishments of modern medicine and science in conquering death and prolonging life, the record is impressive enough. As I write these lines, medicine is close to the discovery of a vaccine against cancer, one of the great killers of our time, and the new genetic medicine can attack viruses and reverse illnesses without side effects. In Mary's time, forty children out of every one hundred died at birth – a statistic particularly real to Mary whose children, with one exception, died before the age of six. Mary herself reached the age of fifty-four (she died of cancer of the brain), a premature death by more than two decades for the average American or European woman. While visiting Romania during the Ceauşescu period, the author visited the internationally known Institute of Geriatrics at Bucharest, headed by the late Dr Ana Aslan, where the life span of many of her patients reached beyond 103 (remember that Konrad Dippel aimed to reach the age of 135 with the help of his blood elixir). Through medicines still half-recognized by the medical profession, Ana Aslan's secret for longevity (Gerovital) or that of the late Dr Niehans at Montreux (he injected his patients with the cells of a newborn lamb), has definitely slowed or set back the clock of time. Is it therefore conceivable that once emancipated from the natural limitations of biology, we may, with proper medical prescriptions or by proper diet, decide the length of our own life?

Lenthening the life span is equally true with regard to the increasing number of successful operations and transplants undertaken by modern surgeons. Except for the brain, virtually every organ, such as the lungs, the liver, the kidneys, limbs, bowels, stomach, pancreas, bones, bone marrow and sexual organs, can be replaced today. So great has been their success that the chief problem is not so much the operation, but the scarcity of available organs – one reason why central clearing houses have been established in the US and various other Western countries which keep hospitals and medical centres informed of the availability of 'spare parts', which are frozen until such time as they can be successfully implanted. The reconstruction or rejuvenation of a face, skin grafts, nose jobs, breast implants, even the implantation of teeth and hair are routine plastic surgery procedures, performed with greater skills than those required for Boris Karloff's famous mask or for de Niro's make-up in the most recent Frankenstein film where scars and sutures followed a careful study of facial musculature. Nor does medical science necessarily have to rely on human parts for such operations; indeed in current medical practice, the artificial organ has many advantages over the cadaver (overcoming the problem of rejection among other things). It uses a great diversity of materials which include nylon, orlon, silicone, plastic alloy and even metal parts. Almost any organ, again with the exception of the brain, can be synthetically manufactured. Many of the more famous artificial spare parts such as the pacemaker, the artificial lung, the kidney and the electronic TV eye have been the object of newspaper headlines; other, such as breast implants, penis extensions, wigs, hearing-devices, or even a dreary set of teeth kept in a glass beside the bed, have become household jokes. Badly disfigured Vietnam veterans, people seriously injured in automobile accidents as well as those severely burned, realize the full tragic yet consoling meaning of the term 'semi-artificial man'.

In a book called *God and Golem*, Norbert Wiener stated that 'a man with a wooden leg represents a system composed of mechanical and human parts'. If such a simple device as a stump can provide an illustration of the man-machine concept, how much more is this true in case of injury where virtually two thirds of the innards and even the external façade of a human needs to be replaced? The replacement of worn-out body parts also resolves the problem of failing health.

Mary obviously had a fleeting dream concerning the importance of the power of electricity in instilling life. Indeed, many of the current artificial organs – the pacemaker and the artificial kidney – rely on electricity to function. Without this 'juice of life' many patients would simply die – one of the reasons why major hospitals always have back-up electrical power plants. Electricity has also been used for reviving patients considered clinically dead. By an odd coincidence one of the most spectacular experiences was reported in the British press in 1818, the very year that *Frankenstein* was published. A well-known criminal, Matthew Clydesdale, had just been condemned to the gallows by a Glasgow court. Two professors from the university, the professor of anatomy, Jeffrey and a chemist, Andrew Ure, obtained the use of the corpse, then infused electrical current in it, with a kind of galvanic battery that Shelley had tried at Eton. The corpse apparently was temporarily animated, shaken by tremors, which so frightened the two learned scientists that they had the victim re-killed by cutting his jugular vein. The experiment, performed in public, awakened much public attention and may have helped to sell Mary's book.

Similar experiments in which men and women were described as chemically dead or in a state of catalepsy, where life has been continued and death cheated for hours, days or even weeks by various artificial means, have been performed in many countries since – and all have raised many basic theological and philosophical questions concerning the morality of these attempts. I refer among many other instances to the question of prolonging former President Truman's and President Tito's lives for several weeks, when to all intents and purposes they were destined to die.

Since we are talking of a partially human, partially mechanical, semi-artificial man, why not link Mary's Frankenstein to the concept of a totally mechanical man? Even though her monster was human, some of the inspiration stemmed from her and Shelley's interest in automatons. The twentieth century has witnessed a most remarkable revolution in the annals of mankind – the cybernetic revolution – with the advent of the information highway likely to transform humanity far more permanently than the industrial revolution of the nineteenth century it has superseded. The man who coined the word 'cybernetics', the title of his first book in 1948, is the mathematical genius Norbert Wiener, whose central theme is a close parallelism between the nervous system of man and the feedback control system of the all-powerful computer. Whereas machines were used for power in the nineteenth century, Wiener conceived them as also having a brain and sensory system. Placing his services in the cause of the allies in World War II (he was a refugee from Nazi Germany), Wiener devised the first electronic military hardware which had the 'brain' to find its objective, no matter how elusive the target – the ancestors of the guided missiles system of today. Since that time, computers have simply ousted men from their occupations in a wide variety of fields, not necessarily limited to war – the computer performs its functions more quickly and more efficiently than the human brain. We use computers for complicated arithmetic, collecting data from space, flying planes and making weather or political forecasts. Computers report the latest Stock Exchange quotations to us. They can play games: the latest American chess computer, Deep Blue, commanded headlines as it came close to beating the international chess champion, Gary Kasparov. Computers can compose music, write books and produce CD-roms. A new computerized generation has been born with machines taking the place of humans, communicating with each other instantly through Internet, reducing the size of the world, and making it safer and more dangerous at the same time. All this represents a fundamental change in the annals of human thinking and its ultimate consequences, at the moment of writing, are hard to predict.

Thus the advent of the information highway has helped develop a new mentality which looks at human problems in mechanistic terms and computers almost in human terms, helping focus on the man-machine analogy first noted by the eighteenth-century philosopers. By stressing the parallel between the function of a human brain and the sensitivity of the nervous system with that of a machine – and given the increasing number of mechanical devices with purposive and self-adaptive characteristics – we may conclude with Norbert Wiener that modes of behaviour 'long held to be peculiar to the living system need not necessarily lie beyond the range of mechanism'. Completing the rapprochement between humans and machines, researchers in a new behavioural science have similarly emphasized that the thinking process, sense perception and the human anatomy could be viewed as mechanistic – the brain after all is composed of many small parts. Therefore, can we say that humans are machines? If machines are like men and since men resemble machines, there is nothing intrinsically illogical in believing that machines, like men, can be affected by illnesses and even by psychic disorders (computer cancer, for instance). If you repress the machine's ego excessively it develops neuroses, a disorder some may have noted with their automobiles, if you do not treat them well.

For the layman, however, this man-machine analogy can have little meaning unless the computer can also look human (I cannot gather any great enthusiasm in 'talking' to a computer as if it were a human being unless it approximates to the shape of a person). From the 1920s onwards, a number of semi-human-like monsters, somewhat suggestive of Mary's own monster, have been constructed that are able to perform a variety or more/less difficult thinking functions. They were given specific names by their inventors, such as the American 'Televox 1 and 2' constructed by the engineer, Wensley of Westinghouse. Their cast even included a 'gossiping woman' and a pistol-packing man who was as quick on the draw as Gary Cooper. An ambitious recent attempt at creating a human-shaped robot occurred in Toulouse, France. Appropriately enough, it was called 'Shakey'. It was designed to accomplish the simple tasks of a three-year-old child, such as walking in the room with several obstacles in its way, finding objects, pushing a box along a rail, etc. In order not to fatigue it excessively, the robot worked only a few days a week – the rest of the time was spent in editing its program, which required the services of two other computers and fifteen programmers. In the end, the French newspaper, *Le*

Monde announced that 'Shakey was dead'. At least this particular program had ended in failure. There is no need, however, to despair of the future. When André Maurois returned
from the United States in the 1960s, he was so impressed by
the information revolution he witnessed in industry and elsewhere that he had a vision of the advent of the completely
mechanical man endowed with vision, hearing, touch, smell,
arms and legs resembling 'the rough synthesis of man'.
Shakey's failure, notwithstanding, it is perfectly conceivable
in the not too distant future to envisage the possibility of a
mechanical monster, a kind of a household electronic slave
that would wake us up with a rubdown and breakfast in the
morning and prepare our meals, fix our cocktails, perform
our household chores by using our washing machines and
vacuum cleaners, fix our hardware more efficiently than a
human repair man, keep our lawns manicured, even drive us
to work – and perform all these tasks in a fraction of the time
it would take a human. There is nothing Utopian about the
notion of the 'robot, soldier, sailor or airman' (the airmen and
astronauts already exist) who would fight for our nation. The
robot-soldier's advent on the battlefield holds great promise
for the conscientious objector; so does the robot-judge that
will always hand out a fair sentence (no mis-trial will be possible); the robot-physician who will make no mistake in diag-
nosis (no mis-read mammograph); the robot-surgeon that will
never leave a piece of cotton wool inside an incision (no need
for malpractice insurance); the robot-teacher that will come
close to Socrates in his logic (no need for remedial reading
courses) and why not the robot-President that will invariably
make judicious political decisions (no possibility of
Watergate or Whitewater). The very mention of such
possibilities introduces a spectre which has been presaged in
current literature of a new class of Frankenstein mechanical
monsters taking over our planet and reproducing themselves,
while humanity, with emasculated strength and diminishing
brain, is gradually reduced to the role of servant by these
monsters, the former slaves of humans. This frightening
vision may indeed have been foreseen by Mary Shelley's

scientist, Victor Frankenstein, when he decided to break the promise he had made to the monster and refused to proceed with the manufacture of a mate for fear that the world would be populated by monsters!

In lengthening life, by conquering diseases, replacing organs or using artificial implants, using electrical devices or even creating a mechanical man, the Frankensteins of today have not as yet trespassed upon the moral law, though they may have come dangerously close to 'playing God'. However, other recent experiments point to a more definite presumption. Artificial insemination and developments in *in vitro fertilization* have made Aldous Huxley's Utopia seem more real than ever. Another un-Godly approach to the presumption of creation – we should say 're-creation' – which in some ways approximates Konrad Dippels' Frankenstein approach, is that of Doctor C W Ettinger, professor of physics at Highland Park Community College (Michigan), founder of the Cryogenic Society of America and author of the book *The Prospect of Immortality* (first published by Doubleday in 1964; reprinted in 1966 and 1969). In essence, Professor Ettinger proposed to freeze dead bodies at very low temperature, −270 degrees centigrade. According to him this super freezing can preserve bodies like mummies during indefinite periods of time without impairing any of the organs. Given the progress of medicine, Professor Ettinger believed that at some point in the not too distant future, when medical science will have progressed to the point of conquering all diseases, it will become possible to thaw out these cadavers and bring them back to life. In the decade after his book was published some twenty cadavers were frozen with some such intent. Like Huxley's vision, Ettinger's prospect of immortality when first published in 1964 seemed little more than science fiction. The two subsequent editions of the book indicated that an increasing number of readers were beginning to take Professor Ettinger's prospect of immortality more seriously.

Are we to conclude then that the age-old dream of the alchemist – the idea of procreation without sex or the renewal of the life of a cadaver – which had so obsessed Mary

Shelley, is on the verge of becoming a reality? Are the twentieth-century scientists succeeding where the alchemists failed? The answer to this problem hinges upon whether we believe in a mechanistic philosophy of life, such as that preached by Oxford University philosopher Gilbert Ryle, who published his controversial book *The Concept of Mind* in 1949 in which he dismissed the idea of a human soul. This theory is also propounded by many cyberneticists, biologists, geneticists, behaviourists, physicists and physicians. Those who profess to be science-minded, typically impressed by the man-machine analogy, believe 'machines can think' and their slogans attract an increasing number of adepts. Inevitably this parallel contains a grain of truth. Our body could well be considered a biological container within which there operates a very subtle machine, capable of all kinds of reflexes and responses – and with mechanistic rules of their own. We do know, for instance, that unless our digestive tract is linked to the œsophagus in a certain way – of which Vaucanson was well aware when he built his 'digestive duck' – the body will cease to operate.

Nonetheless, when all is said and done, our human 'machine' cannot be dissected into its component parts, however essential these might be to life. People are clearly more than brain, heart, liver, kidney, lungs and digestive tract. What precisely that additional ingredient which established man's intrinsic humanness is, is yet to be defined. That is why such imperfect words as 'soul', 'spirit', 'vital forces', 'will', 'consciousness', and 'mind' have been used to describe the completeness and uniqueness of humans in most religions and philosophies. That point has of late been admirably expressed by philosopher David Chalmers in his book, *The Conscious Mind* (to be published in 1996), which lays emphasis on the existence of pleasure, pain, love and guilt to prove his vitalist interpretation. There is, therefore, something in a human being that eludes a mechanistic interpretation of the universe, defies the cleverest robot and excels the most powerful computer – in much the same manner as in art, where the brilliance of Leonardo Da Vinci reduces the brush stroke of an ape to ridicule, while in science the genius of an

Einstein eclipses the mathematical calculator. Even Deep
Blue, the chess computer which has the power of gauging
more than one million moves a second, could not really
understand the game of chess: the *reason why* Kasparov won.
At a much lower level of intelligence, as Marvin Minsky of
MIT acknowledges, the computer has no common sense. It
cannot make small talk or play simple games. Put in another
way, the sudden cancer cure of a man doomed by his doctors
– just as any other event which we loosely term 'miraculous'
(for lack of a better word) – can never be rationalized or scien-
tifically or mechanistically accounted for. There is in this
puzzle of life a hidden element which belongs to a different
dimension, that lies beyond the capacities of humans to deci-
pher. In this respect the scientist will always fall short of the
ultimate goal – and the man-machine analogy, however
attractively phrased, becomes a matter of semantics.

Science has certainly achieved miracles which, not many
years ago, were within the domain of science fiction, like
walking on the moon. The fact that we can talk intelligently
today about prolonging life by replacing every conceivable
organ either synthetically or by transplant; that we can cure
or reverse disease by genetic manipulation; that we can create
mechanical brains more powerful than the human mind
which can perform a great number of services; that we can
deep-freeze human spare parts and even bodies for an indefinite period of time; that we are able to explore the mysteries
of the reproductive system; that we can create viruses of all
kinds – all this has inclined some to say 'nothing is impossible'. Mary Shelley's *Frankenstein* might be looked upon by
some as remarkably prophetic book presaging many of the
scientific breakthroughs of the twentieth century. Given the
number among us who in our everyday existence have
learned to live with varying spare parts, ranging from
implanted hair to a transplanted kidney, we might conclude,
somewhat lightheartedly that those so affected are at least in
part 'Frankenstein monsters'.

There is, however, a deeper message to *Frankenstein* (no
matter what others have chosen to read into it), a message

that is the more striking since it is often repeated. As Frankenstein agonizes in the cabin of Walton's ship in the distant polar North, a wreck of a man, physically and mentally exhausted, having sacrificed everything, including his life, in the interests of science and the pursuit of a 'loud sounding' monster, who pours his heart's contents to the last before dying on the funeral pyre (no one actually witnesses the suicide), one cannot help but feel pity for this human wretch. But more fundamental than the sense of pity is the moral of the story, one that Victor Frankenstein expressed several times in his lengthy discourse to his captive and captivated audience Captain Walton. 'Learn from me, if not by my precepts at least by my example how dangerous is the acquirement of knowledge and how much happier is that man who believes his native town to be the world than he who aspires to be greater than his nature will allow.'

In a contrite mood, Frankenstein calls himself the 'living monument of presumption and rash ignorance'. He has transgressed the moral law and hence suffers the inevitable retribution for his sins. One wonders to what extent his tragic odyssey (and perhaps Mary's own) may not serve as a lesson to our many presumptuous scientists who should pause before daring to resolve the unsolvable mysteries of life.

Notes

1 The Geographical Background of the Search

1. Boston: *Dracula: Prince of Many Faces* (Little, Brown, 1989); *In Search of Dracula* (London: Robson Books, 1995), both co-authored with Raymond T McNally.

2. The French title is *Fantasmagoriana, ou Recueil d'Histoires d'Apparitions. de Spectres, Revenants, etc.* (Paris: F Schoell, 1812), 2 vols.

3. See note 37, chapter 5, for a more detailed analysis of the controversy over the actual date of Byron's proposal.

4. Eileen Bigland, *Mary Shelley* (London: Cassell, 1959); Richard Church, *Mary Shelley* (London: Gerald Howe Ltd, 1928); Rosalie Glynn Grylls, *Mary Shelley, A Biography* (Oxford: Oxford University Press, 1938); Florence Ashton Marshall, *The Life and Letters of Mary Wollstonecraft Shelley* (London: R Bentley & Son, 1889), 2 vols.; Elizabeth Nitchie, *Mary Shelley, Author of Frankenstein* (New Brunswick, NJ: Rutgers University Press, 1953); Jean de Palacio, *Mary Shelley dans son Oeuvre: Contribution aux études Shelleyennes* (Paris: 1969).

5. Frederick L Jones, ed., *The Letters of Mary W Shelley* (Norman, Oklahoma: University of Oklahoma Press, 1944).

6. (London: T Hookham, 1817).

7. The airy spirit, or Ariel quality is probably a reference to Shelley, or to André Maurois's biography *Ariel, The Life of*

Shelley, trans. Ella D'Arcy (New York: Appleton, 1924). The boat on which Shelley drowned was named the *Ariel*; and one of Shelley's poems begins:

> With a Guitar, to Jane [Williams]
> Ariel to Miranda. – Take
> this slave of Music for the Sake
> Of him who is the slave of thee.
> Poor Ariel sends this silent token
> Of more than ever can be spoken;
> Your guardian spirit, Ariel, who
> From life to life, must still pursue
> Your happiness; for this alone
> Can Ariel ever find his own . . .

Edward Dowden, ed., *The Poetical Works of Percy Bysshe Shelley* (London: Macmillan and Co., 1891).

8. *Causeries d'un Octogénaire Genevois* (Geneva, 1883).

9. The tale was related to us by Dean Gagnebin, a relative of Mayor Guempert.

10. Jones, *The Letters*.

11. For a discussion of the controversy over the dates of the *Tour du Lac*, see footnote 30, chapter 5.

12. See chapter 5, pp. 116–117.

13. Mary Shelley, *Rambles in Germany and Italy in 1840, 1842 and 1843* (London: Edward Moxon, 1844), vol. 1, p. 174.

14. Hansards, *Parliamentary Debates*, New Series, vol. 10 (16 March 1824), column 1103.

15. William A Wheeler, *Dictionary of the Noted Names of Fiction* (1865).

16. Ebenezer Cobham Brewer, *Dictionary of Phrase and Fable* (London, 1897).

17. Walter E Peck, *Shelley, His Life and Work* (New York & Boston: Houghton Mifflin, Co., 1927), vol. 1, p. 55. See Lewis's *Romantic Tales* (London, 1808) and *Tales of Wonder* (London, 1801).

18. Reply to a letter commenting on Samuel Rosenberg's article, 'Horrible Truth About Frankenstein', *Life* Magazine (5 April 1968). See also Donald F Glut, *The Frankenstein Legend* (Metuchen, NJ: Scarecrow Press, 1973), p. 10.

19. (London: Saunders and Otley, 1826).

20. P. 27, footnote 6.

21. The events of the summer of 1816 have been studied and romanticized by, among others, Derek Marlowe, in his admirable little book: *A Single Summer with Lord B.* (New York: Viking, 1969); they have been researched in a more scholarly way by Claire-Elaine Engel in *Byron et Shelley en Suisse et en Savoie Mai–Octobre, 1816, 1930.*

2   The Tomb of Mary Wollstonecraft and St Pancras Cemetery

1. Ralph M Wardle, *Mary Wollstonecraft: A Critical Biography* (Lawrence, Kansas: University of Kansas Press, 1951), p. 306.

2. Elizabeth Robins Pennell, *Life of Mary Wollstonecraft* (Boston: Roberts Brothers, 1884), p. 351.

3. Claire Tomalin, *The Life and Death of Mary Wollstonecraft* (London: Weidenfeld & Nicolson, 1974).

4. Ibid.

5. Pennell, *Mary Wollstonecraft*, p. 15.

6. Coincidentally, in 1775, while the Wollstonecraft family was residing in Hoxton, William Godwin was a student at the Dissenting College in that town, although the two did not meet at the time. Ibid, p. 26.

7. Ibid., p. 33.

8. (London: J Johnson, 1792).

9. An ungenerous team of psychoanalysts, Ferdinand Lundberg and Margina F Famham in *Modern Woman the Lost Sex* (New York and London: Harper & Bros., 1947), pp. 144ff., labelled the pattern of Mary's romantic behaviour as sex without social and moral restraint.

10. Pennell, *Mary Wollstonecraft*, p. 230.

11. (London: J Johnson, 1796).

12. Wardle, *Mary Wollstonecraft*, p. 245.

13. William Godwin, *Memoirs of Mary Wollstonecraft* (London: Constable and Co., Ltd., 1927), p. 84.

14. Ibid., pp. 100–101.

15. The marriage certificate is still in existence and is reproduced in Tomalin, p. 212.

16. (London: C G J and J Robinson, 1793).

17. (London: R Bentley, 1835). The subtitle is *,or things as they are*. Mary Shelley read it no less than five times: twice in 1814, 1816, 1820, and 1821.

18. (London: H Colburn and R Bentley, 1831).

19. (London: F J Mason, 1834).

20. Miss Harriet Lee, a teacher from Bath, Amelia Alderson, who subsequently married the painter Opie, and Maria Reveley, a wealthy widow.

21. Charles Kegan Paul, *William Godwin: His Friends and Contemporaries* (London: H S King & Co., 1876), vol. 2, pp. 231–232.

22. R Glynn Grylls, *Mary Shelley, A Biography* (London: Oxford University Press, 1938), p. 14, fn. 2.

23. *Deutsche Sagen* (Berlin: Cassel, 1816), vol. 1, story 218, pp. 300–301. (See Appendix for a translation of the tale.)

24. Edward Dowden, *The Life of Percy Bysshe Shelley* (London: Kegan Paul, Trench & Co., 1886), vol. 1, pp. 418–419.

25. Eileen Bigland, *Mary Shelley* (London: Cassell, 1959), p. 30.

26. Samuel Rosenberg, 'Happy 150th Dear Frankenstein,' *Life* magazine (15 March 1968).

27. (London: Saunders and Otley, 1837), vol. 1, pp. 6–7.

28. Elizabeth Nitchie, *Mary Shelley: Author of Frankenstein* (New Brunswick, NJ: Rutgers University Press, 1953), p. 97.

29. Ibid., p. 9.

30. *Epipsychidion*, 1. 281. Cf. *Journal*, p. 182.

31. 'Mary Shelley, Traveller', *Keats-Shelley Journal X* (Winter 1961): 29.

32. Dowden, *The Life of Percy Bysshe Shelley*, vol. 1, p. 62.

33. Ibid., vol. 1, p. 18.

34. Ibid., vol. 1, p. 30.

35. Ibid., vol. 1, pp. 30–31.

36. Ibid., vol. 1, p. 64.

37. Ibid., vol. 1, p. 182.

38. Ibid., vol. 1, p. 433.
39. Ibid., vol. 1, p. 218.
40. Ibid., vol. 1, pp. 220–222.
41. Ibid., vol. 1, p. 420.
42. Ibid., vol. 1, pp. 430–431.
43. Ibid., vol. 1, p. 17.
44. Ibid., vol. 1, p. 17.
45. Ibid., vol. 1, p. 37.
46. Frederick L Jones, ed., *Mary Shelley's Journal* (Norman, Oklahoma: University of Oklahoma Press, 1947), p. 3.

3 The Elopement to the Continent: 1814

1. (London: T Hookham, 1817).
2. Edited by Frederick L Jones (Norman, Oklahoma: University of Oklahoma Press, 1947).
3. Edited by Marion Kingston Stocking (Cambridge, Mass.: Harvard University Press, 1968). Unless otherwise indicated, quotations in this chapter will be taken from these three journals.
4. *The History of a Six Weeks' Tour*, p. 76.
5. 'Notes and Corrections to Shelley's Six Weeks' Tour in 1817', *Modern Language Review II* (October, 1906): 61–62. Also see André Koszul, *La Jeunesse de Shelley* (Paris: Bibliothèque de la Fondation Thiers, 1910).
6. Shelley continually suffered from acute attacks of hypochondria. Dowden relates one such instance in vol. 1, page 373. 'Towards the close of 1813 the strange delusion afflicted him that he was attacked by elephantiasis; he had travelled in a mail-coach with a fat old lady, whose legs, the reverse of slender, had horribly fascinated Shelley's gaze and imagination. She must be a victim of that cruel disease which changes the human skin into an elephant's hide; the disease must be contagious, and he himself could not now escape from its invasion. One day at Mr Newton's house in Chester Street, "as he was sitting in an armchair," writes Madame Gatayes, "talking to my father and mother, he suddenly

slipped down on the ground. twisting about like an eel. 'What is the matter?' cried my mother. In his impressive tone Shelley answered, 'I have the elephantiasis.' " '

7. Brothers Grimm, *Deutsche Sagen* (Berlin: Cassel, 1816), vol. 1, story 218, pp. 300–301. Cf. note 23, chapter 2.

8. T Engelmann, *Manuel des voyageurs sur le Rhin* (Paris, 1812), first edition.

9. Mary Wollstonecraft, *Letters Written during a Short Residence in Sweden, Norway, and Denmark* (London: J Johnson, 1796), pp. 183–184.

10. Mary Shelley, *Rambles in Germany and Italy, in 1840, 1842, and 1843* (London: Edward Moxon, 1844), vol. 1, p. 27.

4 Castle Frankenstein and the Alchemist Dippel

1. 'Memoirs of a Campaign along the Rhine in the Years 1792–1795', cited in Karl Esselborn, *Der Frankenstein* (Berlin, 1902).

2. See note 9, chapter 3.

3. Philipp Moritz Scriba, *Geschichte der ehemaligen Burg und Herrschaft Frankenstein und ihrer Herrn (The History of Old Castle Frankenstein, the Estates, and their Rulers)* (Darmstadt, 1853), pp. 490 ff.

4. *In Search of Dracula* (London: Robson Books, 1995), p. 83.

5. 'Untersuchungen zur Genealogie und Besitzgeschichte der Herren von … Frankenstein', in *Archiv für Hessische Geschichte und Altertumskunde* ('Research into the Genealogy and History of the Estates of the Frankensteins', in the *Archives for Hessian History and Archaeology*, New Series), Neue Folge, 28 (1963), pp. 99–114. See also Walther Möller, 'Der Grabstein des Ritters Jörg zu Frankenstein an der Kirche zu Nieder Beerbach', in *Quartalblatter des Historischen Vereins für Hessen* ('The Gravestone of Sir Georg of Frankenstein in the Church of Nieder-Beerbach', in the *Quarterly of the Historical Society of Hesse*) (Darmstadt, 1916), Neue Folge, 6, pp. 366–367.

6. Johann Konrad Dippel, *Eröffneter Weg zum Frieden mit*

Gott und allen Creaturen, durch die Publication der sammtlichen, schriffen Christian Democriti (pseud.) (*The Way Revealed to Peace with God and All Creatures through the Publication of the Collected Writings of Christian Democritus.* pseud.), (Amsterdam, 1709–1735).

7. Karl Ludwig Voss, *Christianus Democritus Das Menschenbild bei Johann Konrad Dippel ein beispiel Christlicher Anthologie Zwischen Pietismus und Aufklärung (Christian Democritus, a Portrait by Johann Konrad Dippel, A Christian Anthology of Pietism and Enlightment)* (Leiden, 1970), p. 42. For other works on Dippel, see the Bibliography.

8. Rudolph Kunz, 'Goldmacher an der Bergstrasse: Drei Alchimistenbriefe' ('The Alchemist on the Bergestrasse: Three Alchemical Documents') in *Die Starkenburg*, 31, no. 6 (1954), p. 59.

9. *Velamen apertum aercanorum a principo mundi reconditorum.*

10. Voss, *Christanus Democritus*, p. 42.

11. Wilhelm Diehl, *Neue Beiträge zur Geschichte Johann Konrad Dippels in der theologischen Periode seines Lebens (New Contributions to the History of Johann Konrad Dippel in the Theological Period of His Life)* (Darmstadt, 1908), p. 183.

12. Ibid.

13. J C G Ackerman, *Das Leben Johann Konrad Dippels (The Life of Johann Konrad Dippel)* (Leipzig, 1858), p. 27.

14. Scriba, *Geschichte*, pp. 499–502.

15. Transcribed by author from parish records.

16. Essellborn, *Der Frankenstein*, pp. 359–360. See also F Ebner. *Darmstadt der Goethezeit (Darmstadt during Goethe's Time)* (Darmstadt, 1963).

17. Cf. Merck, *Goethe, Dichtung und Wahrheit (Goethe, Poetry and Truth)*, vols. 12 & 13. See also H Braüning-Oktavio, 'Goethe und Johann Heinrich Merck' in the magazine *Goethe*, no. 12 (1950), pp. 177–217.

18. Primavesi, *Die Burg Frankenstein in zwölf Abbildungen (Castle Frankenstein in Twelve Pictures)* (Darmstadt, 1819).

19. *Encyclopaedia Britannica* (1768), vol. 2, p. 630.

5   The Haunted Summer of 1816

1. *Disputatio Medica Inuguralis, Quaedam de Morbo Oneirodynia Dicto, Complectens* (Edinburgh, 1815).

2. William Michael Rossetti, ed., *The Diary of Dr John William Polidori* (London: Elkin Mathews, 1911).

3. Ibid., p. 33.

4. Ibid., p. 87.

5. The plaque that can still be seen in front of the park of Mon Repos bears sufficient testimony to the fashionableness of the inn. Apart from Byron, Empress Josephine, Empress Marie Louise, Hortense de Beauharnais, Madame de Récamier, Benjamin Constant, and Queen Victoria all stayed there, before the hotel went bankrupt in 1842. Edouard Chapuisat, *L'Auberge de Sécheron, au temps des princesses et des berlines* (Geneva, 1934), p. 148.

6. Letter to an unknown addressee (17 May), Frederick L Jones, *The Letters of Mary W Shelley* (Norman, Oklahoma: University of Oklahoma Press, 1947), p. 869.

7. R Glynn Grylls, *Claire Clairmont. Mother of Byron's Allegra* (London: John Murray, 1939), pp. 55–56.

8. Derek Marlowe, *A Single Summer with Lord B.* (New York: Viking, 1969), p. 35.

9. Rossetti, *The Diary*, p. 99.

10. Dowden, *The Life of Percy Bysshe Shelley*, vol. 2, p. 12.

11. Rossetti, *The Diary*, p. 101.

12. Thomas Moore, *The Letters and Journals of Lord Byron* (London: John Murray, 1833), Byron to Augusta (8 September 1816).

13. Jones, *The Letters*, vol. 1, p. 12, letter 19 (Campagne Chapuis, 1 June 1816).

14. Ibid., vol. 1, pp. 10–11, letter 18.

15. Ibid., p. 11, letter 18 (Sécheron, 17 May 1816).

16. Moore, *The Letters* (Byron to Thomas Moore, 19 September 1821), letter 453, vol. 5, p. 242.

17. Dowden, vol. 2, p. 14. At the beginning of the century, there was still a small bronze plaque at Diodati that bore the following inscription: 'John Milton, English poet, Secretary of

State of Oliver Cromwell, author of *Paradise Lost*, lived here, the host of John Diodati in 1639.'

18. Jones, *The Letters*, vol. 1, pp. 11–12, letter 19.

19. Ibid., vol. 1, p. 13, letter 19.

20. Frederick L Jones, *Mary Shelley's Journal* (Norman, Oklahoma: University of Oklahoma Press, 1947), p. 80.

21. Mary Shelley, *Rambles*, vol. 1, pp. 139–140.

22. Interview with author.

23. Moore, *The Letters* (25 March 1817), vol. 3, p. 361, letter 637 to Thomas Moore.

24. Balzac was to re-visit Diodati in 1837 with another woman, Madame Caroline Marbouty, while on a business trip to Italy via Switzerland. Noel B Gerson, *The Prodigal Genius: the Life and Times of Honoré de Balzac* (Garden City, NY: Doubleday and Co., 1972).

25. Dowden, *The Life of Percy Bysshe Shelley*, vol. 2, p. 10.

26. Letter to unknown recipient in Jones, *Letters*, vol. 1, p. 12, letter 19.

27. Rossetti, *The Diary*, p. 30.

28. Dowden, *The Life of Percy Bysshe Shelley*, vol. 2, p. 16. Another version has Byron commenting that he would give Polidori 'a damn good thrashing'.

29. Ibid.

30. Again, there is some discrepancy on these dates. Mary Shelley lists the start of the journey as 23 June in her *Six Weeks' Tour*. Dowden concurs with the date of the 23rd in his *The Life of Percy Bysshe Shelley*. The entry in Polidori's Diary for 22 June notes, however, that 'L[ord] B[yron] and Shelley went to Vevay.' I intend to accept the accuracy of Polidori's *Diary*, and assume that the two poets left for the *Tour du Lac* on 22 June, and returned on 1 July.

31. See John Harrington Smith, 'Shelley and Claire Clairmont', *Publications of Modern Language Associations* (September 1939), p. 181. See also Frederick L Jones, 'Mary Shelley and Claire Clairmont', *South Atlantic Quarterly* XLII (1943): 406–412.

32. Shelley went before a magistrate on 27 December 1818 in Naples to declare that Elena Adelaide Shelley had been

born to him and Mary. The Shelleys' maid Elize later related that Shelley had smuggled the child by Claire into a Naples foundling hospital. To this day the real mother of Adelaide is a subject of much controversy.

33. See note 31.

34. Rossetti, *The Diary*, p. 110.

35. Ibid., pp. 134–135.

36. Samuel Rosenberg, *The Confessions of a Trivialist* (Baltimore, Md: Penguin, 1972), p. 58.

37. There is much controversy among scholars over the actual date on which the contest was proposed by Byron. Dowden, in his *The Life of Percy Bysshe Shelley* (Kegan Paul, Trench & Co., 1886), vol. 2, p. 33, places the incident on the night of 18 June. In his edited version of *Frankenstein, or the Modern Prometheus* (Indianapolis: Bobbs-Merrill, 1974), p. 226, fn. 10, James Rieger gives the date as 16 June, when Polidori was laid up with a sprained ankle, and the Shelley party spent the night at Villa Diodati. Polidori, in his *Diary* (William Michael Rossetti, ed., London: Elkin Mathews, 1911), pp. 122–123, notes: 'Up late; began my letters. When to Shelley's. After dinner, jumping a wall my foot slipped and I strained my left ankle. Shelley, etc. came in the evening talked of my play, etc., which all agreed was worth nothing. Afterwards Shelley and I had a conversation about principles, – whether man was to be thought merely an instrument.'

Dowden gives the reading of Coleridge's 'Christabel' and Shelley's hallucination on 18 June the same night that Byron proposed the contest. Polidori's *Diary* for 17 June notes, however, that 'the ghost stories are begun by all but me'.

38. See note 2, chapter 1.

39. Dowden, *The Life of Percy Bysshe Shelley*, vol. 2, p. 34.

40. Rossetti, *The Diary*, p. 126. Coleridge, as we have noted, had been a friend of William Godwin and the poem 'Christabel' was written shortly after Mary Wollstonecraft died. The plot centres upon the story of a young noblewoman whose mother died in the hope that she would live. With memories of the promises made at Mary Wollstonecraft's

grave, is it to be wondered that Shelley, probably under the influence of laudanum, should have left the room, terror-stricken at seeing Mary's or her mothers ghost? (This was not the first apparition in Shelley's life.)

41. pp. 122–123.

42. Sir S H Buxton Forman III, 382.

43. Jones, *Mary Shelley's Journal*, pp. 50–54.

44. A Charles Swinburne, 'Notes on Shelley Text', in *Essays & Studies* (London, 1875).

45. The *London Chronicle* (June 1819).

46. Jones, *Mary Shelley's Journal*, pp. 52–53.

47. Ibid., pp. 52–54.

48. Ibid.

49. Letter to Peacock (23 July 1816).

50. In the same way that they had adapted the story of the dragon-monster at Castle Frankenstein, the Brothers Grimm used some of Monk Lewis's stories.

51. *London Magazine* IX (March 1824): 253–256.

6 A Summer's End

1. Edward Dowden, *The Life of Percy Bysshe Shelley*, vol. II (London: Kegan Paul, Trench & Co., 1886), p. 57.

2. Mary to Shelley (17 December 1816). In Dowden, *The Life*, p. 70.

3. Walter Edwin Peck, *Shelley, His Life and Work* (Boston & New York: Houghton Mifflin Co., 1927), vol. 1, p. 494.

4. Ibid., vol. 1, p. 502.

5. Charles Kegan Paul, *The Life and Letters of William Godwin* (London: Henry S. King & Co., 1876), vol. 2, p. 245.

6. F L Jones, *Mary Shelley's Journal* (Norman, Oklahoma: University of Oklahoma Press, 1947). p. 41.

7. Ibid., p. 105.

8. R Glynn Grylls, *Mary Shelley. A Biography* (Oxford University Press, 1938), p. 101.

9. Dowden, *The Life*, vol. 2, pp. 267–268.

10. Grylls, *Mary Shelley*, p. 110.

11. Ibid., p. 105.

12. William Michael Rossetti, *The Diary of Dr John William Polidori* (London: Elkin Mathews, 1911), pp. 5–6.

13. Ibid., pp. 7–8.

14. F L Jones, *The Letters of Mary W Shelley* (Norman, Oklahoma: University of Oklahoma Press, 1947), vol. 2. p. 95.

15. Ibid., vol. 2, p. 95,

16. Dowden, *The Life*, vol. 2, p. 199.

17. Marion Kingston Stocking, *The Journals of Claire Clairmont* (Cambridge, Mass: Harvard University Press, 1968), p. 227.

18. Marchesa Iris Origo, *Allegra* (London: Hogarth Press, 1935), p. 87.

19. Dowden, *The Life*, vol. 2, p. 494.

20. Grylls, *Mary Shelley*, p. 163.

21. Dowden, *The Life*, vol. 2, p. 500.

22. Ibid., vol. 2, p. 514.

23. Ibid., vol. 2, pp. 515–516

24. Ibid., vol. 2, p. 516.

25. Ibid., vol. 2, p. 507.

26. Ibid., vol. 2, p. 17.

27. Ibid.

28. Mary Shelley claims that the builder of the boat, Captain Roberts, was also on board.

29. Dowden, *The Life*, vol. 2, pp. 525–528.

30. Ibid., vol. 2, p. 529.

31. Ibid., vol. 2, p. 533.

32. Thomas Moore, *The Life of Lord Byron, with His Letters and Journal* (London: John Murray, 1847), p. 1009.

33. Ibid., p. 1034.

34. Ibid., p. 1037.

35. Ibid.

36. Jones, *Mary Shelley's Journal*, pp. 193–194.

37. Ibid.

38. Hobhouse, *Journey to Albania*, vol. 2, chapter 2.

7   Frankenstein: In Print and On Stage

1. Edward Dowden, *The Life of Percy Bysshe Shelley* (London: Kegan Paul Trench & Co., Ltd., 1886), vol. 2, p. 140.

2. Christopher Small, *Mary Shelley's Frankenstein: Tracing the Myth* (Pittsburgh: University of Pittsburgh Press, 1973), p. 21.

3. Vol. 2 (March 1818), pp. 249–253.

4. *New Series*, vol. 18 (March 1818), pp. 139–142.

5. Vol. 2, no. 12 (March 1818), pp. 612–620.

6. *Shelley and Mary* (Privately published, 1882), vol. 2, p. 327.

7. Vol. 3, no. 5 (August–November 1824), pp. 195–199.

8. F L Jones, ed., *Mary Shelley's Letters* (Norman, Oklahoma: University of Oklahoma Press, 1947), vol. 2, p. 353.

9. No. 2 (3 February 1835), p. 3.

10. Allardyce Nicoll, *A History of English Drama: 1660–1900* (Cambridge: Cambridge University Press, 1952–1959), vol. 4, p. 2.

11. Ibid., p. 55.

12. R Glynn Grylls, *Mary Shelley, A Biography* (Oxford University Press, 1938), p. 198.

13. (London: Colburn, 1823), 3 vols.

14. (London: Colburn, 1826), 3 vols.

15. (London: Colburn and Bentley, 1830), 3 vols.

16. (London: Bentley, 1835), 3 vols.

17. (London: Saunders Otley, 1837), 3 vols.

18. Jones, *Letters*, vol. 1, p. 251.

19. Ibid., vol. 1, p. 259.

20. Allardyce Nicoll, *A History of English Drama*, vol. 4, p. 13.

21. *Mary Shelley: Author of Frankenstein* (New Brunswick, NJ: Rutgers University Press, 1953), p. 222.

22. Donald F Glut, *The Frankenstein Legend* (Metuchen, NJ: Scarecrow Press, 1973), p. 54.

8   Mary Shelley and the Gothic Novel

1. Ford K Brown, *The Life of William Godwin* (New York: E P Dutton Co., 1926), p. 366.
2. *Frankenstein, or the Modern Prometheus*, James Rieger, ed. (Indianapolis: Bobbs-Merrill, Co., 1974), p. xviii.
3. Not to be confused with Shelley's friend, Thomas Jefferson Hogg.
4. Christopher Small, *Mary Shelley's Frankenstein: Tracing the Myth* (Pittsburgh: University of Pittsburgh Press, 1972), pp. 96–100.
5. 15 March 1968.
6. *New York Review of Books* (21 March 1974), pp. 24 ff.
7. Robert Kiely, *The Romantic Novel in England* (Cambridge, Mass: Harvard University Press, 1972), p. 156.
8. Winifred Gérin. *Emily Brontë: A Biography* (Oxford University Press, 1971), pp. 215–20.
9. Lowry Nelson, Jr, 'Night Thoughts on the Gothic Novel', *Yale Review* LII (December 1962), pp. 236–57.
10. Bernard Bergonzi, *The Early H G Wells* (Manchester, 1969), p. 18.
11. V S Pritchett, *Balzac* (London: Chatto & Windus, 1933), p. 148.
12. London: Jonathan Cape Ltd, 1973.

10   The Artificial Man

1. Mary Shelley, *Frankenstein*, N K Joseph, ed., p. IX.
2. Frederick L Jones, ed, *Mary Shelley's Journal* (Norman, Oklahoma: University of Oklahoma Press, 1947), p. 73.
3. September 1812, vol. 8, p. 65.
4. Volney, *Ruins of Empire (Les Ruines, ou Méditations sur les Revolutions des Empires)* (1791), p. 142.
5. Peter Tompkins and Christopher Bird, *The Secret Life of Plants* (Harper & Row, 1973).
6. Desmond King-Hele, *Erasmus Darwin* (New York: Charles Scribners Sons, 1963), pp. 40–41.
7. *Botanic Garden* (London: J Johnson, 1791), vol. 1, p. 36.

8. King-Hele, *Darwin*, p. 143.

9. Aram Vartanian, *Diderot & Descartes: A Study of Scientific Naturalism in the Enlightenment* (Princeton, NJ: Princeton University Press, 1953).

10. *Genesis*, ch. 2, p. 7.

11. *Point de Vue* (5 July 1974).

12. Paracelsus, *On the Nature of Things* (London, 1850).

13. William Godwin, *Lives of the Necromancers* (London: F J Mason, 1834), pp. 325–27.

14. *The Temple of Satan* (Paris, 1891).

15. Christianus, *Physical Astronomical Political Treatises on the Essence, Birth, Species, Predictions, and Disappearance of the Comets* (Geissen, 1653).

16. pp. 35–36.

17. See Shelley's letter to Godwin (19 June 1811).

18. Godwin, *Necromancers*, pp. 261–63.

19. Donald Glut, *The Frankenstein Legend* (Metuchen, NJ: Scarecrow Press, 1973), p. 5.

20. Silvio A Bedini, 'The Role of Automata in the History of Technology', *Technology and Culture* V, no. 1 (Winter 1964).

21. Mario Praz, *Three Gothic Novels*, Peter Fairclough, ed. (Baltimore, Md.: Penguin Books, 1968).

22. *Frankenstein, or The Modern Prometheus*, ed. James H Kieger (New York: Bobbs-Merrill, 1974), p. XXVII.

Appendix 1

The Knight and the Dragon-Monster

The dragon, over which the figure of a knight is standing, is an allusion to the patron of the knight, the dragon-killing St George. Since the people did not know what this represented, they made up their own legend. The first record of this legend appeared in the first volume of the Brothers Grimm Collected German Legends (1816); it was handed down orally by a peasant from 'Oberbeerbach'. The legend was told in the following way.

The Dragon by the Well

(As told by a peasant from Oberbeerbach)
In Frankenstein, an old castle 1½ hours away from Darmstadt, there lived three brothers, a long time ago. Their gravestones can still be seen in the church of Oberbeerbach. One of the brothers was named Hans and is portrayed in stone as standing on a dragon. Down in the village there is a well which is used as a water supply by the people from the village as well as the people of the castle. Right by this well a horrible dragon had his resting place and the people could only get water if they daily brought him a sheep or other cattle; as long as the dragon was eating from it, the people could use the well. In order to put an end to this nuisance, Knight Hans decided to wage a battle. He fought a long time, but finally he succeeded in striking off the dragon's head. Then he wanted to pierece with his spear the body of the monster, too, which was still wriggling, but the pointed tail then curled around the right leg of the knight, and stung him right in the hollow of his knee, the only spot not covered by the armour. The dragon was poisonous, and Hans of Frankenstein had to part with his life.

The Grimm delivery of the story is not completely accurate. They

271

*changed Nieder- to Ober-Beerbach and also changed the name of the
knight. Konrad Dahl (1762–1833), in his text on the work of the court
painter Georg Primavesi (1774–1855), tells the legend in a similar way to
the Brothers Grimm. He portrays the dragon, in 'a lair in a cliff' near
Castle Frankenstein, playing havoc among the men and animals, stealing
sheep, etc. to eat, and then being killed by Knight Georg. In substance,
this coincides with the poetical treatment which the Weinheim peda-
gogue, Albert Ludwig Grimm (1786–1872), gives the legend. The collector
of legends, August Nodnagel (1803–1853), tells the story in a similar fashion in his unpublished work 'Hessenspiegel' (Reflection of Hesse), handed
down from reports of the oldest people there.*

A long time ago, up by the spring which gushed from the cliffs above
Nieder-Beerbach and which furnished the castle with the freshest drinking
water, a dragon had his resting place and was doing a lot of harm. The people in the castle and in the valley were accustomed to fetching their water
here because at this time it was supposed to be very healthy. They could
only take it, however, while the dragon was eating a horse or an ox; therefore, every time they took it, they had to sacrifice an animal. Then they
complained to Georg von Frankenstein. He promised help, even if he were
to lose his life. Well-armoured and on horseback, he rode to the little
spring, where the dragon was sunning himself. The horse impeded him in
the small spot, so Georg dismounted and attacked the foe. The dragon,
defending his life, panted, and spewed forth fire and smoke; the castle and
the valley resounded with the clang of the sword. Finally the knight triumphed. Scarcely alive though the dragon was, it happened that he wound
the tip of his tail with the poisonous spike around the knight's leg and
wounded him by piercing the iron bands of his armour. Knight Georg
reached his family castle with difficulty and died from his wounds on the
third day.

*One of the earlier records, which deviated from other versions of the
legend, was told by the pastor Heinrich Eduard Scriba. He had heard it
often in his childhood from the mouths of old people. According to his version, the dragon was located at Katzenborn.*

[The dragon] demanded victim upon victim, and was especially ravenous
for the flesh of young girls. When an old woman prophesied that only
through the sacrifice of the most beautiful girl in the valley could the
dragon be moved to retreat into Katzenborn, the lot fell on the beautiful
forester's daughter, Anne Marie, 'the Rose of the Valley', the secret love of
the knight Georg, who was away at the time. She thought herself already
lost; then she saw three candles being lit at Frankenstein – the sign that her
love had returned. She returned the sign. The next day the knight took up
the fight with the monster, killed it, but was himself mortally wounded,

and the Rose of the Valley died from grief and sorrow. On the holy Advent Sunday, however, three candles glow in that house, and behind them Anne Marie's pale countenance appears, turned toward Frankenstein, beseeching and imploring. The formerly clear and lively brook which flows down from Katzenborn became slow and thick, muddy and lazy from the blood of the dragon, and was therefore given the name 'Dunkelbach' (murky brook).

The pastor's version of the legend also received a poetical treatment in the hands of the talented Georg Wehr (born on 7 March 1884, in Weisenau), who on 15 September 1914, died fighting for his country. This version was published in the 205th volume of the 'Landkalenders für das Großherzogtum Hessen' (Almanac for the Grand Duchy of Hesse).

Appendix 2
Godwin and Shelley Genealogy

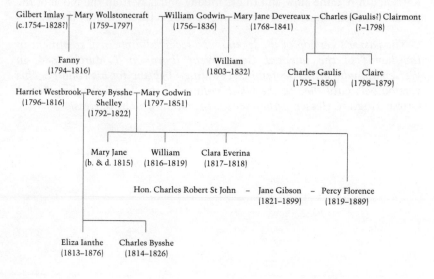

Gilbert Imlay — Mary Wollstonecraft   William Godwin — Mary Jane Devereaux — Charles (Gaulis?) Clairmont
(c.1754–1828?)   (1759–1797)   (1756–1836)   (1768–1841)   (?–1798)

Fanny   William
(1794–1816)   (1803–1832)   Charles Gaulis   Claire
                                                         (1795–1850)   (1798–1879)

Harriet Westbrook — Percy Bysshe — Mary Godwin
(1796–1816)   Shelley   (1797–1851)
                    (1792–1822)

            Mary Jane   William   Clara Everina
            (b. & d. 1815)   (1816–1819)   (1817–1818)

                    Hon. Charles Robert St John   –   Jane Gibson   –   Percy Florence
                                                      (1821–1899)   (1819–1889)

        Eliza Ianthe   Charles Bysshe
        (1813–1876)   (1814–1826)

Appendix 3
Frankenstein Genealogy

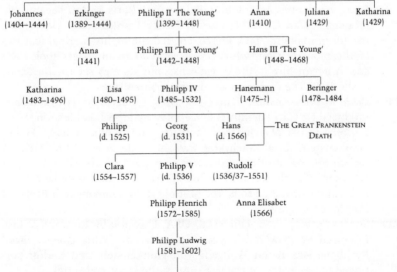

N N von Lützelbach
(ca. 1150–1200)

Conrad Reiz von Lützelbach
(1178–1209)

Conrad I. Reiz von Breuberg
(1222–1239?–42)

Eberhard Reiz von Breuberg
(1239–1282?–86)

Conrad II Reiz von Breuberg

Built Castle Frankenstein ca. 1252

FRANKENSTEIN LINE

Conrad I.
von Frankenstein
(1266–1292)

Ludwig
von Frankenstein
(1268–1275)

Friedrich
von Frankenstein
(1268–1292)

Erkinger
(1309–1321)

Conrad
(1321–?)

Conrad II

YOUNGER LINE

Johann I. 'The Old'
(1363–1401)

Johannes
(1404–1444)

Erkinger
(1389–1444)

Philipp II 'The Young'
(1399–1448)

Anna
(1410)

Juliana
(1429)

Katharina
(1429)

Anna
(1441)

Philipp III 'The Young'
(1442–1448)

Hans III 'The Young'
(1448–1468)

Katharina
(1483–1496)

Lisa
(1480–1495)

Philipp IV
(1485–1532)

Hanemann
(1475–?)

Beringer
(1478–1484

Philipp
(d. 1525)

Georg
(d. 1531)

Hans
(d. 1566)

THE GREAT FRANKENSTEIN
DEATH

Clara
(1554–1557)

Philipp V
(d. 1536)

Rudolf
(1536/37–1551)

Philipp Henrich
(1572–1585)

Anna Elisabet
(1566)

Philipp Ludwig
(1581–1602)

END OF YOUNGER LINE

Appendix 4

Filmography

1910 *Frankenstein*. Edison, USA. A one-reel version (975 ft. in 35 mm), featuring Charles Ogle, a member of the Edison stock company, as a hunchbacked monster. No known prints of the film have ever been discovered.

1915 *Life Without Soul*. Ocean Film Company, USA. A five-reel version of the story featuring the English actor, Percy Standing, as a much more sympathetic monster.

1931 *Frankenstein*. Universal, USA. Directed by James Whale. Produced by Carl Laemmle. Adapted from a play by Peggy Webling based on the Shelley novel. Screenplay by Garrett Fort and Francis Edward Faragoh (adaptation by John L Balderston). Boris Karloff became the monster, Colin Clive became Dr Henry Frankenstein. Universal's master of make-up, Jack Pierce, created the highly original features of the monster from which most subsequent monsters took their cue. A horror film in the truest sense, purists may see the influence of the 1920 *The Golem* in the design of this film.

1935 *Bride of Frankenstein*. Universal, USA. Directed by James Whale. Produced by Carl Laemmle. Screenplay by John L Balderston. Boris Karloff again played the monster and Colin Clive, Henry Frankenstein. Elsa Lanchester was the bride of the film's title. A superb original musical score was composed for the film by Franz Waxman. The photography by John D Mescall was exemplary. *Bride* is usually considered to be the best of all the Frankenstein films – a classic of its genre.

1939 *Son of Frankenstein*. Universal, USA. Directed by Rowland V Lee. Produced by Rowland V Lee. Screenplay by Willis Cooper. Basil Rathbone was Baron Wolfgang von Frankenstein and Karloff portrayed the monster for the last time in the Universal series.

1942   *The Ghost of Frankenstein*. Universal, USA. Directed by Erle C Kenton. Produced by George Waggner. Screenplay by W Scott Darling based on an original story by Eric Taylor. Sir Cedric Hardwicke was Dr Ludwig Frankenstein and Lon Chaney, Jr portrayed the monster. Bela Lugosi, who had also appeared in *Son*, again played Ygor.

1943   *Frankenstein Meets the Wolf Man*. Universal, USA. Directed by Roy William Neil. Produced by George Waggner. Screenplay by Curt Siodmak. Bela Lugosi portrayed the monster, and he managed to do a very bad job of it. Lon Chaney, Jr played Wolf Man.

1944   *House of Frankenstein*. Universal, USA. Directed by Erle C Kenton. Produced by Paul Malvern. Screenplay by Edward T Lowe. Karloff played a mad doctor, Lon Chaney, Jr was the Wolf Man, John Carradine assumed the cloak of Dracula, J Carrol Naish was a murderous hunchback and Glenn Strange (primarily a leading heavy in B-Westerns) became the Frankenstein monster.

1945   *House of Dracula*. Universal, USA. Directed by Erle C Kenton. Produced by Paul Malvern. Screenplay by Edward T Lowe based on a story by George Bricker and Dwight V Babcock. Another quintet of deformities: Lon Chaney, Jr as the Wolf Man, John Carradine as Dracula, Onslow Stevens as the mad doctor, Jane Adams as a hunchback and Glenn Strange as the monster. The film closed the horror series for Universal.

1948   *Abbott and Costello Meet Frankenstein*. Universal, USA. Directed by Charles T Barton. Produced by Robert Arthur. Screenplay by Robert Lees, Frederic Rinaldo and John Grant. A good score by Frank Skinner. Lon Chaney, Jr was the Wolf Man, Bela Lugosi returned to the screen as Dracula (although he had played similar vampire-types in earlier non-Universal films) and Glenn Strange played the monster for the final time on Universal City property.

1957   *The Curse of Frankenstein*. Hammer Films, Great Britain. Directed by Terence Fisher. Produced by Anthony Hinds. Executive Producer Michael Carreras. Associate Producer, Anthony Nelson-Keyes. Screenplay by Jimmy Sangster. The first colour production of the famous tale. Peter Cushing was Baron Victor Frankenstein and his monstrous creation was portrayed by Christopher Lee. A gory though exquisitely designed film.

1957   *I Was a Teenage Frankenstein*. American-International, USA. Directed by Herbert L Stock. Produced by Herman Cohen. Story and screenplay by Kenneth Langtry. Whit Bissell was Professor Frankenstein and Gary Conway, the monster created from the parts of dead teenagers.

1958   *The Revenge of Frankenstein*. Hammer Films, Great Britain. Directed by Terence Fisher. Produced by Anthony Hinds. Executive Producer, Michael Carreras. Associate Producer, Anthony Nelson-Keyes. Screenplay by Jimmy Sangster with additional dialogue by

H Hurford Janes. In this second Hammer film Cushing changes his name to Dr Victor Stein and creates a new monster via a transplanted brain. (Michael Gwynn played the creature.)

1958   *Frankenstein–1970*. Allied Artists, USA. Directed by Howard W Koch. Produced by Aubrey Schenck. Screenplay by Richard Landau and George Worthing Yates, based on a story by Aubrey Schenck and Charles A Moses. Boris Karloff played the disfigured Victor Frankenstein, a victim of Nazi torture, who brings back his ancestor's earlier creation by means of an atomic device.

1959   *Frankenstein's Daughter*. Astor Pictures, USA. Directed by Richard Cunha. Produced by Marc Frederic. Screenplay by H E Barrie. A very low-budget quickie that deserves little attention. John Ashley played John Bruder (supposedly the son of Frankenstein) who created Sandara Knight as his monster.

1961   *Frankenstein, the Vampire and Company*. Mexico. Directed by Benito Alazraki. Attempts to be a remake of *Abbott and Costello Meet Frankenstein*. Some things can never be duplicated.

1963   *El Infierno del Frankenstein*. Mexico. No credits available.

1964   *El Testamento del Frankenstein*. Mexico. Directed by José Luis Madrid. In the cast were Gerard Landry and George Vallis. No other credits or information available.

1964   *The Evil of Frankenstein*. Hammer Films, Great Britain. Directed by Freddie Francis. Produced by Anthony Hinds. Screenplay of John Elder (Anthony Hinds). Third in the Hammer series (and to many the best of the series) found Peter Cushing as Baron Frankenstein creating a new monstrosity played by Kiwi Kingston.

1965   *Furankenshutain Tai Baragon*. Toho, Japan. (Released in the USA as *Frankenstein Conquers the World*.) Directed by Inoshiro Honda. Cast featured Nick Adams, Tadao Taksahima and Kumi Mizuno. Grotesque make-up (unlike English versions) and many rubber props and creatures. Very unnoteworthy.

1965   *Frankenstein Meets the Space Monster*. Vernon Films, USA. (Released in Great Britain as *Duel of the Space Monsters*.) Directed by Robert Gaffney. In the cast of this exploitation-type cheapie were Robert Reilly, Jim Karen and Nancy Marshall.

1965   *Jesse James Meets Frankenstein's Daughter*. Embassy Pictures, USA. Directed by William Beaudine. Produced by Carroll Case. Story and screenplay by Carl H Hittleman. Still another cheapie filmed in colour but with awful acting and a terrible plot. Narda Onyx acted like an unskilled amateur as she created a very human monster in the person of Cal Bolder.

1967   *Frankenstein Created Woman*. Hammer Films, Great Britain. (Co-produced with Seven Arts Productions, USA.) Directed by Terence Fisher. Produced by Anthony Nelson-Keyes. Screenplay by John Elder (Anthony Hinds). This fourth in the Hammer series once again found Peter Cushing as Baron Frankenstein. He was brought back to life in time to revive a drowned girl (Susan Denberg), and implant her boyfriend's brain in her skull so that she could engage in acts of revenge.

1967 *Mad Monster Party*. Embassy Pictures, USA. Directed by Jules Bass. Produced by Arthur Rankin, Jr. Screenplay by Len Korobkin and Harvey Kurtzman (of *Mad* magazine fame). Music and lyrics by Maury Laws and Jules Bass. A full-length animated cartoon feature with all the usual monsters; the Wolf Man, Dracula, the Mummy, etc. Boris Karloff supplied the voice of the Frankenstein monster.

1969 *Frankenstein Must be Destroyed*. Hammer Films, Great Britain. Directed by Terence Fisher. Produced by Anthony Nelson-Keyes. Screenplay by Bert Blatt based on a story by Anthony Nelson-Keyes and Bert Blatt. Peter Cushing was Baron Frankenstein, and Freddie Jones was the unfortunate victim of a brain transplant. Released in the USA by Warner Bros–Seven Arts.

1970 *Horror of Frankenstein*. Hammer Films, Great Britain. (Released in USA by MGM–EMI.) Directed by Jimmy Sangster. Produced by Jimmy Sangster. Screenplay by Jeremy Burnham and Jimmy Sangster. Victor Frankenstein was portrayed by Ralph Bates and his creation by David Prowse.

1970 *Frankenstein on Campus*. Directed by Gil Taylor. Simon Ward as a descendent of Dr Frankenstein turns his fellow classmates into monsters in this youth-oriented flick.

1971 *Dracula vs Frankenstein*. Independent–International Films, USA. Directed by Al Adamson. Produced by Al Adamson and Samuel M Sherman. Screenplay by William Pugsley and Samuel M Sherman. Zandor Vorkov was Count Dracula and John Bloom, the Monster. This film marked the final screen appearances of Lon Chaney, Jr and J Carrol Naish. Kenneth Strickfaden, who had created the laboratory effects for the 1931 Frankenstein film did the special effects for this low-budget horror film.

1971 *Frankenstein's Bloody Terror*. Directed by Enrique L Equiluz. A Spanish film that has nothing to do with Frankenstein but something to do with werewolves and vampires.

1972 *La Marcha del Hombre Lobo*. Spanish. (Released in the USA as *Frankenstein's Bloody Terror* by Independent–International Films.) Directed by Enrique L Equiluz. A Maxper Production. Screenplay by Jacinto Molina. Filmed in 70 mm and 3-dimension.

1972 *Frankenstein*. (Made for TV by Dan Curtis Productions.) Directed by Glenn Jordan. Screenplay (Part 1) by Sam Hall. (Part 2) by Richard Landau. Robert Foxworth was Dr Victor Frankenstein; Bo Svenson the monster.

1972 *Frankenstein 80*. Gorgon–MPI. Directed by Mario Mancini. Low-budget Italian retelling of the legend. Lots of blood and sexy women.

1973 *Frankenstein: The True Story*. Universal TV, USA. Directed by Jack Smight. Produced by Hunt Stromberg, Jr. The teleplay was by Christopher Isherwood and Don Bachardy, freely adapted from the Shelley classic. This 180-minute television film was probably the most faithful rendering the screen has yet seen. Dr Frankenstein was played by Leonard Whiting and Michael Sarrazin his inquiring and childlike creation. The film was produced at Pinewood Studios.

1973 *Blackenstein*. Media. Produced and written by Frank Saletri. Directed by William Levey. Ultra low-budget rip-off of the far superior *Blacula*. Does not even work on an unintentional comic level.

1974 *Flesh for Frankenstein*. French–Italian. (Released in the USA as *Andy Warhol's Frankenstein*.) A Carlo Ponti–Andrew Braunsberg–Jean Pierre Rassam Production. Directed and written by Paul Morrissey. USA release was by Bryanston Pictures. Another 3-dimension Frankenstein and a real stomach-turner. Udo Kier was The Baron and Srdjan Zelenovic was the farmer-monster.

1974 *Frankenstein and the Monster From Hell*. Hammer Films, Great Britain. (Released in the USA by Paramount.) Directed by Terence Fisher. Produced by Roy Skeggs. Screenplay by John Elder (Anthony Hinds). Peter Cushing was Baron Frankenstein. David Prowse played the monster for a second time (first in *Horror of Frankenstein*).

1974 *Young Frankenstein*. 20th Century-Fox, USA. A Gruskoff/Venture/Crossbow/Joner Production. Directed by Mel Brooks. Produced by Michael Gruskoff. Screenplay by Gene Wilder and Mel Brooks. A devastatingly funny satire on the Frankenstein legend with Gene Wilder as Dr Frederick Frankenstein and Peter Boyle as his tap-dancing monster. Use was made again of Kenneth Strickfaden who supplied some of the original *Frankenstein* (1931) special effects and equipment. The film was photographed in moody black and white.

1975 *The Rocky Horror Picture Show*. CBS–Fox. Written by Jim Sharman and Richard O'Brien. Directed by Jim Sharman. Ultra-cool rock and roll 'transvestite' musical. Tim Curry as Frank-n-Furter, an alien from the planet 'Transexualvania' creates the perfect blond-haired, blue-eyed, muscle-bound playmate, Rocky Horror, while seducing two stranded lovers with car trouble played by Barry Bostwick and Susan Sarandon. Super fun all around.

1977 *Frankenstein–Italian Style*. Directed by Armando Crispino. X-rated spoof with well-endowed monster seeking out and being sought out by the women of the countryside.

1981 *Frankenstein Island*. Monterey. Produced and directed by Jerry Warren. So bad it is almost unwatchable except for some appearances by some well known has-beens including Cameron Mitchell, Patrick O'Neil, Andrew Duggen and John Carradine's floating head.

1984   *Frankenstein.* Lightening/Alive Video. US/British TV version shot in the annoying clarity of video tape. Robert Powell stars as Victor, Carrie Fisher as his sister, Sir John Gielgud as the Blind Man in the forest and David Warner as the Monster.

1984   *Frankenstein.* Vestron Video. Japanese animated version. Outrageous over the top, extremely gory. In step with most animated Japanese films.

1984   *Frankenstein 88* (aka *The Vindicator*). Key. Directed by Jean-Claude Lord. Not bad Canadian, action sci-fi fantasy where mad doctor takes an accident victim and transforms him into a Robocop-type cyborg that turns evil because of bad programming. Nice surprise, well worth a look.

1984   *Frankenweenie.* Disney. Produced by Julie Hickson. Directed by Tim Burton. The director of *Batman* and *Beetlejuice* conjures up a Frankenstein tale for kids. In this short film Barret Oliver plays young Victor Frankenstein whose pet dog is killed in an accident. He, of course, digs him up and resurrects him complete with stitching scars and neck bolts. A little scary for young children but fun for the entire family.

1985   *Frankenstein's Great Aunt Tillie.* Video City. Writer-Director Myron J Gold. When the family castle is threatened because of tax evasion along comes Victor Jr played by Donald Pleasance and his 109-year-old Great Aunt Tillie, played by Yvonne Furneaux, to the rescue. Nothing funny's goin' on here. Look for an appearance by Zsa Zsa Gabor.

1985   *Weird Science.* Written and directed by John Hughes. Amiable teen sex comedy where two computer nerds played by Anthony Michael Hall and Ilan Michael Smith create a woman, Kelly le Brock, with their keyboards. Bill Paxton is hysterical as the tyrannical older brother.

1985   *The Bride.* Columbia Pictures. Directed by Franc Roddam. Sting and Jennifer Beals do their best to destroy this remake of *The Bride of Frankenstein* as the Doctor and his Bride. Clancy Brown as the Monster and David Rappaport as his midget companion do their best to save it.

1986   *Gothic.* British. Written and directed by Ken Russell. The story of the night during which Mary Shelley conceived her novel *Frankenstein* turned into a horror story. Adult, thought provoking and stylish, with a stellar cast which includes Gabriel Byrne, Julian Sands, Natasha Richardson and Timothy Spall.

1986   *Deadly Friend.* Warner Brothers. Written and directed by Wes Craven. Teen, Matthew Laborteaux, loses girlfriend, Kristy Swanson, and decides to resurrect her by implanting computer chips and a little electricity. Not bad. Some good frights and an emotional payoff.

1988 *Frankenstein General Hospital.* Video/Laser: New Star. Directed by Deborah Roberts. Mark Blankenfield of *Jekyll and Hyde . . . Together Again* tries again and fails again.

1988 *Haunted Summer.* Cannon Films. Directed by Ivan Passar. Once again the story of the summer during which Mary Shelley conceived her *Frankenstein* novel is told. This time it is more historically accurate but much less stylish or enjoyable. This slow moving picture stars Phillip Anglim, Eric Stoltz, Alex Winter, Laura Dern and Alice Krige.

1989 *Frankenhooker.* Shapiro Glickenhaus. Directed by Frank Henenlotter of *Basket Case* fame. A cult 'midnight movie' full of gore and twisted humour with James Lorinz as the mad doctor/electrician boyfriend and Patty Mullen as his street walking creation.

1990 *Frankenstein: A Cinematic Scrapbook.* Rhino. Written and directed by Ted Newsom. A collection of movie trailers from most of the Universal and Hammer Films with a few oddball independents thrown in for good measure. Also features rare behind the scenes footage.

1990 *Frankenstein Unbound.* Written by F X Feeny from Brian W Aldiss's novel. Directed by Roger Corman. John Hurt as time traveller gets sent back to the summer that Mary Shelley conceived her novel *Frankenstein.* However, this time the novel turns out to be fiction. Excellent cast headed by Raul Julia's stupendous performance as Dr Frankenstein. Also Bridget Fonda, Jason Patrick and Michael Hutchence of the rock group INXS. Not bad, but takes itself too seriously to be fun.

1991 *Frankenstein: The College Years.* Fox Television. Directed by Tom Shadyac. William Ragsdale tries to do for Frankenstein what he did for vampires with *Fright Night.* He can't.

1993 *Frankenstein.* Turner. Writer, producer, director David Wicks. Patrick Bergen stars as Dr Frankenstein and Randy Quaid as his creation. Nothing noteworthy but not entirely bad.

1994 *Mary Shelley's Frankenstein.* Columbia Pictures. Written by Frank Darabount. Produced by Francis Ford Coppola, James V Hart and Kenneth Branagh. Directed by Kenneth Branagh. Set up to be the Frankenstein of the century. It doesn't come close. Wasted talent all around, especially Robert de Niro as the monster. Branagh is awful as Victor. Exceptional cameo by John Cleese of *Monty Python* as Dr Waldman. Excellent supporting cast includes Ian Holm, Helena Bonham Carter, Cherie Lunghi and Tom Hulce.

Appendix 5

Bibliography

Aldiss, Brian W, *Frankenstein Unbound*, London: Jonathan Cape Ltd, 1973
  Trillion Year Spree, London: Gollancz, 1986
Armistead, C Gordon, *Allegra: The Story of Byron and Miss Clairmont*,
  London: Methuen and Co Ltd, 1927
Baldick, Chris, *In Frankenstein's Shadow: Myth, Monstrosity and
  Nineteenth-century Writing*, Oxford: Oxford University Press, 1987
Bann, Stephen, *Frankenstein, Creation and Monstrosity*, London: Reaktion
  Books, 1994
Bennett, Betty T, *Letters to Mary Wollstonecraft Shelley*, 3 vols, Baltimore:
  Johns Hopkins University Press, 1980, 1983, 1988
  and Robinson, Charles E, *Mary Shelley Reader*, New York: Oxford
  University Press, 1990
Bigland, Eileen, *Mary Shelley*, London: Cassell, 1959
Blumberg, Jane, *Mary Shelley's Early Novels: This Child of Imagination
  and Misery*, Iowa City: University of Iowa Press, 1993
Botting, Fred, *Making Monstrous*, Manchester: Manchester University
  Press, 1991
  (ed), *Frankenstein: Mary Shelley*, London: Macmillan (New Casebook
  series), 1995
Brown, Ford K, *The Life of William Godwin*, London: Dent, 1926
Butler, Marilyn (ed), Mary Shelley, *Frankenstein or the Modern
  Prometheus: The 1818 Text*, London and Oxford: Oxford University
  Press, 1993; Oxford World's Classics paperback, 1995
Cantor, Paul, *Creature and Creator: Mythmaking and English
  Romanticism*, Cambridge University Press, 1984
Church, Richard, *Mary Shelley: A Biography*, London: Gerald Howe Ltd,
  1928. Also in *Six Women of the World*, London: Gerald Howe Ltd, 1930

Crouch, Laura, 'Davy, *A Discourse*: a possible scientific source of *Frankenstein*', *Keats–Shelley Journal*, 27 (1978) 35–45

Dowden, Edward, *The Life of Percy Bysshe Shelley*, 2 vols, London: Kegan Paul, Trench & Co, Ltd, 1886
The Poetical Works of Percy Bysshe Shelley, London: Macmillan & Co, 1891; shortened version, London: Routledge, 1951

Elshtain, J, *Public Man, Private Woman*, Oxford: Robertson, 1981

Engel, Claire-Elaine, *Byron et Shelley en Suisse et en Savoie Mai-Octobre, 1816* (unpublished). Paris: Chambéry, 1930

Feldman, Paula R, and Scott-Kilvert, D, *Journals of Mary Shelley, 1814–1844*, 2 vols, Oxford: Clarendon Press, 1987

Fisch, Audrey A, Mellor, Anne K, and Schor, Esther H, *The Other Mary Shelley, Beyond 'Frankenstein'*, Oxford and New York: Oxford University Press, 1993

Forman, Buxton H, ed, *The Letters of Edward John Trelawny*, London: O O Pierce, 1910

Forry, Steven Earl, Hideous Progenies: *Dramatizations of Frankenstein from Mary Shelley to the Present*, Philadelphia: University of Philadelphia Press, 1990

Friedman, Lester D, 'Sporting With Life: *Frankenstein* and the Responsibility of Medical Research', *Medical Heritage*, 1 (May–June 1985), 181–5

Fuller, Jean Overton, *Shelley: A Biography*, London: Jonathan Cape, Ltd, 1968

Gerson, Noel Bertram, *Daughter of Earth and Water: A Biography of Mary Wollstonecraft*, New York: William Morrow, 1973

Gilbert, Sandra, and Gubar, S, *Madwoman in the Attic*, New Haven, Connecticut: Yale University Press, 1979

Gittings, Robert, and Manton, Jo, *Claire Clairmont and the Shelleys, 1798–1879*, Oxford and New York: Oxford University Press, 1992

Glut, Donald F, *The Frankenstein Legend: A Tribute to Mary Shelley and Boris Karloff*, Metuchen, New Jersey: The Scarecrow Press, 1973

Godwin, William, *Memoirs of Mary Wollstonecraft*, London: Constable & Co, Ltd, 1927
Complete Novels, ed Mark Philp, London: Pickering & Chatto, 1992

Graham, William, *Last Links with Byron, Shelley & Keats*, London: Leonard Smithers & Co, 1898

Grylls, Rosalie Glynn, *Claire Clairmont: Mother of Byron's Allegra*, London: John Murray, 1939
Mary Shelley: A Biography, Oxford: Oxford University Press, 1938
William Godwin and his World, London: Odhams Press Ltd, 1953

Hill-Miller, Katherine C, *My Hideous Progeny: Mary Shelley, William Godwin and the Father–Daughter Relationship*, London: Associated University Presses, 1915; Newark: University of Delaware Press, 1995

Ingpen, Roger, *Shelley in England*, New Facts and Letters from the Shelley–Whitton Papers, London: Kegan Paul, Trench, Trubner & co, Ltd, 1917

Johnson, Barbara, 'My Monster/Myself', *Diacritics* 12 (1982), 117–61

Jones, Frederick L (ed), *The Letters of Mary W Shelley*, 2 vols, Norman, Oklahoma: University of Oklahoma Press, 1944
Mary Shelley's Journal, Norman, Oklahoma: University of Oklahoma Press, 1947

Ketterer, David, *Frankenstein's Creation: The Book, the Monster and Human Reality*, English Literary Studies, University of Victoria, Australia, 1979

Koszul, André, 'Notes and Corrections to Shelley's *History of a Six Weeks' Tour* (1817)', *MLR* 2 (October 1906): 61–62

Koszul, L, *La jeunesse de Shelley*, Paris, 1907

Lecercle, J J, *'Frankenstein', mythe et philosophie*, Paris: Presse universitaire de France, 1988

Leighton, Margaret (Carver), *Shelley's Mary: The Life of Mary Godwin Shelley*, New York: Farrar, Straus & Giroux, 1973

Levine, G, and Knoepflmacher, U C, *The Endurance of 'Frankenstein'*, Berkeley, California: University of California Press, 1979

Luke, Hugh J, 'Sir William Lawrence, Physician to Shelley and Mary', *Papers on English Language and Literature*, I (1965), 141–52

Marlowe, Derek, *A Single Summer with Lord B*, New York: Viking, 1969

Marshall, Florence A, *The Life and Letters of Mary Wollstonecraft Shelley*, 2 vols, London: Richard Bentley & Sons, 1889

Maurois, André, *Ariel: a Shelley Romance*, London: Bodley Head, 1924; published in the United States as *Ariel: The Life of Shelley*, trans Ella D'Arcy, New York: Appleton, 1924

Mellor, Anne K, *Mary Shelley: Her Life, Her Fiction, Her Monsters*, London: Routledge, 1988

Moers, Ellen, 'Female Gothic: The Monster's Mother', *The New York Review of Books*, 21 March 1974

Moore, Helen, *Mary Wollstonecraft Shelley*, Philadelphia: Lippincott & Co, 1886

Murray, E B, 'Shelley's Contribution to Mary's *Frankenstein*', *Keats–Shelley Bulletin*, 29 (1978), 50–60

Nelson, Lowry, Jr, 'Night Thoughts on the Gothic Novel', *The Yale Review* 52, Winter 1963: 236–57

Nicoll, Allardyce, *A History of English Drama: 1600–1900*, 6 vols, Cambridge: Cambridge University Press, 1952–59

Nitchie, Elizabeth, *Mary Shelley: Author of Frankenstein*, New Brunswick, NJ: Rutgers University Press, 1953
'Mary Shelley', *Times Literary Supplement* 1801 (30 April 1938): 296
'Mary Shelley, Traveler', *KSJ* 10 (Winter 1961): 29–42

'The Stage History of *Frankenstein*', *South Atlantic Quarterly* 41 (October 1942): 384–98

O'Flinn, Paul, 'Production and Reproduction': The Case of *Frankenstein*, *Literature & History* (Autumn 1983), 194–213

Origo, Iris, Marchesa, *Allegra*, London: Hogarth Press, 1935

Palacio, Jean de, 'Mary Shelley and *The Last Man*: A Minor Romantic Theme', *Revue de Littérature Comparée* 42 (January–March 1968): 37–49
Mary Shelley dans son Oeuvre: Contribution aux études Shelleyennes, Paris: Editions Klincksieck, 1969

Paul, Charles Kegan, *William Godwin: His Friends and Contemporaries*, London: Henry S King & Co, 1876

Peck, Walter Edwin, 'The Biographical Element in the Novels of Mary Wollstonecraft Shelley', *PMLA* XXXVIII (1923): 196–219
Shelley: His Life and Work, 2 vols, London: Benn, 1927; Boston and New York: Houghton Mifflin Co, 1927

Pennell, Elizabeth Robins, *Life of Mary Wollstonecraft*, Boston: Roberts Brothers, 1884; published in the UK as *Mary Wollstonecraft Godwin*, London: W H Allen, 1885

Poovey, Mary, *The Proper Lady and the Woman Writer*, Chicago: Chicago University Press, 1984

Rieger, James, 'Dr Polidori and the Genesis of *Frankenstein*', *Studies of English Literature* 3 (Autumn 1963): 461–72
(ed), Mary Shelley, *Frankenstein, or the Modern Prometheus: the 1818 Text*, Indianapolis: Bobbs-Merrill Co, 1974; Chicago: University of Chicago Press, 1982

Rosenberg, Samuel, *Frankenstein, or Daddy's Little Monster: The Confessions of a Trivialist*, New York: Prentice-Hall, 1970; London and Baltimore, Maryland: Penguin Books, 1972
'The Horrible Truth about Frankenstein', *Life* LXIV, 11 (15 March 1968): 77

Rossetti, Lucy Madox, *Mrs Shelley*, London: W H Allen & Co, 1890

Rossetti, William Michael, ed, *The Diary of Dr John William Polidori 1816: relating to Byron, Shelley etc*, edited and elucidated by W M Rossetti, London: Elkin Mathews, 1911

Sherwin, P, '*Frankenstein*: Creation as Catastrophe', *PMLA* 96 (1981), 883–903

Small, Christopher, *Ariel Like a Harpy: Shelley, Mary and 'Frankenstein'*, London: Gollancz, 1972. Published in the US as *Mary Shelley's Frankenstein – Tracing the Myth*, Pittsburgh: University of Pittsburgh Press, 1973

Smith, Johanna M (ed), *Mary Shelley: 'Frankenstein'*, Boston: Bedford Books; New York: St Martin's Press, 1992

Spark, Muriel, *Mary Shelley*, London: Constable & Co, 1987; paperback, 1993 (A complete revision of *Child of Light: A Reassessment of Mary*

Wollstonecraft Shelley, London: Tower Bridge Publications, 1951)

Spector, Judith A, 'Science Fiction and the Sex War', *Literature and Psychology*, 31 (1981), 21–32

Stocking, Marion Kingston (ed), *The Journals of Claire Clairmont*, Boston: Harvard University Press, 1968

Sunstein, Emily, *Mary Shelley: Romance and Reality*, Boston, Toronto and London: Little, Brown, 1989

Tomalin, Claire, *The Life and Death of Mary Wollstonecraft*, London: Weidenfeld & Nicolson, 1974; New York: Harcourt Brace Jovanovich, 1974

Vasbinder, Samuel H, *Scientific Attitudes in Mary Shelley's 'Frankenstein'*, Ann Arbor, Michigan: UMI Research Press, 1976

Veeder, William, *Mary Shelley and 'Frankenstein': the Fate of Androgyny*, Chicago: University of Chicago Press, 1986

Wardle, Ralph Martin, *Mary Wollstonecraft: A Critical Biography*, Lawrence, Kansas: University of Kansas Press, 1951

Wolf, Leonard, *The Annotated 'Frankenstein'*, New York: Clarkson N Potter, 1977

Essential Frankenstein, Los Angeles: Plume, 1995. (Wolf served as consultant to Branagh's film.)